BI 0709065 X

9203978
LEAA

KU-545-472

Towards a New Education System: The Victory of the New Right?

Dedication

To Joan and Brian who first awakened my
interest in the politics of educational change,
and without whose support and encouragement,
this book would never have been written.

Towards a
New Education System:
The Victory of the New Right?

by Clyde Chitty

The Falmer Press
(A member of the Taylor & Francis Group)
London • New York • Philadelphia

UK   The Falmer Press, Falmer House, Barcombe, Lewes,
          Sussex, BN8 5DL

USA   The Falmer Press, Taylor & Francis Inc., 242 Cherry
          Street, Philadelphia, PA 19106-1906

1989 © C. Chitty

*All rights reserved. No part of this publication may be
reproduced, stored in a retrieval system, or transmitted in
any form or by any means, electronic, mechanical,
photocopying, recording or otherwise, without permission
in writing from the Publisher.*

First published 1989

**British Library Cataloguing in Publication Data
available on request**

**Library of Congress Cataloguing-in-Publication Data
available on request**

Typeset in 10½/13 California by
Chapterhouse, The Cloisters, Formby L37 3PX

Printed and bound in Great Britain by Taylor & Francis
(Printers) Ltd, Basingstoke.

Contents

... The Bishop of London said he was very strongly of the opinion that the centre of England's greatness, and the whole source of England's life, consisted in the persistent and regular development of local self-government. There was no increase of municipal activity which ought not to be a source of unmitigated rejoicing.

Mandell Creighton, Bishop of London, speaking at the opening of the Art and Technical Schools in Leicester, reported in *The Standard*, 6 October 1897.

We tend to forget that local government is also a cornerstone of freedom, as every dictator realises when, on getting into power, he abolishes it (Napoleon in France, Mussolini in Italy, Hitler in Germany).

Henry Morris writing in 1943. Harry Ree (Ed.) (1984) *The Henry Morris Collection*, Cambridge, Cambridge University Press, p. 86.

The return of a Conservative government today will mean the break-up of the state education system that has existed since 1944.

Peter Wilby writing in *The Independent*, 11 June 1987.

INFORMATION SERVICES

BOOK No. 0709065X

SUBJECT No. 379.42 Chi

ADDED SUBJECT No.

Birmingham Polytechnic

Preface

This book is largely an account of two attempts (in 1976/77 and 1987/88) to change the character and direction of the education system of this country, with particular reference to the secondary school curriculum. It is chiefly concerned with the situation in England and Wales, with only occasional references to factors that also embrace Scotland and Northern Ireland; and this should be taken into account if the word 'Britain' creeps into the text.

The study has, in fact, grown with the accumulation of developments affecting education over the past twelve years. It began life as a dissertation for a higher degree on the eight-year period from 1976 to 1984: to be precise, the period from James Callaghan's Ruskin College speech in October 1976 to Sir Keith Joseph's speech to the North of England Education Conference meeting in Sheffield in January 1984. With its more limited scope, its original title was 'The road from Ruskin to Sheffield' taken from an article by George Walker in *The Times Educational Supplement* (27 January 1984). Curiously, the Sheffield speech seems less significant now than it did in 1984, meriting only the occasional reference in the chapters that follow. The final phase of Sir Keith's five-year period at the DES has, of course, been overshadowed by the truly momentous nature of the changes wrought by his successor.

Some of the material in the chapters that follow has already appeared in papers published within the last two years. Chapter 4 is a revised and extended version of a paper which first appeared in Bedford Way Paper 33, *The National Curriculum*, published by the Institute of Education in April 1988; chapter 5 develops themes and ideas which were first explored in an article in *History of Education*, 17, 4, December 1988. Where ideas developed in other earlier papers are either endorsed or repudiated, this is acknowledged in the text or in the accompanying notes.

I should like to express my sincere thanks to two of my colleagues at the Institute of Education, University of London, Janet Maw and Professor Denis Lawton, who jointly supervised the thesis upon which this book is based. My thanks are also due to Professor Ivor Goodson of the University of Western Ontario and Malcolm Clarkson, Managing Director of the Falmer Press, for first suggesting that the theme of that thesis would make a useful subject for a book. I would also like to thank the following friends and colleagues for many hours of often heated discussion about the issues dealt with in the following chapters: Richard Aldrich, Denis Baylis, Caroline Benn, Tony Benn, Shane Blackman, Joyce Broomhall, Derek Gillard, Caroline Gipps, Peter Gordon, Andy Green, Pauline Green, Janet Harland, Richard Harris, Maurice Holt, Jean Jones, Peter Keelan, Alex McLeod, Sally Poplar, Stewart Ranson, Helen Simons, Jim Thawley, Paddy Walsh, John White and Michael Young. In addition, the Editorial Board of *Forum*, which meets at least three times a year, has been a constant source of ideas and fresh avenues of enquiry. Finally, I wish to acknowledge a special debt to Joan and Brian Simon for their unstinting support and encouragement over the past twenty-five years, culminating in their close involvement with the present project. It is to them that this book is dedicated with gratitude and much love.

Clyde Chitty
London
September 1989

Introduction: Education, Politics and the State

The Education Sub-Government[1]

Ranson (1980) has succinctly summarized the main problems facing education since the early 1960s, drawing particular attention to the changed circumstances created by the economic recession of 1974/75:

> Education has perhaps been the most complex and burdened of services. As the keystone of public policy-making and social reform in the post-war period, education has been expected to fuel economic growth, facilitate equality of opportunity and afford some social justice to the deprived: to educate has been to bring a new world out of the old. To accomplish this burdensome collective vision, education has had to manage the most complex network of relationships which cuts across communities, services, authorities and levels of government. A rising birth-rate, economic growth and political will coalesced in the expansion of the education service during the 1960s and early 1970s. But education now occupies a changed and more fragmented world: the confluence of forces has altered. Demographic and economic contraction, eroded beliefs about the contributions which education can make and the disquiet of parents and politicians have combined to produce a more severe and pessimistic context for education. This changing context is having enormous implications for the management of the service. Its vision and objectives are being questioned and simplified, while the complex, often ambiguous, traditional framework of decision-making — with its assumptions about *who* should be involved, *whose* values should count, *how* decisions should be arrived at — is being clarified, concentrated and centralized: in short, the traditional balance of autonomy, power and accountability in education is being redefined. (p.3)

Although written nearly a decade ago, the main points of this analysis have lost none of their relevance. The 'redefinition' referred to in the final sentence is still taking place, and the debate has acquired a sharper focus with the passing of the 1988 Education Act.

According to Briault (1976), all education systems have a number of characteristics in common:

> Any educational service is necessarily provided through a large number and considerable range of separated institutions, and many decisions are necessarily taken within the individual institution and indeed by individual teachers and others within the school or college. For the most part, however, such day-to-day decisions are taken within a framework laid down elsewhere and relate to resources of different kinds, the extent and distribution of which has been decided elsewhere. Power and responsibility within an educational system relate chiefly to the extent and nature of the resources provided, the curriculum and teaching methods, the character and purpose of individual institutions and the internal organization of these institutions. Significant decisions may be taken at national level; at State or, to use the phrase used in the United Kingdom, local education authority level; or at the level of the individual institution. (p. 430)

It was Briault's contention that the system of administration of schools in England and Wales could be viewed as a 'triangle of tension', the three points of the triangle being central government, local government and the individual schools. Where there was conflict, it usually concerned competing priorities for resources. Yet, providing the sides held, the tension could be seen as constructive and valuable in preventing the dangers which would arise if too much power became concentrated at one point of the triangle (*ibid.*, p.431).

The 'triangle of tension' model is one of a number of theoretical models which have been put forward over the years to explain the relations between the DES, local education authorities and schools. It may be more useful than the concept of 'partnership' favoured by, among others, Smith (1957) and Hall (1985) because it acknowledges the existence of conflict inherent in the system, but it has been criticized by Lawton and Gordon (1987a, p. 109) for over-simplifying the situation in assuming that there are only three 'sides' and that there is no conflict *within* each corner. It is also over-simplified in suggesting that money is the major, perhaps even the only, source of conflict. For obvious reasons, since it was elaborated in the mid-70s, it is unable to take account of the major changes which are the subject of this book.

Waddington (1985) has found it useful to adopt key features of the so-called 'loose-coupling' model of educational management as a means of understanding the framework for curriculum control that has existed in this country since 1944. As developed by Weick (1976), the loose-coupling model is an ambiguity perspective which stresses uncertainty and unpredictability in organizations and systems. As with all ambiguity models, organizational structure is regarded as problematic. There is uncertainty over the relative power of the different parts of the system. The effective power and influence of each element within the structure is said to vary with the issue and according to the level of commitment of the individuals concerned. According to Weick:

> Loose coupling also carries connotations of impermanence, dissolvability and tacitness, all of which are potentially crucial properties of the 'glue' that holds organizations and systems together. (*ibid.*, p.3)

Yet for our purposes the usefulness of this model is also undermined by the emergence of significant trends towards greater central control of the school curriculum in the years since 1976.

In a lecture delivered in 1978, Professor Denis Lawton argued that it was necessary to distinguish between five levels of decision-making in the British educational system: national, regional (local education authority), institutional (school), departmental and individual (the teacher in the classroom). At that time, it was still possible to argue that effective power rested with the teacher in the classroom:

> It must be accepted that teachers ultimately have the greatest control because they make the most crucial decisions facing the pupils in the classroom. But they need to make these individual decisions about lesson content and teaching methods in accordance with the syllabus decisions made by their departmental colleagues, and in accordance with the 'whole curriculum' decisions made by the rest of their colleagues in the school. Some schools do this already, but let us not pretend it is a very common practice: far too many teachers work in complete isolation from their colleagues. It is also the case that as yet few schools have an adequate machinery for discussing the curriculum as a whole and making decisions about it (Lawton, 1979, p.20; 1982, p.18).

At this stage, Lawton was talking of the central authority in terms of the Secretary of State, the officials of the DES and HMIs, without attempting to make a sophisticated analysis of their differing sets of beliefs,

3

values and tastes. A later model (1984) concentrating on the structure and
dynamic of the central authority itself (often referred to ambiguously as the
DES) attempted to identify the conflicting ideologies at the centre as well as
the picture presented to the outside world. The three groups postulated in
the Lawton model, each with its distinct ideology, were: the politicos
(ministers, political advisers, etc.); the bureaucrats (DES officials); and the
professionals (HMI). It was, of course, accepted that reality might not be as
neat as the model: some DES officials might behave more like professionals; and some members of HMI might have views close to those of DES
civil servants or even of Conservative politicians. At the same time, the
standpoint of political advisers would clearly be closely related to the
political complexion of the party in power. Nevertheless it was argued that
there would still be sufficient differences between the three factions to
make sensible generalizations about them as groups. From the three
ideologies could be derived different views on particular issues or policies.
On curriculum policy, for example, one might find evidence of the politicians' addiction to standards, the DES concern for specified objectives,
contrasted with HMI support for a common-culture curriculum of high
quality. Instead of being seen as a monolithic body, the DES would emerge
as a site of competing interests. It would be revealed as a 'tension system',
not as a consensus.

It is Lawton's concept of a 'tension system' at the centre which will
serve as a useful theoretical model for the discussion which follows. The
next section will examine the role and philosophy of each of the three main
groups which constitute the central authority: the DES bureaucracy, HMI,
and the group of influential advisers to the Prime Minister brought together
within the Downing Street Policy Unit.

The Central Authority as a 'Tension System'

The Department of Education and Science was created as a single department, responsible for education, science and the universities, in April 1964
when the Ministry of Education and the Office of the Minister for Science
were amalgamated and took in various responsibilities from other departments. In 1974, a small team of investigators from the OECD (Organization for Economic Cooperation and Development) was appointed by the
DES to review educational planning in England and Wales and concluded
that 'although the powers of government with regard to educational
planning are formally limited . . . the central Department of Education and

Science is undoubtedly the most important single force in determining the direction and tempo of educational development' (OECD, 1975)[2].

The OECD document paid particular attention to the role played by the Civil Service in determining that direction and tempo:

> The permanent officials of the DES, in the tradition of British Civil Servants, are non-political in their function. In no country, it is safe to say, does the Civil Service govern itself more closely by a code of loyalty to whatever government is in power. The protections in the British System against the Civil Service's being captured by a political party go very far . . .
>
> A permanent officialdom possessing . . . external protections and internal disciplines becomes a power in its own right. A British department composed of professional civil servants who have watched the ministers come and go is an entity that only an extremely foolish or powerful politician will persistently challenge or ignore.
>
> The prestige, acquaintanceships, and natural authority of leading civil servants give them a standing in the civil forum often superior to that of their *de jure* political superiors. They are, in the continental phrase, *notables*, whose opinions must be given special weight, whether or not votes in the next election will be affected.
>
> There has also to be taken into account the momentum of thought and action within a department composed of career officials who have long known one another, who have the same training and prospects, and who work within a common tradition and point of view. An essential part of their ethos is to serve their 'political masters'. They interpret this as imposing upon them the obligation to remain at all times sensitive to the changing realities of political pressures and to endeavour to identify in all situations a social consensus as to the priority issues towards which policy planning could be directed.

The OECD investigators went on to make the following points in relation to recent policy-making in the Department:

> . . . the United Kingdom offers an example of educational planning in which the structures for ensuring public participation are limited. This has at least two consequences. One is that in certain cases policy is less likely to be understood and therefore less likely to be wholeheartedly accepted when the processes which lead up to its formulation are guarded as arcane secrets. The

second is that goals and priorities, once established, may go on being taken for granted and hence escape the regular scrutiny which may be necessary for an appropriate realignment of policy.

This latter consequence is discernible in the White Paper's posture of acquiescence towards existing goals. The method of planning it evinces as it sets forth its programme for the allocation of resources, directed towards effecting incremental improvements within existing structures, derives from the assumption that the basic directions of educational development are largely foreclosed; determined, one infers, by historical circumstances, demographic trends, and changes in public attitudes.

The White Paper under discussion here was *A Framework for Expansion*, published in 1972 during Margaret Thatcher's period as Education Secretary. The OECD team noted that, though designed to provide a 'framework for expansion' for the 'British educational service', it seemed to be rather more a 'framework of expansion' for certain pre-selected areas. The problems associated with the areas chosen were said to be treated with 'admirable clarity, technical expertise, and straightforwardness'. There seemed, on the other hand, to be certain other areas — such as provision for the 16–19 age group and for adult education — which had been wholly or partly omitted, without adequate explanation of the selection criteria and procedure. By restricting itself largely to quantitative projections and proposals for resource allocation, the White Paper could be said to be implicitly accepting the existing institutional framework and thereby discouraging the raising of fundamental questions of education purpose, content or method:

> Departmental perspectives, the self-interpretation of the role of civil servants as apolitical, or in any case neutral, servants of the state, and the views of the content of education as a matter for local self-government, that is for teachers or local authorities, seem to preclude the possibility of interpreting the role of education as an agent for innovation and social progress.

The concluding summary of the OECD appraisal was particularly critical of the Department's concern to minimize controversiality and reduce the planning process to a matter of resource allocation:

> The chief features of the bases for its policy formation seem to be characterized by attempts to: minimize the degree of controversiality in the planning process and its results; reduce possible

alternatives to matters of choice of resource allocation; limit the planning process to those parts of the educational services and functions strictly controlled by the DES; exploit as fully as possible the powers, prerogatives and responsibilities given to the DES under the 1944 Education Act; understate as much as possible the full role of the government in the determination of the future course of educational policy and even minimize it in the eyes of the general public... The preservation of this powerful position, by combining the task of coherent planning with defensive tactics, excluding an open planning process, public hearings or, even, participation, seems to an outside observer as a mixture of strength and weakness... What we miss... is the use of greater daring in the delineation of new paths of learning and of new institutional and administrative developments which would allow education to respond and at the same time contribute to changes in society.

In the same year that the findings of the OECD investigators were made public (1976), another report critical of the DES was published, this time the work of the Parliamentary Expenditure Committee[3]. The two main complaints in this document were that the DES was excessively secretive and that it lacked an adequate planning organization. The preparation of the confidential Yellow Book in 1976 was probably a good example of the Department's *modus operandi* at that time, with the publication of a number of curriculum documents in the years that followed being indicative of the gradual development of a more open stance in policy-making.

It is sometimes suggested that the criticisms levelled at the DES in 1976 caused the bureaucrats to start making better use of HMI in the planning process. In fact, it could be argued that a much more positive participation by HMI in educational planning had already been initiated by H. W. French, Senior Chief Inspector in the period 1972–74, and then continued vigorously by his strong-minded successor Sheila Browne. According to Lawton and Gordon (1987a, p.25), this is only one example of a large number of misunderstandings concerning the role and influence of the Inspectorate:

As an institution, Her Majesty's Inspectorate of Schools is unique. No other country possesses a group of professional educational advisers who operate independently from the controlling central authority — the Department of Education and Science. HMI has a different status from the civil servants at the DES, partly because inspectors are professional educationists and partly because they are appointed, for historical reasons, by Order of the Queen in Council — on the recommendation of the Secretary of State. HM Inspectors are an extremely influential professional group. But their position is much misunderstood: their role is often confused with that of advisers and inspectors employed by local education authorities; their relationship to the DES is complex and ambiguous; their much proclaimed independence has frequently been challenged; on several occasions, the need for their continued existence has been questioned (*ibid.*, p.1).

Certainly, the relationship of the Inspectorate to the DES bureaucracy seems to have undergone a number of changes since 1944, with the status of the inspectors as independent professionals often coming under critical scrutiny from outside observers. When, for example, the Inspectorate was investigated by the 1967–68 Parliamentary Select Committee, the idea of its effective independence from the Department was soundly rejected:

Throughout our enquiry, we heard a good deal of evidence about the independence of the Inspectorate. We do not consider appointment by Her Majesty in Council to be of any great significance, although we recognize that it 'delights the people who enjoy it'. That HMI is wholly independent of the Department is a myth: the Department and the Inspectorate are a very integrated body. (Report of the Select Committee on Education and Science, p.xi)

Yet three years later, it was possible to argue that:

It is a basic weakness that the Department of Education and Science is not manned by persons with educational experience. Among comparable countries, our Department of Education is the only one devoid of educationists. I know that, when challenged, the Department point out that there is the Inspectorate, but the Department always makes a virtue of the in-dependence of the Inspectorate; and the plain fact is that the Inspectorate remains isolated from the administrative processes and decisions of the Department (Willey, 1971, p.2).

In a book written after the period of the Great Debate, Salter and Tapper described the inspectors as the 'organic intellectuals' of the DES. It was difficult, they argued, to avoid the impression that since 1976, the Inspectorate had become 'much more directly responsive to the Department's policy-making needs and much more alive to providing the right information at the right time' (Salter and Tapper, 1981, p.213). Although HMI was wary of becoming too obviously a slave of DES needs, its traditional independence from the Department was, in fact, being steadily eroded. As the 'organic intellectuals' of the Department, the Inspectors had the responsibility for ensuring that DES policies were legitimized in advance by the presentation of the appropriate evidence and arguments (*ibid.*, p.216). In short, HMI could be seen as part of the growing system of central control:

> If there is doubt . . . about the Department's ability to orchestrate policy change, where does that leave its territorial force, Her Majesty's Inspectorate? How far can HMI be regarded as the willing tool of the DES in its attempts to impose central definitions of desirable policy shift and how far is HMI an independent body with opinions and values of its own? Its position in the educational system as authoritative supplier of information both to the LEAs and schools on the one hand, and the DES on the other, is undoubtedly critical. At the local level, HMIs have the functions of inspectors of schools and colleges, interpreters of Department policy to the LEAs, and are members of numerous committees such as examination boards and regional advisory councils for further education . . . At the central level, they act as professional advisers to the DES, drawing on their network of local contacts, contribute to Department publications and staff Department courses for teachers. Any move by the DES to systematize further the process of policy construction is therefore dependent upon HMI to acquire and to disseminate the right information at the right time. This would imply that from the Department's point of view the closer the ties between itself and HMI the better . . .
>
> As the DES moves further in the direction of policy-making enclosure, so it must rely more on its internal means of information collecting rather than on information supplied by external groups. In this respect, the role of HMIs as the field representatives and data collection agents of the DES is bound to be crucial in its efforts to sustain this move . . . Suffice it to say . . . that whatever independence the Inspectorate still retains is likely to be further eroded in response to the requirements of the new style of policy-making; though the myth of autonomy may well be retained as long as possible, since it enhances the supposed objectivity of the information on which the Department rests its policy proposals. (*ibid.*, pp.109–11)

The 1981 Salter and Tapper thesis has been criticized by Lawton and Gordon (1987a, p.113) on the grounds that after 1976 HMI independence was, in fact, steadily increasing, not diminishing. This could be seen principally in the increasing confidence with which the Inspectorate published its views on the school curriculum, even though these were clearly at variance with the curriculum model favoured by the DES bureaucracy[4]. According to Lawton and Gordon (and it is a finding borne out by the research for this book), this was not a chance difference of opinion, but 'a fundamental question of educational as opposed to bureaucratic values' *(ibid.)*. Commentators have generally shown little understanding of the essential differences between a bureaucratic and a professional model of a national curriculum when they write as though a common and a core curriculum amount to the same thing in practice (see Chitty, 1988).

The third element in Lawton's central 'tension system' with an important role to play in educational policy-making is comprised of ministers and political advisers. For the purposes of this study, the all-important body is seen to be the Downing Street Policy Unit containing as it does some of the Prime Minister's most trusted political aides. It will be shown that educational reform has always been one of this body's chief concerns and that it has not been frightened to challenge DES orthodoxy.

The creation, in March 1974, of a Policy Unit, separate from the Central Policy Review Staff (CPRS) created by Edward Heath in 1970, has been described by Peter Hennessy (1986) as 'Harold Wilson's most important and, to date, durable innovation' (p.82). Under the direction of Dr. Bernard (now Lord) Donoughue from 1974 to 1979, it became, in Hennessy's words, 'a prime-ministerial cabinet in all but name' *(ibid.)*[5].

Donoughue himself was well aware of the potential role of the Unit as the 'eyes and ears' of the Prime Minister (which was Harold Wilson's own concept):

> The Policy Unit was the newest part of the Downing Street machine. Previous Prime Ministers had employed individual advisers. However, until Harold Wilson created the Policy Unit in 1974 there was no systematic policy analysis separate from the regular civil service machine and working solely for the Prime Minister. These are the three characteristics which distinguished the Policy Unit from what had existed before: it was systematic, it was separate from the Whitehall machine and it was solely working for the Prime Minister. This strengthening of the supportive mechanisms serving the Prime Minister has proved an important reform among the several contributions which Harold Wilson made to the effectiveness of British central government. It

is significant that not only did James Callaghan retain the Policy
Unit, but his Tory successor, Margaret Thatcher, continued and
strengthened it. (Donoughue, 1987, p.20)

The press release on the new Policy Unit issued from Downing Street
in 1974 stated that the Unit would 'assist in the development of the whole
range of policies contained in the government's programme, especially
those arising in the short and medium term'. This was an attempt to
distinguish it from the Central Policy Review Staff based in the Cabinet
Office which was more, although not exclusively, orientated to longer-term
policy horizons. Members of the Unit were specifically encouraged to
maintain regular liaison with the CPRS, with other special advisers
working for individual departmental ministers, with the chairmen of
policy committees of the Parliamentary Labour Party and with policy
specialists in party headquarters. An internal memorandum to Unit
members, drafted by Donoughue and cleared by Harold Wilson, described
the Unit's functions in detail:

> The Unit must ensure that the Prime Minister is aware of what is
> coming up from departments to Cabinet. It must scrutinize
> papers, contact departments, know the background to policy
> decisions, disputes and compromises, and act as an early warning
> system. The Unit may feed into the system ideas on policy which
> are not currently covered, or are inadequately covered . . . The
> Unit should feed in 'minority reforms' which departments may
> overlook, or which fall between departmental boundaries, or
> which are the subject of worthy but unsuccessful Private
> Members Bills. This is especially the case with issues which
> concern ordinary people (and of which Whitehall may be
> unaware).

The political dimension in the Unit's work was underlined:

> The Prime Minister has assumed responsibility as custodian of the
> Labour manifesto. The Unit must assist in that role, making sure
> that the manifesto is not contravened, nor retreated from,
> without proper discussion and advance warning . . . Throughout
> its policy work the Unit will clearly be aware of the political
> dimension in Government. It must maintain good relations with
> the party organization. The individual ministries must not be
> allowed to become isolated from the Government as a whole and
> lapse into 'traditional departmental views'. (*ibid.*, pp.21–2).

When Margaret Thatcher became Prime Minister in 1979, her initial inclination was to rely for political advice on her ministers and, by implication, for policy advice on their departments. She cut down the number and seniority of her political aides at No. 10 and reduced the size of the Policy Unit. Over the period of her term of office, however, she has revised this earlier judgment. Since the 1983 election, the role of the Policy Unit has widened considerably as part of the calculated move away from collective to presidential government. With the abolition of the CPRS in 1983, the Unit has developed into what Hennessy (1986) calls 'a shadow Whitehall' (p.194), with each of its members, led since 1985 by Professor Brian Griffiths[6], covering a clutch of subject areas — a distinct change from the free-ranging approach of the Unit's early days. These members now tend to be young, mainly in their 20s or 30s, with experience as civil servants, or in commerce or industry, or in the Conservative Research Department or in the Centre for Policy Studies. The person who held the education and training portfolio in the Unit in the period before the 1987 election was Oliver Letwin, who had previously been special adviser to Sir Keith Joseph at the DES[7].

These, then, are the three elements — the DES bureaucracy, the Inspectorate and the Downing Street Policy Unit — making up the central 'tension system' in the period under discussion in this book. The views of these three bodies have obviously changed over time. For our purposes, it is important to understand their general outlook at two key points: in 1976–77 and in 1987–88.

The educational outlook of the Policy Unit in 1976 was very much dominated by the views and personality of Donoughue himself. His chief concern was that the Right was making too much political capital out of a perceived decline in educational standards:

> My political finger-tips told me that unless we did something very soon, the whole state and comprehensive system would be discredited by its own failures. And that we had to pull it together pretty sharp[8].

Much of the blame, in Donoughue's view, lay with the teachers' unions in general and with the National Union of Teachers in particular:

> Educational policy was conducted by the local authorities and the teachers' unions with the Department of Education . . . being little more than a post-box between the two. A further problem was that each Minister was burdened with party policy commitments which were based on the assumption that all education problems would be solved by simply throwing money at them or, to be more precise, giving the cash to the teachers' unions. In fact

the latter, and especially the National Union of Teachers, had become a major part of the problem. In all my many dealings with the NUT . . . I never once heard mention of education or children. The Union's prime objective appeared to be to secure ever decreasing responsibilities and hours of work for its members, and it seemed that the ideal NUT world would be one where teachers and children never entered a school at all — and the executive of the NUT would be in a permanent conference session at a comfortable seaside hotel. (Donoughue, 1987, p.110)

These strong views about teachers and teaching standards, allied to equally strong criticisms from leading industrialists and employers, helped to convince Callaghan that something had to be done to rescue the comprehensive system from the grip of militants and progressives.

By 1987/88, the views of the Policy Unit had, of course, changed considerably. The consensus created by the Ruskin speech of October 1976 and confirmed by the publication of *Better Schools* in March 1985 (DES, 1985c) — built around more central control of the curriculum, greater teacher accountability and the more direct subordination of secondary education to the perceived needs of the economy — was hardly considered appropriate to the new radical thrust of the third Thatcher administration. For the Griffiths Policy Unit — which is said to act as a conduit between a number of right-wing pressure groups, particularly the Centre for Policy Studies, and the Prime Minister herself (see Gow, 1988)[9] — the chief objective of current policy-making would seem to be the complete privatization of the education system.

Turning to the second element in the 'tension system', the concern of the DES civil servants in 1976 for greater control of the school curriculum could be seen as part of their new-found interest in policy, efficiency and value for money. They felt the need to make themselves accountable for the state of the nation's schools. A senior DES civil servant, interviewed in the late 1970s, argued that the Secretary of State and the DES had to be accountable to the nation for the quality of the education service. And clearly no such accountability was possible without a central responsibility for standards and the curriculum:

Education is a national service (it is the first thing we teach our Secretary of State) and there are therefore legitimate concerns about education which are too great to allow to continue the present extent of local control and discretion. The other partners must accept the recent centralizing initiatives because the Secretary of State is the public embodiment of national expectations of central control and accountability. (Quoted in Ranson, 1980, p. 10)

At the same time, external economic circumstances complemented the internal bureaucratic dynamic by inspiring a widespread belief (to which the DES had to respond) that education should be geared more closely to the needs of the economy. There is evidence to suggest (see chapter 6) that the DES bureaucracy came to share the politicians' concern that, in a time of economic crisis, the views of employers and industrialists could no longer be ignored. The school curriculum in general, and the secondary-school curriculum in particular, could not, however, be channelled in new directions without the introduction of new lines of management planning and control.

It is not clear whether the DES bureaucracy has come to fully accept the politicians' desire to create a new consensus in the late 1980s. From the bureaucratic point of view, the creation of greater differentiation and choice clearly poses a number of serious administrative problems. Speaking at the Society of Education Officers' meeting at Lancaster in July 1988, Nick Stuart, Deputy Secretary at the DES, was enthusiastic about preparations for the National Curriculum but was anxious to play down the advantages for schools of seeking grant-maintained status (Hugill and Surkes, 1988).

The curriculum outlook of the Inspectorate would seem to have remained fairly consistent in the period under discussion. Many of the views on curriculum planning and construction to be found in *Curriculum 11–16*, the first of the so-called HMI Red Books published in March 1978 (DES, 1977c), can also be found in the Curriculum Matters pamphlet *The Curriculum from 5 to 16*, published in March 1985 (DES, 1985a)[10]. Yet it can be argued that the Inspectorate has been effectively marginalized since the resignation of Sir Keith Joseph as Education Secretary in May 1986 and that there is little sign of HMI influence in the construction of the framework for the 1987 National Curriculum. As late as April 1987 (the consultation document was published in July), Eric Bolton, Senior Chief Inspector since 1983, was arguing in vain that politicians and administrators should make greater use of HMI expertise:

It is silly politicians indeed who fly totally in the face of the best professional advice they can get. (Reported in *The Times Educational Supplement*, 17 April 1987)

Recent attacks by New Right pressure groups on the role and independence of HMI have caused Lawton and Gordon (1987a) to argue that:

One of the advantages of a national Inspectorate is that it can, and should, remain outside the realms of party politics. In recent years, there has been a tendency for education to become increasingly politicized, and it would be easy for HMI to be used by the government of the day for the implementation of political doctrines. It is most important that HMI retain their traditional independence in such matters, and also that they use their ability to pursue lines of enquiry, even if these are liable to cast doubt upon some aspects of government policy. (p.151)

In the light of the differing views of the bodies at the Centre and of the complex nature of centre-local relations, it is important to ask how and why educational policies have come to be formulated and implemented.

According to Sir William Pile, who was Permanent Under-Secretary of State at the DES from 1970 to 1976, moral, social and economic forces have been the main determining factors in the post-war history of the education service:

The history of a department of state like the Department of Education and Science cannot help but be largely a history of a developing education system and service. Looking back now over the thirty or so postwar years, the main determinants of educational development might be thought to have been successive ministers bringing with them into office explicit political commitments (and occasionally educational convictions), or the permanent officials who advise ministers during their terms of office from a base of professional skills, accumulated knowledge and a concern for the continuity of things. Yet in the final analysis, this is not perhaps the right first conclusion. Certainly ministers, and occasionally officials, by personal characteristics like clarity of mind, strength of character or instinctive tactical skills, have made distinctive contributions to the shaping of events. But in the matter of objectives, and often of the means to those ends, they have themselves been shaped by more deep-seated forces. The obscure tides of moral, social and economic change which have run with singular strength in the postwar years have in this sense been the main determining factors. (Pile, 1979, p.228)

Yet, while there is obvious merit in the Pile thesis, the view put forward in the chapters that follow is that at the two key points of 1976/77 and 1987/88, it was the politicians, or rather the government's political advisers, who took the lead in determining educational policy.

The Downing Street Policy Unit was certainly very active in 1976. It was the Policy Unit which secured the replacement of Sir William Pile by James Hamilton as Permanent Secretary at the DES (Donoughue, 1987, p.110); which drafted the questions to be asked of Fred Mulley by the Prime Minister at the interview which took place in May (Callaghan, 1987, p.409); which coordinated the various drafts of the Ruskin speech delivered by James Callaghan in October. It was the Policy Unit which initiated the idea of a Great Debate in education, even though the 1977 Green Paper in its final form was not as challenging and assertive as Donoughue himself would personally have wished[11].

The DES appeared to gain the ascendancy in the early 1980s when the civil servants successfully blocked Sir Keith Joseph's proposal for a new scheme of education vouchers. Yet, as Wilby has pointed out (1987, p.56), it is not clear whether Sir Keith was actually *defeated* by his civil servants or whether he himself came to realize that a 'market' in compulsory education was a logical impossibility[12].

If the arguments put forward by the DES bureaucracy did triumph over the pressures exerted by a number of right-wing political groups, it was a short-lived victory. The educational policies carried out by Kenneth Baker and his ministerial team since 1986 have been greatly influenced by the writings and speeches of a number of educationists, philosophers and economists often referred to collectively as the New Right. This body of thinkers, dispersed among a host of influential pressure groups, has a history going back to the 1950s, but it has pursued its objectives with exceptional vigour in the past ten years, aided by its easy access to the Downing Street Policy Unit and Prime Minister Margaret Thatcher and a friendly relationship with large sections of the media. It claims to have a coherent strategy for the economic and moral regeneration of Britain, in which education clearly has an important role to play. So great is its influence that many believe that any defence of the old orthodoxies will henceforth be a damage limitation exercise fought on the New Right's terms[13].

Salter and Tapper (1988) have traced the process by which the Right has sought since the early 1970s to reverse what Sir Keith Joseph described in a speech to the Oxford Union in December 1975 as 'the left-wing ratchet' (Joseph, 1976, p.21). In the 1970s, this largely meant reversing the *ideological* ratchet and two groups had a particularly important role to play in the process: the Centre for Policy Studies founded in 1974 by Sir Keith Joseph, Margaret Thatcher and Alfred Sherman and the Conservative Philosophy Group formed in the spring of 1975 by Roger Scruton and John Casey — then two academics at Peterhouse, Cambridge[14]. With the

election of a Conservative government in May 1979 the Right was in a
position to move beyond purely ideological struggle into the arena of
practical politics; although it was to be another eight years before the
Thatcher government felt strong enough to draft a bill incorporating all its
ideas for restructuring the education service. As Maclure (1988) has argued,
the Downing Street Policy Unit had an important role to play in the final
process of translating New Right ideology into practical policies:

> What eventually emerged in the 1987 election manifesto — and
> therefore ultimately in the 1988 Act — was assembled in secret in
> the nine months before the 1987 General Election. There was a
> determined effort *not* to consult either the DES or the civil
> servants or chief education officers or local politicians. Under the
> discreet eye of Professor Brian Griffiths, Head of the Prime
> Minister's Policy Unit, the outline of a radical reform was set
> down in bold lines from which there was no going back. (p.166)

The consensus created in 1976/77 had lasted for little more than ten
years. By 1988, the Government was so confident of its ability to crush all
opposition, there was no longer any need to create consensus.

Notes

1 The term 'education sub-government' was the one used by Manzer (1970, pp.1–2)
to describe what he called a 'tripartite structure' between the DES, local education
authorities and organized teachers. He argued that this structure was a sub-system
of the modern British political system and was the one in which most decisions
about national educational policy were made.
2 This OECD report was first published in *The Times Higher Educational
Supplement*, 9 May 1976 and is reprinted in Raggatt, P. and Evans, M. (Eds.)
(1977) *Urban Education 3: The Political Context*, pp.149–69.
3 Extracts from the Tenth Report of the Expenditure Committee are also reprinted in
Raggatt, P. and Evans, M. (Eds.) (1977) *Urban Education 3: The Political
Context*, pp.170–91.
4 These differences are explored at some length in chapter 4.
5 An interesting description of the Donoughue Policy Unit can be found in Jones,
G. W. (1985) 'The Prime Minister's Aides' in King, A. (Ed.) *The British Prime
Minister*, especially pages 82–4. Dr. Donoughue, former journalist, political
historian and lecturer at the London School of Economics had the status of a
temporary civil servant, paid from public funds.
6 A former Dean of the City University Business School, Professor Brain Griffiths is
also a Director of the Bank of England and Chairman of Christian Responsibility
in Public.
7 Oliver Letwin's somewhat eccentric views on the chief purposes of education can
be discovered in the Centre for Policy Studies pamphlet *Aims of Schooling: the
Importance of Grounding*, published in March 1988.

17

8 Interview with Bernard Donoughue, 16 January 1986. A fuller version of this section of the interview is to be found in chapter 2.

9 According to David Gow (1988), the CPS pamphlet *Correct Core* prepared by Sheila Lawlor was 'compulsory bedtime reading' for the Prime Minister in March 1988.

10 This is discussed at some length in chapter 4.

11 All these issues are discussed in greater detail in chapters 2 and 3.

12 This is discussed further in chapter 7.

13 The composition and views of the various New Right pressure groups were analysed by Peter Wilby and Simon Midgley in an article entitled 'As the New Right wields its power' published in *The Independent*, 23 July 1987.

14 Roger Scruton moved on to become the editor of *The Salisbury Review*, a quarterly of extreme Conservative thought founded in 1982, and a prominent member of the Hillgate Group. In an interview published in *The Times Higher Educational Supplement* (22 July 1988), he argued that 'the Education Bill grew out of discussion by the Hillgate Group, which itself grew out of *The Salisbury Review*'. His educational ideas are analysed in chapter 8.

Chapter 1

The Evolution of the Comprehensive School: 1944–76

It can be argued that the post-war campaign for comprehensive education in Britain has passed through a number of phases — not all of them directly related to the political complexion of the government in power. Over forty years have now elapsed since the passing of the Butler Education Act of 1944, and in that time a number of new theories and practices have surfaced to acquire a transient popularity, while many others have been discredited and effectively discarded. Having said that, it is, of course, highly dangerous to suggest that any reform movement can be divided up into neat periods each with its own distinct flavour and outlook. If we think in terms of phases or periods — and this chapter makes use of 1965 as a suitable turning-point in the analysis — they are clearly to a large extent arbitrary, and can be justified only as an artificial device for making a complex subject more manageable.

The 1944 Act established secondary education for all pupils as an integral part of an educational system which was to be seen as a continuous process — ranging from the primary sector to further education (Education Act, 1944). The twenty years following its implementation down to 1965 — the first of our arbitrary phases — saw the comprehensive movement very much in its infancy, when a number of committed teachers and educationists campaigned for the abolition of the 11 + and for the introduction of the common secondary school. It was also very much a grass-roots movement, with no encouragement, and often fierce opposition, from central government. A number of the urban comprehensives built during this period were very large institutions (one or two with over 2000 pupils), since only large schools were thought to be capable of producing sixth-forms of a viable size, with the added 'bonus' that a wide assortment of options could then be offered to pupils in years 4 and 5. Yet by 1960, the number of pupils in comprehensive schools in England and Wales still amounted to less than 5 per cent of the secondary school population (Benn and Simon, 1972, p. 102).

The morale of the reformers and innovators was obviously given a marked boost by the election in October 1964 of a Labour government (albeit with a tiny majority) returned on a programme which included a promise to introduce comprehensive education. Yet the period 1965 to the early 1970s began with the acceptance of comprehensive reorganization as a largely *institutional* reform, as if comprehensive schools were simply a good thing *in themselves.* Circular 10/65, for example, declaring the Government's intention 'to end selection at 11+ and to eliminate separatism in secondary education', was concerned primarily with the *mechanics* of reorganization — with outlining the various schemes which would be acceptable as comprehensive systems (DES, 1965, pp.1–6).

What was clearly lacking in the late 1960s and early 1970s was a national debate about the kind of education a comprehensive school could be expected to provide. It is true that a number of teachers were anxious to plan new courses, particularly for those children labelled 'non-academic' or 'Newsom' (following the publication of the *Newsom Report* in 1963); but there was comparatively little evidence of the development of radically new approaches to the secondary school curriculum. The Schools Council for Curriculum and Examinations had been established in 1964, but, while initiating some innovative projects, was predisposed towards a piecemeal, subject-centred view of the curriculum with most of its schemes designed for only *part* of the ability range. Even books and articles welcoming the movement towards mixed-ability teaching and flexible grouping had little to say about the content and purpose of the curriculum *as a whole* (see, for example, Chitty, 1969, pp.2–8).

Then in 1976, the so-called Great Debate inaugurated by James Callaghan's Ruskin College speech, and the campaign to 'preserve' educational standards, coincided with the start of a concerted effort by the DES and HMI to win teachers and local authorities over to the idea of a more unified curriculum for the comprehensive school. Although it has been argued by a number of commentators (for example: CCCS, 1981, p.218; Hargreaves, 1982, p.219; Dale, 1983, p.243; Ball, 1984, p.7) that the Callaghan initiative was little more than a thinly-disguised attempt to wrest the populist mantle from the Conservatives, pandering to perceived public disquiet at the alleged prevalence of soft-centred progressivism, the result was, in fact, to wean a number of comprehensives away from the narrow curriculum traditions derived from the grammar and modern schools (for example see Holt, 1983a, pp.109–67). Ten years or so later, it remains, of course, to be seen whether or not school-based curriculum development can come to terms with a national curriculum framework imposed from the centre.

It is the aim of this introductory chapter to look at the first two phases in the history of the comprehensive school (1944–65 and 1965–76) in some detail — and particularly from the point of view of curriculum development — in order to provide an historical framework for the material that follows in later chapters.

Yet it needs to be stated, right at the outset, that a serious problem presents itself to anyone contemplating a brief historical survey of the secondary school curriculum. Any historical treatment has, of necessity, to take account of at least two major developments: the evolution of DES and HMI thinking on the curriculum as outlined in official documents and circulars; and the implementation of change within the schools themselves as some ideas are taken up and others are ignored or rejected. As Donald has pointed out (Donald, 1979, p.13), 'the obvious disparities between what the Department of Education and Science says ought to be happening and what is actually going on in schools are usually explained in common-sensical terms of a time-lag, or of the incompetence and/or obstruction of teachers, administrators and students'. Yet we, in fact, know very little about the relationship between the *formulation* of policy and its actual *implementation*. It is all too easy to assume either that all new theories are eventually translated into practice or that all DES policy statements are viewed at classroom level with cynicism and mistrust. Salter and Tapper (1981) have argued that 'in the present-day redefining of the educational system, the increasing power of the DES stems from its ability to provide some substance as to what the new goals of schooling should be and how the educational system should be reshaped to fulfil these' (p.43). In their view, educational change occurs within three inter-related arenas:

> The first is the redefinition of the social ends of education and the restructuring of the experiences of schooling designed to achieve them. The second is the allocation of resources which will flow in the direction of those schooling experiences which apparently achieve those goals defined as necessary, and away from those schooling experiences deemed to be either redundant or at least not meriting state support. The third is the struggle between institutions for educational power. (*ibid.*, p.45)

Yet this essentially macro view of the forces behind educational change tells us little about the *effectiveness* of government initiatives, particularly in relation to the curriculum where, until recently, the DES has not been in a position to exercise direct control and has been forced to rely instead on exhortatory documents.[1]

The fact is that full-scale investigations into secondary schooling in general, or comprehensive schooling in particular, have been remarkably few in number: the NFER (National Foundation for Eductional Research) surveys of the late sixties and early seventies written up in three reports (Monks, 1968 and 1970; Ross, Bunton, Evison and Robertson, 1972); the research carried out by Caroline Benn and Brian Simon for the two editions of their book *Half Way There* (Benn and Simon, 1970 and 1972); and the HMI survey of secondary schools (grammar and secondary modern as well as comprehensive) published in December 1979 (DES, 1979a). Case studies of individual schools tell us little about general trends; and can be used only to illustrate developments which other sources tell us are widespread. The following account attempts to avoid the pitfall of assuming that the schools most written about (see, for example, Fletcher, Caron and Williams, 1985) are representative of the comprehensive movement as a whole.

From the 1944 Act to *Circular 10/65*

The 1944 Act sought to extend educational opportunity by providing free secondary education for all. It has been described as 'probably the greatest single advance in English educational history, its provisions showing real breadth of outlook and considerable educational vision' (Evans, 1985, p.109). Yet it is easy to exaggerate its beneficial effects. Although it came to be regarded by many as a cornerstone of the Welfare State, it could be argued that it had a number of weaknesses and shortcomings which undermined its good intentions. Above all, it provided no clear definition of the *content* or *structure* of secondary education. It has been pointed out that 'the word "curriculum" does not appear in the 1944 Act. There is no statutory requirement for the inclusion of any subject in the school timetable except that of religious education' (Aldrich and Leighton, 1985, p.55). With regard to structure, the initial assumptions favoured a bipartite or tripartite system, even though comprehensive schools were not officially proscribed. One interpretation of section 8, referring to the provision of opportunities for all pupils 'in view of their different ages, abilities and aptitudes, and of the different periods for which they may be expected to remain at school', ensured that secondary reform of a radical nature was deferred for many years. At the same time, the ambiguity in the wording of the Act meant that when the pressure for reform became almost irresistible in the 1960s, it could be carried out by reinterpreting the formula without the need for further legislation. Attention was drawn to this possibility, even while the Bill was under discussion, by an experienced educational administrator, J. Chuter Ede, the Labour Parliamentary

Secretary to the Board of Education. 'I do not know where people get the idea about three types of school', he said, in a speech in April 1944, 'because I have gone through the Bill with a small toothcomb, and I can find only one school for senior pupils and that is a secondary school. What you like to make of it will depend on the way you serve the precise needs of the individual area in the country' (*The Times*, 14 April 1944 quoted in Rubinstein and Simon, 1973, p.31).

The absence of any curriculum guidelines in the 1944 Act was defended by R. A. Butler (since 1941, President of the Board of Education) in a debate in the House of Commons on the grounds that general responsibility for running the secondary schools rested with headteachers, governing bodies and local education authorities:

> I will begin by saying that the local education authority, as I see it, will have responsibility for the broad type of education given in the secondary schools . . . The governing body would, in our view, have the general direction of the curriculum as actually given from day to day, within the school. The headteacher would have, again in our view, responsibility for the internal organization of the school, including the discipline that is necessary to keep the pupils applied to their study, and to carry out the curriculum in the sense desired by the governing body . . . We . . . suggest that, in future, major changes in the curriculum should be brought formally before the local education authority and the governors, and not done in some chance way. (*Hansard*, H. of C., Vol. 397, Cols. 2363-4, 10 March 1944)

With the removal of the constraints of the Regulations which had operated since 1902, the 1944 Act ushered in what Lawton has called 'the Golden Age of teacher control (or non-control) of the curriculum' (Lawton, 1980, p.22). This lasted for at least twenty years; and if it was not a great age of curriculum innovation, that was partly because any individual initiatives would have to be severely limited in scope owing to the very nature of the divided system itself.

That system was, in fact, justified in that it reflected admirably the view outlined in the *Norwood Report* of 1943 that there were three 'rough groupings' of children with different 'types of mind'. For these three groups three types of curriculum were needed each with its own particular bias:

> In a wise economy of secondary education, pupils of a particular type of mind would receive the training best suited for them and that training would lead them to an occupation where their capacities would be suitably used; that a future occupation is

already present to their minds while they are still at school has been suggested, though admittedly the degree to which it is present varies. Thus, to the three main types . . . there would correspond three main types of curriculum, which we may . . . attempt to indicate.

First, there would be a curriculum of which the most characteristic feature is that it treats the various fields of knowledge as suitable for coherent and systematic study for their own sake apart from immediate considerations of occupation, though at a later stage, grasp of the matter and experience of the methods belonging to those fields may determine the area of choice of employment and may contribute to success in the employment chosen.

The second type of curriculum would be closely, though not wholly, directed to the special data and skills associated with a particular kind of occupation; its outlook and its methods would always be bounded by a near horizon clearly envisaged. It would thus be closely related to industry, trades and commerce in all their diversity.

In the third type of curriculum, a balanced training of mind and body and a correlated approach to humanities, natural science and the arts would provide an equipment varied enough to enable pupils to take up the work of life: its purpose would not be to prepare for a particular job or profession, and its treatment would make a direct appeal to interests, which it would awaken by practical touch with affairs.

Of the first, it may be said that it may or may not look forward to university work; if it does, that is because the universities are traditionally concerned with the pursuit of knowledge as such. Of the second, we should say that it may or may not look forward to the universities, but that it should increasingly be directed to advanced studies in so far as the universities extend their orbit in response to the demands of the technical branches of industry. (SSEC, 1943, p.4)

Significantly, the *Norwood Report* goes on to say: 'we have treated secondary education as that phase of education in which differences between pupils receive the consideration due to them' (*ibid.*, p.4).

It might be thought that the philosophy behind such statements would be totally unacceptable to a large section of the working-class and trade union movement. In 1942 both the Labour Party Conference and the Trades Union Congress had, after all, given their official support to the idea of a common school as the basis for secondary education for all (Evans, 1985, p.115). Yet the divided system sanctioned by the findings of the *Norwood Report* was not effectively challenged largely owing to a lack of enthusiasm for the common or comprehensive school on the part of the Labour leadership which saw the state grammar school (now at last opened completely to talent) as providing the best answer to the competition of the independent public schools.

Despite a reputation for strong radical sympathies, Ellen Wilkinson, the first Labour Minister of Education in the Attlee post-war administration, made little attempt to challenge the prevailing philosophy of her Ministry which embraced a firm commitment to a tripartite system of secondary education (grammar, technical and modern schools) and a deep mistrust of multilateral and comprehensive schools. The new Minister was herself a working-class product of the state education system; and it has been argued that this probably coloured her outlook (Simon, 1974, p.284). Whatever the motivation, she made her position perfectly clear soon after her appointment, at a meeting in London. It was not her intention 'to destroy the grammar schools. They were the pioneers of secondary education and . . . it would be folly to injure them. The most urgent need in the field of new development was an adequate number of modern secondary schools because more than half the children of secondary age would attend these schools' (*Education*, 2 October 1945 quoted in Fenwick, 1976, p.54).

The new Minister did little to appease her critics by her refusal to repudiate the views expressed in *The Nation's Schools*, the first pamphlet issued by the post-war Ministry. This had actually been written *before* Ellen Wilkinson took office; but its publication in 1945 provoked a deep rift between the Minister and her more radical supporters. For one thing, it echoed the conclusions of the *Norwood Report*, advocating 'three broad types' of secondary school to meet 'the differing needs of different pupils'. But it went even further by declaring that the education of vast numbers of children in the secondary modern schools was to be determined by the fact that their 'future employment will not demand any measure of technical skill or knowlege'. Where multilateral schools were concerned, these should be restricted to 'sparsely populated districts', though there might be room for 'judicious experiments' elsewhere (Ministry of Education, 1945, pp.13, 21 and 22–3).

The document came in for bitter criticism at the 1946 Labour Party Conference where the Minister suffered a major defeat and was forced to concede that it would not be reprinted. Nevertheless, the pamphlet which eventually replaced it voiced substantially the same opinions. *The New*

Secondary Education, as it was called, published in 1947, once more summarized the Norwood Committee's theories about the three types of mind, and stressed the need for the corresponding three types of school. This pamphlet clearly reflected Ministry thinking over a considerable period, and was reprinted unaltered as late as 1958 (Rubinstein and Simon, 1973, p.36).

According to Morgan (1984) 'Ellen Wilkinson embodied Labour's instinctive faith in the grammar schools, the bright working-class child's alternative to Eton and Winchester' (p.174). She was certainly not prepared to respond to pressure from the National Union of Teachers or from the National Association of Labour Teachers to indulge in multi-lateral or comprehensive experiments on a large scale. 'I want to make it clear', she told the House of Commons in 1946, 'that there is no antagonism in my mind to the idea of multilateral or bilateral schools . . . but I do want to see the proposals are properly worked out and that the schools do not become unreasonably large' (*Hansard*, H. of C., Vol. 424, Cols. 1811–2, 1 July 1946 quoted in Vernon, 1982, p.217). Nor did she accept the argument, common on the Left, that the tripartite system was socially and education-ally divisive. In her view, the provision of one-third of a pint of milk free to all pupils under 18 could be seen as 'a culmination of our (the Labour Party's) promise to do away with class distinction'. And this was a point she re-emphasized at the 1946 Labour Party Conference where she declared: 'Free milk will be provided in Hoxton and Shoreditch, in Eton and Harrow. What more social equality can you have than that?' (quoted in Vernon, 1982, p.214).

Ellen Wilkinson's successor in office, George Tomlinson, followed the same general policies. It has been pointed out (Fenwick, 1976) that 'the new Minister went out of his way, in the 1947 (House of Commons) debate on the education vote, to emphasize "that it is no part of our policy to reduce in any way the status or standing of the grammar school" ' (p.57). In 1950 Tomlinson warned that 'the (Labour) Party are kidding themselves if they think that the comprehensive idea has any popular appeal' (quoted in Parkinson, 1970, p.47). As far as curriculum matters were concerned, his attitude appears to have been one of complete indifference and he is remembered chiefly for his often quoted remark on the Minister's lack of a role in school curriculum planning[2]. According to his biographer, Fred Blackburn (1954), he had a limited vision of his task at Education, so that during his term as Minister from 1947 to 1951, the general lines of government policy were invariably determined by Ministry officials. When the Labour government fell in 1951, *The Times Educational Supplement* wrote, approvingly, that it was 'extremely doubtful whether Mr.

Tomlinson ever once lifted a hand' to increase the number of comprehensive schools (19 October 1951, quoted in Rubinstein and Simon, 1973, pp.39–40). In fact, six years of Labour rule had resulted in the actual establishment of some thirteen comprehensive schools which accounted for less than 0.5 per cent of the secondary school population (Evans, 1985, p.115).

Yet, despite the wholesale approval it received in official documents, the tripartite system was never fully realized in practice. Priority was given to establishing the new system of secondary modern schools, while the majority of local authorities were reluctant to spend the money necessary to develop secondary technical schools. This caution may have resulted from a certain amount of confusion as to the exact function of these schools, or it may have been due to the cost of the equipment required. Whatever the reason, as late as 1958, secondary technical schools still accounted for less than 4 per cent of the secondary age-group. The structure that emerged was, therefore, in reality, a bipartite system comprising grammar schools on the one hand and modern schools on the other — the former taking, in 1950, one in five of all children at 11 (Rubinstein and Simon, 1973, pp.40–1).

At the same time, the introduction of common or comprehensive schools was being actively discouraged. Experimentation was to be restricted to the development of a few multilateral schools where 'grammar' and 'secondary modern' pupils (and sometimes 'technical' as well) would be educated on the same site while following different curricula and possibly housed in separate buildings. The Ministry further stipulated that multilateral schools must be large establishments of at least 1600 pupils. Circular 144, issued in June 1947, argued that a multilateral school must provide effective education of all three types; to do this, it needed as a minimum a ten-form entry of around 300 pupils, divided into two 'grammar' streams, two 'technical' streams and six or seven 'modern' streams. Comprehensive schools, if they were to offer a sufficient variety of courses, must be of a similar size — although the terms 'grammar', 'technical' and 'modern' would not be required (Ministry of Education, 1947, p.3). When Middlesex proposed a rapid transition to comprehensive education by making use at first of existing buildings, the plan was rejected by the Ministry in 1949 for two main reasons: first, the schools proposed were too small and second, the 'logical' way of dealing with different 'types' of children was by providing different 'types' of school. London, on the other hand, was able to press ahead, in 1946/47, with the establishment of five 'interim' comprehensive schools by merging selective central schools with modern schools and making use of existing buildings, each school comprising about 1200 pupils (Rubinstein and Simon, 1973, p.47).

It would, of course, be wrong to suggest that the Labour government was being subjected to enormous pressure to promote 'comprehensive' or 'multilateral' experiments throughout the country, or, indeed, that curriculum reform was a priority for any particular political party or interest group. Radical opinion was vocal but it was not widespread. According to Vernon (1982) 'in all fairness, there was no groundswell of enthusiasm for multilateralism within the Labour Party as a whole' (p.217). In his survey of policy-making in secondary education from 1944 to 1970, Fenwick (1976) suggests that:

> The most significant aspect of parliamentary pressure for comprehensive schools at this time (1945–51) is its relative insignificance; no more than half a dozen Labour MPs came out in support of comprehensive schools throughout the first Labour government. (p.58)

Fenwick goes on to concede that 'the supporters of comprehensives could look to Labour Party conferences for support when they claimed that "we shall never let this issue die; we shall always raise it" '. But even here, it seems, the influence of the radicals was not overwhelming. A few years later, in October 1953, Richard Crossman noted how Labour Party Conference delegates were relatively 'conservative' on educational matters: 'nearly all the delegates either were at grammar school or have their children at grammar schools, and are not quite so susceptible to the romantic Socialism of the 1920s' (quoted in Morgan, 1981, p.270).

The post-war Labour Party was clearly in considerable confusion over the exact meaning and implications of the concept of 'secondary education for all'. The principal kind of school providing a secondary education in the inter-war period had, after all, been the grammar school. As long ago as 1922, the Socialist thinker R. H. Tawney had argued, in his influential *Secondary Education for All*, that there was no defence for a system whereby only middle-class children had the opportunity to benefit from a grammar school education. In his words 'the very assumption on which it (the system) is based, that all that the child of the workers needs is "elementary education" — as though the mass of the people, like anthropoid apes, had fewer convolutions in their brains than the rich — is in itself a piece of insolence' (Tawney, 1922, p.33). Part of the antagonism aroused by the 1945 document *The Nation's Schools* (Ministry of Education, 1945) can be attributed to its assertions that there was no need to expand the provision of grammar school places beyond the pre-war limit — and that there was actually something to be said for making a reduction.

For all those who equated the concept of a 'secondary education for all' with one of a 'grammar school education for all', this was sheer heresy. The grammar school was seen by many as 'the main avenue of occupational and social mobility for working-class children' (Parkinson, 1970, p.48).

What happened to those who were not suited to a strictly academic secondary education was hardly taken into consideration. Consciously or not, the aim was, as Vaizey (1966) has put it, 'to identify the one clever child in a big group and rescue it' (p.115). This would seem to be a variation of Tawney's wry description of social inequality as an endorsement of 'the Tadpole Philosophy' whereby 'intelligent tadpoles reconcile themselves to the inconveniences of their position' by reflecting that character and hard work can enable a select few of their number to 'rise to be frogs' (Tawney, 1951, p.105). In these circumstances, there was a sense in which radicals in the Labour Party who advocated the idea of common, unsegregated secondary education were seen as actually *betraying* the interest of those working-class children who wanted to climb the 'ladder of opportunity'.

The cautious approach of the Attlee government at least ensured that, nationally, the organization of secondary education was not a source of conflict between the main political parties in the early post-war years. The comprehensive school did not figure in the 1950 election manifestoes and was an issue of only minor importance in the second election of 1951 which gave victory to the Conservative Party (Rubinstein and Simon, 1973, p.50). It was, in fact, only in 1951, when they were on the verge of electoral defeat, that the Labour leadership produced *A Policy for Secondary Education* and came out (albeit somewhat hesitantly) in favour of comprehensive education, thereby turning the issue into one of party politics (Fenwick, 1976, pp.62-3 and 73; Evans, 1985, p.115).

Yet, despite the hostile attitude of the 1945-51 Labour government and of the Conservative administrations which followed it (at least until the appointment of Sir Edward Boyle as Minister of Education in July 1962), the number of comprehensive schools in England and Wales steadily grew, from the ten that had been created by 1950 to the 262 in existence in 1965 (Benn and Simon, 1972, p.102). According to Simon (1985):

> It is worth noting ... that comprehensive secondary education was originally a grass-roots movement in Britain, the first schools being established in the late 1940s or early 1950s by certain advanced local authorities in opposition to government policy and advice, whether that government was Labour (as it was from 1945 to 1951) or Tory (1951 to 1964). (pp.26-7)

At the time local autonomy did not always go unchallenged. In 1954, for example, the Minister of Education, Florence Horsbrugh, refused to permit the London County Council to close Eltham Hill Girls' Grammar School and transfer these 'selected' pupils to Kidbrooke School, its first new purpose-built comprehensive (Simon, 1955, p.45; Fenwick, 1976, pp.97–9; Pedley, 1978, p.48). Her successor, Sir David Eccles, shortly after taking office late in 1954, took an early opportunity to reassure the grammar school lobby that reorganization was not acceptable to the Conservative Party. In setting the pattern of secondary education, he said:

> One must choose between justice and equality, for it is impossible to apply both principles at once. Those who support comprehensive schools prefer equality. Her Majesty's present government prefer justice. My colleagues and I will never agree to the assassination of the grammar schools. (*The Schoolmaster*, 7 January 1955 quoted in Rubinstein and Simon, 1973, pp.70–1)

It has to be emphasized that respect for the grammar school tradition and the grammar school curriculum was by no means confined to the Conservative Party and its representatives at Westminster. It continued to be an important feature of Labour Party thinking — even after the first tentative endorsement of the comprehensive school in 1951. Indeed, it was evident right through the period of the 1950s — despite the publication of *Challenge to Britain* in 1953 and *Learning to Live* in 1958 which embraced more positive proposals for the reorganization of secondary education along comprehensive lines (Fenwick, 1976, pp.76 and 109). Since Labour leaders had fought so hard to provide grammar school places for the children of the working classes, these institutions — middle-class in ethos though many of them might be — were not to be surrendered lightly. A grammar school education was something to be proud of — not a source of shame. Lloyd George had, after all, once described Pengam Grammar School as the 'Eton of Wales' (quoted in Morgan, 1981, p.106). Opposition to plans for comprehensive reorganization was expressed with some vigour in a bitter comment on the thinking of some Labour politicians by the late Emmanuel (Manny) Shinwell in a letter he wrote to *The Times* in June:

> We are afraid to tackle the public schools to which wealthy people send their sons, but at the same time we are ready to throw overboard the grammar schools, which are for many working-class boys the stepping-stones to universities and a useful career. I would rather abandon Eton, Winchester, Harrow and all the rest of them than sacrifice the advantage of the grammar school. (Letter to *The Times*, 26 June 1958 quoted in Parkinson, 1970, p.85)

The writer and broadcaster Edward Blishen taught in a secondary modern school in a neglected, deprived part of London from 1949 until the late fifties, and he was made well aware of working-class admiration for what the grammar schools had to offer.

> What does 'secondary education' mean? In the districts with which I am familiar, the people, justly enough, take it to mean grammar-school education. ('I mean, this isn't a secondary school', said a parent to me once, stubbornly incognisant of the signboard at the school entrance.) And they don't precisely mean grammar-school education in its every detail. They have in mind the fact that grammar schools take their pupils somewhere, strengthen them, and add to them, palpably and measurably. The grammar school has managed to become something much more than a place to which you have, by law, to send your child for a specified period. It's a road that forks out in many directions, not one that comes to a single dead end. (Blishen, 1957, p.75)

These illuminating comments were later confirmed by Taylor (1963):

> It is clear that, for the working-class child, the grammar school not only provides education that makes upward social and occupational mobility practicable, but also furnishes an educational and social environment which encourages the formulation of upwardly mobile vocational aspirations. (p.80)

The secondary modern schools seem, by contrast, to have had very few supporters. Indeed, they were dismissed as failures almost as soon as they were born. A common criticism in the post-war period claimed that they were merely the old elementary schools writ large. As contemporary observers made clear (for example: Dent, 1958; Taylor, 1963), they faced a real problem in that, unlike the grammar and public schools, they lacked a clear sense of their aims and objectives. Should they opt for a diluted version of the traditional grammar school curriculum, particularly for their more able pupils, or should they plan something completely different with little or no regard to the demands created by entering youngsters for external examinations?

The dilemma was highlighted in a special inset devoted to secondary modern schools in *The Times Educational Supplement* of 8 June 1956. The teachers, it said, had had 'to fashion a new sort of school, knowing all the while that it was being measured against the old . . . to build a new Jerusalem with one hand and fend off the critics with the other'. Clearly, there was no shortage of opinions as to what the secondary modern school should be trying to achieve:

Never were labourers in the vineyard subject to so much advice. The secondary modern school has been the target of every new-fangled theory, every half-digested, ill-assorted idea . . . if ever it has seen a settled objective, half the busybodies in the world of education have rushed in to save it from itself. Turn out citizens. Turn out literates. Turn out technicians. Be more vocational. Prepare for leisure. Stick to the wider view . . . The wonder is that with all this, and with all the difficulties of the post-war world, the secondary modern schools have got anywhere at all . . . But they have. (*The Times Educational Supplement*, 8 June 1956 quoted in Dent, 1958, pp.xi–xii)

For some educationists and politicians, there was simply no room in the modern school curriculum for the acquisition of the cognitive-intellectual skills associated with the grammar schools. And this attitude was clearly implicit in a contribution from the Conservative politician Quintin Hogg (now Lord Hailsham) to a debate in the House of Commons in January 1965:

I can assure Hon. Members opposite that if they would go to study what is now being done in good secondary modern schools, they would not find a lot of pupils biting their nails in frustration because they had failed the 11 + . The pleasant noise of banging metal and sawing wood would greet their ears and a smell of cooking with rather expensive equipment would come out of the front door to greet them. They would find that these boys and girls were getting an education tailor-made to their desires, their bents and their requirements . . . I am not prepared to admit that the party opposite has done a good service to education, or to the children of this country, by attacking that form of school, or seeking to denigrate it. (*Hansard*, H. of C., Vol. 705, Cols. 423–4, 21 January 1965)

Yet it would be quite wrong to suggest that the secondary modern curriculum was totally dominated by practical and vocational activities. From the outset, a number of these schools had sought to prepare their more able pupils for the School Certificate; and after 1951 entries for the new GCE 'O' level examination steadily grew. The inevitability of this development has been highlighted by Broadfoot (1979):

With all their manifest disadvantages, the central role of external examinations in determining career opportunities made it impossible for the secondary modern schools to remain uninvolved in the competition, for not only did parents and pupils push for at least the chance to compete, the status and morale of the school itself became increasingly dependent on how well its pupils did academically, in a vain imitation of the traditionally high status grammar school. (p.40)

As Taylor has confirmed (1963), it was clearly a situation which encouraged the development of the modern school as a meritocratic institution:

> The widespread acceptance of examinations in modern schools, whilst enabling the school to enhance its prestige as an educational institution and to satisfy the aspirations of many parents and pupils, has also tended to encourage a degree of competition between and within schools, and perhaps too great a dependence upon 'paper qualifications' as an index of success. (p.28)

At the same time, the successes secured by secondary modern candidates had the obvious and immediate effect of exposing the fallibility of the 11+ selection procedure. It was now clear that it was quite impossible to say, from the results of mental tests applied at the age of 10 or 11, what a child's future accomplishments might be. It was also difficult to argue that every child was born with a given quota of 'intelligence' which remained constant throughout his or her life and that this key quality was a direct product of genetic endowment and not therefore susceptible to any educational influence.

One secondary modern school for girls serving a working-class district in a large industrial city, which took in only pupils who had failed to get into either a grammar or a selective central school, entered two girls for the GCE examination in 1954 both of whom gained five passes; one had had an IQ of 97 on entry to the school in 1949, the other an IQ of 85. (An IQ of 115 or over was generally considered necessary in order to profit from examination courses.) Other schools were soon in a position to tell similar success stories, so that it became increasingly difficult to uphold the standpoint of the psychometrists (Simon, 1955, pp.64–6). Even *Black Paper Two*, published in the 1960s, carried an article by Dr Rhodes Boyson accepting, albeit in cautious terms, the case against selection:

> There is no doubt that the 11+ test made considerable mistakes, that very many secondary modern school pupils can undertake academic work and that the arrangements for transfer within the tripartite system were unsatisfactory. (Boyson, 1969, p.57)

This was one of the factors which helped to create a climate of opinion favourable to widespread acceptance of the solution offered by the common secondary or comprehensive school. At the same time, a number of sociological surveys (notably: Glass, 1954; Floud, Halsey and Martin, 1956) revealed a direct relationship between social class and educational opportunities and made it clear that the selective system resulted in a great wastage of ability. This was at a time when technological change and economic advance were making new demands on the educational system and emphasizing the need to raise the educational level of the population as a whole. In other words, the divided system of secondary education was both socially disruptive and at the same time an anachronism in an age which demanded an educated workforce and put a premium on skills and specialization. As Hunter (1984) has observed, isolating economic prosperity as the determining factor:

> In a period of growing GNP, it was possible to support the two potentially opposing objectives: that secondary schooling should work towards creating greater social justice and equality within society *and* be an investment in creating a more efficient work-force. (p.274)

Yet it can be argued that it was the concern of middle-class parents about the shortcomings of the divided system and the hazards of selection which was to prove *the* decisive factor in the move to comprehensive education, and that it was middle-class support for change which largely influenced the *precise nature* of the comprehensive reform once the Labour Party was returned to power in 1964.

In a conversation with Professor Maurice Kogan, written up in *County Hall: The Role of the Chief Education Officer* published in 1973, a chief education officer for Leeds agreed that 'pressure for comprehensive schools came from middle-class parents anxious that their children might not get selective education and therefore wanting to do away with the 11+' (Kogan, 1973, p.172). Further support for this viewpoint came from Sir Edward Boyle, Conservative Minister of Education from 1962 to 1964, who also argued that 'the pressure for a comprehensive system has come largely from within the broad middle band of society (Boyle, 1972, p.36). In his 1972 article, he recalled reducing a Monday Club audience to momentary silence by asking: 'How many of you know, personally, a single professional-class parent who allows his child to attend a secondary modern school when he can buy him out of it?' To Edward Boyle, it seemed obvious that it was the growth of a 'middle income' society which would make a bipartite system less politically viable and that it was in

Conservative areas that the changes would have to be made. The creation of more grammar schools would further depress the neighbouring secondary moderns; and the only other means, in Boyle's view, of preserving a bipartite system would have been the encouragement of GCE courses in *all* secondary modern schools *from the first*.

In that respect, the Conservative government's 1958 White Paper, *Secondary Education for All: A New Drive*, with its new awareness of greater attainment potential among the mass of children of secondary school age, simply came too late. Reforming and improving the secondary modern schools was no longer the answer. A significant number of 'middle income' parents now realized that they could clearly become the chief 'beneficiaries' of reorganization provided the new comprehensives could be organized along lines which suited the perceived requirements of their children.[3]

In 1960 a group of middle-class parents in Cambridge formed an Association for the Advancement of State Education. Aware of the shortcomings of selection and of the low esteem enjoyed by the vast majority of secondary modern schools, they made it their business to focus public attention on the need to reorganize the state system. They were generally well-informed about educational issues and articulate in expressing their views. So great was their influence that other associations were soon formed in various parts of the country, eventually joining together in the Confederation for the Advancement of State Education (CASE). Pressure on local officials and councillors, on politicians and other public figures, was applied steadily and with growing effect. At last parents were demanding and getting a real say in the kind of education provided for their children. In Pedley's view:

> It was these knowledgeable middle-class parents who . . . built up the necessary national impetus for action. By the time Labour came to power, the country was not only willing to accept comprehensive reorganization: it was demanding it. (Pedley, 1978, p.55)

Leading members of the Labour Party were indeed prepared to exploit the public alarm concerning the iniquities of the 11+ and the general shortage of grammar school places. Yet being aware of the continued popularity of the grammar schools among a large section of their traditional supporters, they were also anxious to play down the suggestion that comprehensive reorganization entailed one type of school being *abolished* in order to create another. Hugh Gaitskell, the Labour leader from 1955 to 1963, rejected Emmanuel Shinwell's accusation that the grammar schools were being 'thrown overboard' when he himself wrote to *The Times* in July 1958:

> It would be nearer the truth to describe our proposals as 'a grammar-school education for all' . . . Our aim is greatly to widen the opportunities to receive what is now called a grammar-school education, and we also want to see grammar-school standards in the sense of higher quality education extended far more generally. (Letter to *The Times*, 5 July 1958 quoted in Fenwick, 1976, p.109)

This view of Labour Party education policy was repeated by Harold Wilson (Gaitskell's successor as Party leader from 1963 onwards) in the period leading up to the 1964 General Election. Despite the embarrassment caused to committed educationists — particularly those Party members who for a decade or more had supported the comprehensive principle for educational and egalitarian reasons and were aware of the limited value of the grammar school model — the slogan of 'grammar schools for all' in fact served a number of useful functions: it silenced the opponents of reorganization within the Party itself; it appealed to growing demands for a more meritocratic system of secondary education; and it dispelled the fears of parents who placed their trust in the traditional grammar school curriculum. Hargreaves (1982) has summed up its appeal in the following way:

> The slogan was a sophisticated one for it capitalized on the contradictions in the public's mind: parents were in favour of the retention of the grammar schools and their public examinations but opposed to the 11 + selection test as the basis of a 'once-for-all' allocation. (p.66)

At the same time, it was important to emphasize the direct economic advantages that could be gained from a system of unsegregated education. This style of presentation was very much favoured by Harold Wilson who, in his 'science and socialism' speech to the 1963 Labour Party Conference, laid great stress on the point that the Party opposed a segregated, elitist secondary system, not only because it was unjust and socially divisive, but also because, by failing to capture talent at the point of entry to secondary education, it held back Britain's technological development and operated against our success in economic affairs:

> To train the scientists we are going to need will mean a revolution in our attitude to education, not only higher education but at every level . . . It means that as a nation, we cannot afford to force segregation on our children at the 11 + stage . . . As Socialists, as

democrats, we oppose this system of educational aparthied because we believe in equality of opportunity. But that is not all. We simply cannot as a nation afford to neglect the educational development of a single boy or girl. We cannot afford to cut off three-quarters or more of our children from virtually any chance of higher education. The Russians do not, the Germans do not, the Americans do not, and the Japanese do not, and we cannot afford to either. (Reprinted in Bell, Fowler and Little, 1973, pp.192–4)

In October of the following year, the Labour Party was returned to power on a programme which included a promise to introduce comprehensive education.

From *Circular 10/65* to the Ruskin Speech

It has already been observed that throughout the period of Conservative administrations from 1951 to 1964, a number of comprehensive schools were created in different parts of the country without the support of central government. Yet towards the end of this period, the generally hostile Conservative approach was modified by Sir Edward Boyle who made it clear in the pamphlet *Educational Opportunity*, published in 1963, that:

> None of us believe in pre-war terms that children can be sharply differentiated into various types or levels of ability; and I certainly would not wish to advance the view that the tripartite system, as it is often called, should be regarded as the right and normal way of organizing secondary education, compared with which everything else must be stigmatized as experimental. (Quoted in Fenwick, 1976, p.118)

Boyle was instrumental in allowing Bradford to become the first English city to abolish selection at 11 — in September 1964. His Foreword to the Newsom Report, *Half Our Future*, (Ministry of Eduction, 1963) shows that he accepted the view that 'intelligence' could be 'acquired' and was not therefore a fixed quantity impervious to any educational influence: 'the essential point is that all children should have an equal opportunity of acquiring intelligence, and of developing their talents and abilities to the full' (p.iv). At the same time, it has to be conceded that the Minister was well aware of his exposed position on the 'liberal' wing of his party; he could make common cause with the diehard opponents of change only to the extent that he shared their antagonism to any form of compulsion.

As it turned out, *Circular 10/65*, issued in July 1965, did not, in fact, *compel* anyone to do anything, and is somewhat reminiscent of the type of 'permissive legislation' much favoured by Disraeli. 'Permissive legislation is the characteristic of a free people', he declared in June 1875 (quoted in Blake, 1966, p.554). Such a view might have commanded widespread support among Conservative politicians in the 1870s; but it seems likely that many of the proponents of comprehensive reform would have welcomed something more *dirigiste* in 1965. For one thing, although it was the new government's declared objective 'to end selection at 11 + and to eliminate separatism in secondary education' (DES, 1965, p.1), *Circular 10/65* had no statutory power. Local education authorities were simply *requested* to prepare plans for the reorganization of their secondary schools on comprehensive lines, and to submit them to the new Department of Education and Science for approval within twelve months. Then again, the range of patterns which would be considered acceptable — even if only on a temporary basis — as comprehensive schemes was so great as to create the well-founded suspicion that the resulting system would resemble a patchwork quilt of uneven quality. Above all, the Circular made no mention of what might be considered an appropriate curriculum for the new schools. The emphasis throughout was on buildings, staffing and the need to take account of specific local circumstances. The inclusion of middle schools, for example, as one of six acceptable forms of comprehensive organization owed little to a belief in the *educational* advantages of such schools. According to Hargreaves (1986), they were, to a large extent, 'a direct result of comprehensive reorganization at the secondary level under conditions of severe economic stringency' (p.41). In the view of another commentator, they were an administrative convenience, 'created for the best of all educational reasons — because they were cheap' (Doe, 1976, p.22).

Pressure groups such as the Comprehensive Schools Committee (CSC), launched in September 1965, and campaigning journals like *Forum*, which had been founded in 1958, soon became alarmed that many LEA reorganization plans were not genuinely comprehensive, and this became a matter of overriding importance. Tony Benn, who joined the Wilson Cabinet as Minister of Technology in July 1966, concedes that in the 1960s a fair amount of campaigning energy had to be absorbed in simply monitoring the comprehensive reform against a background of half-hearted DES commitment.[4] In his view, there was certainly very little support for reorganization at Prime Ministerial level. Harold Wilson's 'science and socialism' speech appeared progressive and forward-looking in 1963, but it was not followed up by a genuine commitment to policies promoting equality of opportunity or enhanced opportunities for hitherto deprived working-class children. In Benn's view: 'Wilson used to make speeches in the Conference sounding like Nye Bevan and in the Cabinet sounding like Reg Prentice'.

According to Kirsten Tait, one of a team of Assistant Principals at the DES working on reorganization plans following the publication of *Circular 10/65*, there was pressure from above to push through schemes despite any shortcomings they might have[5]. At the same time, very little thought was given to the curriculum implications of the move away from selection:

> . . . I felt that we were all working with the unknown . . . Because of the general lack of knowledge and experience . . . everyone was asked to make judgments with totally inadequate instruments in the interests of an important policy . . . As to curriculum, what we put a lot of stress on was: would children really get a chance to have access to more subject choices than had previously been the case? We fixed on something tangible because it was very difficult to judge the intangibles. It seems to me, in the light of what has happened since, that one of the major weaknesses of secondary re-organization was that it was not combined with a really important debate as to what a comprehensive curriculum would look like . . . When schools were reorganized as comprehensives, they took with them into the new system a sort of watered-down version of the old grammar-school curriculum. And, with hindsight, I think that that was a mistake, and that enormous possibilities were lost, particularly in the area of technical education . . . We did not see it in those terms then, but, in my view, we should have been more aware of curriculum issues. It was, after all, the dawn of a new age; and we simply thought that if you made a major effort to bring all these children together in comprehensive schools, the best of everything would slightly rub off on all of them. We thought that the fact that you had children coming together from all sorts of backgrounds meant that everything would eventually sort itself out.

The idea of promoting comprehensive schools as 'grammar schools for all', with the clear implication that a grammar school curriculum could now be made more widely available, was enshrined in the introduction to *Circular 10/65* which made reference to a motion passed on 21 January 1965 in which government policy had been endorsed by the House of Commons:

This House, conscious of the need to raise educational standards at all levels, and regretting that the realization of this objective is impeded by the separation of children into different types of secondary schools, notes with approval the efforts of local authorities to reorganize secondary education on comprehensive lines which will preserve all that is valuable in grammar-school education for those children who now receive it and make it available to more children. (DES, 1965, p. 1; *Hansard*, H. of C., Vol. 705, Col. 541, 21 January 1965)

Clearly, no account of the evolution of the comprehensive school curriculum can ignore the importance and durability of the grammar school tradition. In the forties and early fifties, 'secondary education for all' had been interpreted by many as meaning a 'grammar school education for all'. In the late fifties and early sixties, influential members of the Labour Party promoted comprehensive schools as ensuring a 'grammar school education for all'. Both concepts had obvious shortcomings and could not bear critical examination. Yet there was a very real sense in which, to begin with at least, comprehensive schools *did* become the new grammar schools in that many of them were content to perpetuate the assumptions of the grammar school curriculum. As Elliott (1983) has pointed out: 'through the growth of comprehensive reorganization and people's attempts to legitimate it in terms of a grammar school education for all, secondary education in Britain became "grammarized" ' (p. 119). As late as 1976, the confidential Yellow Book, prepared for the Prime Minister by a group of civil servants within the DES, was using grammar school teaching as a yardstick by which to measure teaching performance in comprehensive schools:

> Formal qualifications apart, because of its recent and rapid expansion, the teaching force contains a disproportionate number of young and inexperienced teachers... In the less definable qualities of skill and personality, while the best teachers are up to very high standards, the average is probably below what used to be expected in, for example, a good grammar school (DES, 1976a, p. 9).

A number of factors help to account for the hegemony of the grammar school curriculum. In the first place, it has been suggested (Hargreaves, 1982, p. 51) that while senior pastoral posts in the new comprehensives usually went to ex-secondary modern school teachers, heads of department were drawn almost exclusively from grammar schools. It was perhaps inevitable that the heavy emphasis on the cognitive-intellectual skills and abilities of the traditional school subjects should be retained if the curriculum was largely in the hands of ex-grammar school teachers whose only experience had been with the 'top' 20 per cent of the school population. A study published in 1971 showed that even in schools going comprehensive from a secondary modern base, a deliberate attempt was made to ensure that all major academic departments should be led by well-qualified graduates with suitable experience (Clark, 1971, pp.14–17).

These new heads of department were not, however, alone in creating a meritocratic ethos for the early comprehensive schools; research shows that they could rely on the support of the vast majority of first generation comprehensive headteachers. The Second NFER Report *Comprehensive Education in Action*, published in 1970, revealed that in the crucial matter of the distribution of additional staff salary allowances for posts of responsibility, grammar-type structures tended to persist in comprehensive schools and particularly in those derived from a selective base. Headteachers were clearly anxious to use the allowances at their disposal to secure experienced graduates for key academic posts, giving special preference to mathematics and science. On average, 50 per cent of allowances in the schools included in the survey went to teachers of prestige academic subjects; compared with 17 per cent to teachers of practical subjects and only 3 per cent to those responsible for the education of the 'less able' and the 'remedial' (Monks, 1970, pp.31–3). The pattern of a school's allowance structure clearly reflects to a large extent the school's sense of priorities, which, in turn, owes much to the educational philosophy of the headteacher. For those responsible for guiding the comprehensive schools of the 1960s, academic achievement tended to be the single criterion of 'success'.

This thesis is ably demonstrated in a number of case studies published since 1970. Writing in *The Fight for Education: Black Paper 1975*, Professor Bantock described his visits to Highbury Grove School in London which had been opened by Dr. Rhodes Boyson in 1966 with the declared object of developing 'a full academic tradition in a disciplined and regulated framework':

> Highbury Grove School . . . is a highly meritocratic institution where the emphasis is on disciplined, structured learning and achievement in examination terms. I have visited the school myself on several occasions during Dr. Boyson's headmastership. Discipline was firm but cheerful; attention was paid to social matters; but the aim of the headmaster was undisguisedly and unashamedly academic in the sense that learning took first priority. (Bantock, 1975, p.17)

The Headmaster in Burgess's study of Bishop McGregor School, *Experiencing Comprehensive Education* published in 1983, devised a rigidly differentiated curriculum which established academic excellence as the central tenet of the value system of the school. In his talks to parents before the school was opened in 1969, he explained that he would take technical courses and Newsom-type options from the secondary modern school and streaming, setting and high standards from the grammar school (Burgess, 1983, pp.31–3).

In Ball's study of a large mixed comprehensive school, *Beachside Comprehensive* published in 1981, the aims of the school as expressed by the headmaster stress primarily the maximization of the pupils' academic potential. Despite the introduction of mixed-ability forms in the first year, Beachside Comprehensive School clearly approximates to the ideal type of a meritocratic comprehensive:

> Success at Beachside . . . is measured in terms of examination passes, the size of the sixth form, and the size and type of university entrance; these measures are reflected throughout the school in the evaluation of the social worth of individual pupils. In the classroom, teaching is formal, with the teacher as dispenser and mediator of knowledge; chalk and talk is the most common classroom technique. There is regular homework for all children, with a planned timetable for every year group. Marking is competitive, and there are twice-yearly examinations, although overall form positions are not used or calculated. (Ball, 1981, p.21)

A third factor with regard to the 'grammarizing' of the comprehensive school curriculum was the powerful external pressure exerted by the examination boards. By 1965, the GCE 'O' level examination had been in existence for fourteen years; and it was very much associated in the minds of parents with high standards and a grammar school education. The plans for the new examination for the ability range immediately below the 20 per cent thought capable of tackling the GCE were approved in 1963; and pupils were entered for the Certificate of Secondary Education (CSE) for the first time in 1965. Many teachers were delighted by the possibilities afforded by CSE Mode 3 which allowed them to devise and examine their own programmes of work. For ambitious candidates, on the other hand, it simply became essential to secure a grade 1 pass which was deemed to be the equivalent of an 'O' level pass grade.

The 1979 survey of secondary education by Her Majesty's Inspectors of Schools, *Aspects of Secondary Education in England*, reported that public examinations were a major preoccupation of the schools inspected and that preparing pupils for them was a dominant feature of the work of years 4 and 5. Perhaps inevitably, a number of schools were thought to be making unrealistic demands on their pupils with consequent deficiencies in the quality of learning.

> It was evident that in some schools, pupils were being entered for examinations inappropriate to their particular abilities and some embarked on examination courses who would have been better suited by non-examination courses. Elsewhere, the range of programmes offered to some groups of pupils, usually the more able, was narrowed: these pupils were thought to have no time to spare for creative and aesthetic subjects and non-examination courses. Careers education, health education and religious education also tended to be excluded. The work attempted in the classroom was often constrained by exclusive emphasis placed on the examination syllabus, on the topics thought to be favoured by the examiners, and on the acquisition of examination techniques. (DES, 1979b, p.217)

With the grammar school model seemingly unassailable after 1965, and in the absence of a clear concept of the *educational* purpose of the comprehensive school, objectives that were primarily *social* soon acquired considerable popularity, particularly among 'reformist' and Fabian elements within the Labour Party. Many of the earlier supporters of comprehensive education had believed in the concept of 'equality of opportunity', but they had taken it to mean that in each school, all pupils should have equal access to all the opportunities offered. Now the concept of 'equality' was widened to apply to situations in the wider world outside the school walls. Many genuinely believed in the early days of the 1964–70 Labour government that capitalist society *could* be reformed, and that comprehensive schools would be a step on the road to achieving greater equality — greater equality in the sense that working-class children would be able to move into 'white-collar' occupations or proceed to higher education. Halsey, for example, argued in 1965 that:

> Some people, and I am one, want to use education as an instrument in pursuit of an egalitarian society. We tend to favour comprehensive schools, to be against public schools, and to support the expansion of higher education. (p.13)

Others simply believed in the theory of the 'social mix' which looked forward to the *amelioration* of social class differences through the pupils' experience of 'social mixing' in a common secondary school. This view can be found, for example, in the first *Where* supplement on streaming, written by two prominent Fabians and published in 1965, where the comprehensive reform is described as having two linked purposes:

> These are to end selection, at any rate at the early ages at which it has been practised in England and Wales, and thereby to raise the standard of education of the great majority of children; and to bring about more social unity between people of different abilities, in different occupations, and in different social classes. (Young and Armstrong, 1965, p.3)

Comprehensive reorganization, then, was seen by many as a means of ameliorating the more obvious inequalities in society, or at least of producing a greater degree of social harmony, without in any way disturbing the basic class structure of the capitalist system. As Wilby (1977) has observed, linking education reform with economic growth:

> Educational equality was an attempt to achieve social change by proxy. More and better education was more politically palatable and less socially disruptive than direct measures of tackling inequality. So was economic growth. Even the most complacently privileged could hardly object to children attending better schools and to the nation producing more wealth. Equality of educational opportunity had an altogether more agreeable ring to it than any other form of equality, such as equality of income or equality of property. With its overtones of self-improvement, it could even appeal to the more conservative elements in society. Its beauty was that, while many must gain, it did not imply that any must lose. Ugly words such as redistribution and expropriation did not apply to education — or nobody thought they applied. Education was a cornucopia, so prolific of good things that nobody would need any longer to ask awkward questions about who got what. (p.358)

This preoccupation with social objectives, however, had the simple effect of setting up convenient targets for the opponents of reorganization to aim at. It was easy to argue, as did Pedley in the first Black Paper, *Fight for Education*, published in 1969, that supporters of the comprehensive reform were using schools 'directly as tools to achieve political objectives'. It was easy for him to ridicule 'that Utopia of equality where the Duke lies down with the docker, and the Marquis and the milkman are as one'. Moreover, in his view, there was evidence to suggest that social divisions were actually perpetuated and strengthened inside the comprehensive school: '4A doesn't mix with 4P, and the Cabinet Minister's son (or daughter) shows no particular eagerness to bring the bus conductor's child home to tea' (Pedley, 1969, p.47). When Ford's researches in the late sixties (Ford, 1969) led her to support the view that comprehensive schools do not necessarily promote social unity, this was promptly hailed by the editors of *Black Paper Three* as a major condemnation of the whole system (Cox and Dyson, 1970).

Benn and Simon (1972), on the other hand, argued that no one should expect comprehensive reorganization to solve all the tensions inherent in modern capitalist society: 'a comprehensive school is not a social experiment; it is an educational reform' (p.110). Yet the theory of the artificial 'social mix' persisted, particularly when it was obvious that re-organization did not *by itself* produce greater equality in any sense that was strictly measurable (see Chitty, 1981, pp.4–6). The Headmaster of Beachside Comprehensive in Ball's case study offers a personal view of comprehensive education which clearly falls into the 'social engineering' category:

> I still have the idea that an education system can have some impact on a society. Some people say that's a bit naive; on the other hand, I look at the impact on people that the public school set-up has. It's social manipulation, it's social engineering; but I think in ten years' time, then one could examine the structure of the adult society in this country, and see, given the fact that the majority of young adults would be products of the comprehensive system, whether the school system can be considered to be one of the reasons for the nature of that society. I think it will be. I do see a much more cohesive society coming out of our comprehensive schools. I think it is already there in this school: there is a great social cohesiveness in this school getting more obvious as the kids get older. (Ball, 1981, p.12)

In the light of the preoccupations of the sixties and early seventies, it can be argued that comprehensive reorganization in this country was not marked, at least initially, by an emphasis on new possibilities for intellectual development, despite the obvious needs of those pupils who had been classified as 'failures' under the old selective system. Owing to the confusion over objectives, there was little attempt either to demolish the assumptions surrounding intelligence and learning or to grasp the curriculum opportunities afforded by the admittedly partial abolition of selection. The chief concerns were instead to reduce the wastage of the human abilities so urgently required as a result of technological change and economic advance and to promote social cohesion in a class-divided society. As such, the comprehensive reform could be said to be, in part, a response to profound conservative instincts. As Simon has pointed out (1978, p.30), the comprehensive school was seen to be 'necessary', in some senses at least, 'for the maintenance and smooth functioning of the existing social order'.[6]

In the meantime, it was clearly not considered necessary to devise a new curriculum model for this new type of school. Even the Schools Council, established in 1964 and potentially an important agent for curriculum planning and development, failed to produce any kind of basis for a new curriculum for the early comprehensives. As late as 1973, Lawton could lament 'the consistent failure to re-think the curriculum and plan a programme which would be appropriate for universal secondary education' (p.101).

There were, admittedly, a number of curriculum innovations in the 1960s, but they were strictly limited in scope and application. On the whole, discussion at all levels tended to be restricted to two related issues of immediate significance: the provision of a large number of subject options for 'able' pupils, particularly in years 4 and 5, and the creation of 'suitable' courses for 'ROSLA' pupils in those years who were not to be entered for public examinations.

Two years before the promulgation of *Circular 10/65*, a report appeared which was to have a profound impact on the internal organization and curriculum structure of the early comprehensive schools. *The Newsom Report* (Ministry of Education, 1963) lent itself to being interpreted as an argument in favour of non-academic, 'life-adjustment' courses for pupils in the 'bottom' streams of the fourth and fifth years: those who before 1973 could leave school at 15. The fact that so many schools simply opted for 'Newsom courses' for non-academic 'Newsom' children was, in itself, indicative of staff-room attitudes towards the seemingly 'less able'. The 'Newsom' pupils at Bishop McGregor School in Burgess's case study were always described in crudely negative terms. They were the pupils who 'deviated' from the academic and behavioural patterns of those 'normal' fourth- and fifth-year students who took public examinations and conformed to their teachers' expectations. According to the Headmaster, 'Newsom' pupils required a special programme 'designed to develop and strengthen those talents in the non-academic which will be most useful to that youngster in society — job-wise, marriage-wise, recreation-wise'. Yet the course carried the stigma that it was designed for pupils who had 'failed' the conventional school programme in the first three years. This was the clear inference of the Headmaster's definition of 'Newsom' as 'work on non-examination material designed for pupils for whom the maximum expectation of success in public examinations seems likely to be three CSE grade 5s or less' (Burgess, 1983, p.125).

The 1979 HMI survey of secondary education showed that even in comprehensives without 'Newsom' groups, curricular differentiation usually operated from the *third* year onwards. Pupils in the 'higher' streams were often given the opportunity to start one or more additional foreign languages — additional, that is, to French; while their 'less able' contemporaries were encouraged to drop French altogether. Similarly, a select group of pupils might be studying separate physics, chemistry and biology; while the 'science' on offer to the 'bottom' streams could be general science, rural science or science incorporated into 'environmental studies'. Again, only the 'less able' were thought to profit from extended contact with the creative/aesthetic area of the curriculum. Whatever form the differentiated curriculum then took in the fourth and fifth years — whether organized around completely segregated courses or a bewildering variety of option schemes — it was obvious that, in reality, the 'top' streams had taken over the traditional grammar school curriculum with its emphasis on the cognitive-intellectual skills and abilities of the academic school subjects; while all those below were following either a diluted version of the curriculum or programmes of work much influenced by the *Newsom Report* and the practical and vocational aspects of the curriculum of the early secondary modern schools (DES, 1979a, pp.14–21).

At the time this survey was published, there were signs that the situation was already beginning to change. By the early 1970s, a number of groups and individuals had begun to address the problem of devising a secondary school curriculum which would be genuinely and demonstrably comprehensive. Lawton, for example, was writing in terms of an integrated curriculum (1969) or a common culture individualized curriculum (1973), acknowledging his debt to the work of Broudy, Smith and Burnett in America (1964) and to the more accessible writings of Raymond Williams in England (1958 and 1961). A small group within Her Majesty's Inspectorate was working towards its own model of a common curriculum based on the concept of 'areas of experience'; and civil servants within the DES were thinking in terms of a core or common-core curriculum based on an irreducible 'core' of essential subjects and disciplines. At the same time, a small but influential group of schools was earnestly engaged in the search for a unified, not divisive curriculum (see, for example, Holt, 1978; Chitty, 1979; Galton and Moon, 1983; Moon, 1983).

Much of this new thinking was made available to a wider audience at the time of the so-called Great Debate of 1976/77. Paradoxically, it was

James Callaghan's Ruskin College speech of October 1976, with its emphasis on standards and the need to see education as a means of servicing the manpower needs of industry, which gave political recognition to the importance of the new curriculum developments. With its curious mixture of traditional and innovative thinking, it set the tone of the educational debate for the next ten years. It will be discussed at greater length in the following two chapters.

Notes

1 Speaking to the Executive Committee of the National Association of Inspectors and Educational Advisers (NAIEA) in June 1988, Sir David Hancock, Permanent Secretary at the DES, said that experience over the past decade had shown that very little of the DES and HMI output was either read or understood by teachers. 'The Department's contacts with teachers and schools have shown how little of what we have already published is known about and understood... Sending schools documents is clearly not enough. The teachers need to be taken through them and given the opportunity to ask questions and debate the issues among themselves. Heads should take the lead in this, but local inspectors may have to start the process off'. (Reported in *The Times Educational Supplement*, 24 June 1988)

2 The origins of the comment attributed to Tomlinson are obscure, as indeed is the exact wording. The version to be found in Smith (1957, p.162) is 'Minister's now't to do with curriculum'; Lawton's version (1980, p.31) is 'Minister knows now't about curriculum'. Aldrich and Leighton (1985) adopt the Lawton version (p.57). There is no reference to the remark in Fred Blackburn's 1954 biography of Tomlinson.

3 The recently-published official papers for 1955 indicate that, ten years after the end of the second World War, there was genuine concern in governmental circles about parental opposition to the 11 + examination. It was in that year that the Minister of Education, Sir David Eccles, advised the Eden Cabinet that opposition (that is, Labour) proposals for introducing a large measure of comprehensive reorganization would gain electoral support if the government did not quickly produce an alternative to assuage the resentment of middle-class parents whose children had failed to secure entry to grammar schools. These parents would demand either selection for none or genuine opportunities for all. Selection for none would be ensured by comprehensive schools for all, with parental choice virtually abolished and grammar schools eventually closed. Opportunities for all, he advised, could be ensured by enabling some secondary modern schools to develop specialisms and more 'vocational' courses to construct 'an alternative route' to that offered by the grammar schools and one that would take pupils at secondary modern and technical schools to well paid jobs, via colleges of technology. (Reported by David Walker in *The Times*, 4 January 1986)

4 Interview with Tony Benn, 3 July 1986.

5 Interview with Kirsten Tait, 24 September 1987.

6 As late as March 1988, James (now Lord) Callaghan was arguing in a speech to the National Council for Educational Standards that it was the social harmony produced by comprehensive schools which would be undermined by the opting-out proposals of the 1988 Education Reform Act, since these changes would 'create one more division between classes of children in our country, at a time when social cohesion is under strain and the gap between the best-off and the poorest is growing wider'. (Reported in *The Independent*, 7 March 1988)

Chapter 2

The Comprehensive System Under Attack: 1970–76

The End of Consensus

The policy-makers of the 1960s had seen a direct and indisputable corre-
lation between educational reform and economic prosperity: a skilled and
educated workforce would facilitate economic growth which would, in
turn, constitute a firm basis for continuing educational expansion.
Theodore W. Schultz had argued in his Presidential Address to the
American Economic Association in 1960 on the theme 'Investment in
human capital' that the process of acquiring skills and knowledge through
education was to be viewed not as a form of consumption, but rather as a
productive investment. 'By investing in themselves, people can enlarge the
range of choice available to them. It is the one way free men can enhance
their welfare' (Schultz, 1961, p.2). According to this analysis, investment in
human capital not only increased individual productivity, but, in so doing,
also laid the technical base of the type of labour force necessary for rapid
economic growth. This superficially attractive message secured keen
converts across the whole political spectrum in America. As Karabel and
Halsey (1977) have pointed out, it even made a direct appeal to pro-
capitalist ideological sentiment through its insistence that:

> The worker is a *holder of capital* (as embodied in his skills and
> knowledge) and that he has the *capacity to invest* (in himself).
> Thus in a single bold conceptual stroke, the *wage-earner*, who
> holds no property and controls neither the process nor the product
> of his labour, is transformed into a *capitalist* ... We cannot be
> surprised, then, that a doctrine re-affirming the American way of
> life and offering quantitative justification for vast public
> expenditure on education should receive generous sponsorship in
> the United States. (p.13)

Human capital theory also exerted a profound influence on a significant number of sociologists and economists in Britain (see Simon, 1985, pp.15–16), and provided the intellectual justification for the Labour government's commitment (however half-hearted) to comprehensive reorganization.

The period of the 1960s can, then, be fairly characterized as one of optimism and expansion. According to Gordon (1986, p.16), the main features of the period were an increasing school population, increasing expenditure, expansion of teacher training, and the spread of comprehensive reorganization:

> Against this material background occurred developments affecting teaching, learning and organization in schools; and future commitments seemed clear. In the spirit of optimism, an education system appropriate for a technological society was being forged; advancement and steady growth were assumed; traditional education seemed inappropriate. The children and youth of the 'nation' were looked at in eager anticipation of this future. Children's potential was emphasized; poverty and deprivation had not yet been 'rediscovered'. New CSE examinations with greater teacher control and curriculum-determined examinations were welcomed ... Comprehensive reorganization gathered momentum through *Circular 10/65*. (*ibid.*, pp.16–17)

All this was to change in the 1970s. The full force of the reaction was not to be felt until the middle years of the decade, following the economic crisis of 1974/75; although there were already signs of a profound disenchantment with the comprehensive reform and the perceived consequences of educational expansion as early as 1969/70. Indeed, Ball (1984) sees the publication in March 1969 of the first Black Paper, *Fight for Education*, as marking neatly and symbolically 'the beginning of the end of the period of optimism' (p.4). While this first pamphlet was dominated by concerns about the 'collapse of community' in higher education, following the widespread student unrest of 1968, it also represented the first of a series of sustained attacks on the associated concepts of comprehensive education, egalitarianism and 'progressive' teaching methods[1].

The contributors to the first three Black Papers (Cox and Dyson, 1969a and 1969b; Cox and Dyson, 1970) were seen as wanting to put the clock back: to the days of formal teaching methods in primary schools, of academic standards associated with a grammar school education and of well-motivated, hard-working and essentially conservative university students. The articles they produced were devoid of radical, forward-looking ideas; theirs was clearly the voice of the past. A critique of the first two Black Papers which appeared in *Tribune* in November 1969 with the significant title 'Blackwards' argued that there was really very little to fear from the hysterical outpourings of tired reactionaries. Using the Victor Hugo maxim that 'nothing is so powerful as an idea whose time has come', it was further argued that the comprehensive school was here to stay and that the Black Paper authors found themselves in the position of having always to react to a radical agenda drawn up by an educational establishment from which they felt themselves to be permanently estranged. Their ideas would be rejected, as they doubtless realised, because of the radical, democratic nature of the society that the comprehensive school was helping to create:

> The enemies of reform have probably realised that with the raising of the general level of education for all, made possible by secondary reorganization, and the consequent widening of experience and opportunity, may come a new generation which will be less subservient to the ruling elites in our society, less prepared to know its place, more knowledgeable, more able, more ready to face the challenges of the last quarter of the twentieth century . . . The authors of the Black Papers are scared men and women — scared of the future, scared of change. The principles enunciated in their dismal essays amount to nothing more nor less than a blue-print for a stagnant, unthinking society, perpetuating itself through a rigid hierarchy of educational establishments. (Chitty and Rein, 1969)

It was, perhaps, rather too easy in 1969 to be arrogant and complacent about the self-evident virtues of the comprehensive reform!

In the late 1960s and early 1970s, the Right in Britain was on the defensive, fighting a rearguard action against an educational consensus of which it heartily disapproved. But this was not a lasting phenomenon; the optimism of the reformers was ill-judged. It has been largely overlooked that there were, in fact, significant differences between, on the one hand, the Black Papers published in 1969 and 1970 and, on the other, those of 1975 and 1977 (Cox and Boyson, 1975; and 1977)[2]. By 1975, it had been decided that it was not enough simply to *react* to the proposals put forward by others. This was made clear in the editorial introduction which took the form of a 'Letter to MPs and parents':

> It is time . . . that we in the Black Papers not only criticized, but suggested what should be done. Let us look at each section of education and make positive suggestions which the educational

administration and the politicians could apply. (Cox and Boyson, 1975, p.3)

A clear example of the positive nature of the new thinking could be found in the changing attitude towards privatization. In 1969, it had simply been argued that 'the need for the times is to extend the possibility of private education to more and more people by making loans and grants available to those who qualify for entrance but cannot afford fees' (Cox and Dyson, 1969b, p.14). In 1975, the editors were urging the introduction of the educational voucher in at least two trial areas (Cox and Boyson, 1975, p.4); and the Paper included a special essay by Dr. Boyson on 'The developing case for the educational voucher' (*ibid.*, pp.27–8)[3]. Support for the voucher was reiterated in the editorial introduction to *Black Paper 1977* which again took the form of a 'Letter to Members of Parliament':

> The possibilities for parental choice of secondary (and primary) schools should be improved via the introduction of the educational voucher or some other method. Schools that few wish to attend should be closed and their staff dispersed. (Cox and Boyson, 1977, p.9)

The new emphasis was on choice and competition and parental control of schools. From being on the defensive at the beginning of the 1970s, the Right was preparing itself to go on to the offensive with the floating of radical ideas for the future organization of the education service[4]. In fact, it could be argued that in the eight years from 1969 to 1977, the thinking of the Old Right gave way to that of the New; the politics of *reaction* gave way to the politics of *reconstruction*. It would be another ten years before a Conservative government felt strong enough to put the new ideas into practice, but the process of making them respectable began with the Black Papers of 1975 and 1977.

In the meantime, there were other signs in the early 1970s that the consensus of the 1960s was apparently coming to an end. Of these, the pursuit of new themes in academic research, particularly in the sociology of education, was of special significance in further undermining the cosy optimism of the first two Wilson administrations.

The publication of *Knowledge and Control* in 1971 (Young, 1971) was a key factor in the birth of what came to be known as the New Sociology of Education which marked the end (or temporary suspension) of approaches in sociological enquiry which were obviously amenable to practical policy implementation. The main preoccupation of educational sociologists in the 1950s and 1960s had been to illuminate the relationship between formal schooling and social stratification (see, for example, Glass, 1954; Floud,

Halsey and Martin, 1956; Halsey, Floud and Anderson, 1961; Douglas, 1964). The extent of working-class access to formal schooling was a key area of concern for these academic researchers anxious to make the case for equality of educational opportunity. There was, moreover, a clear commitment to creating educational experiences which would facilitate social mobility for working-class children; but the actual *processes* of schooling were largely taken for granted. After 1971, interest in the related problems of educational opportunity and achievement was replaced by a new and rigorous concentration on the experience of schooling itself. By the middle years of the decade, there was something of a divide in this New Sociology of Education between those interested in the minutiae of classroom experience from a phenomenological and interactionist viewpoint (see, for example, Hargreaves, 1972; Stubbs and Delamont, 1976; Woods and Hammersley, 1977; Woods, 1979) and those who, using a macro approach, saw education as simply reproducing capitalist divisions and hierarchies in society (see, for example, Althusser, 1971; Carnoy, 1974; Bowles and Gintis, 1976; Bourdieu and Passeron, 1977). The first approach concentrated heavily upon patterns of interpersonal relations and the implications of the hidden curriculum; the second appeared to suggest that teachers and other workers within the field of education were inevitably subsumed as agents of ideological domination and could do nothing to change the *status quo*. Neither approach saw any role for education as a tool for social change, thereby undermining the legitimization for relatively massive educational advances undertaken in the previous decade. As Hunter has observed (1984) 'the axis of agreement on comprehensive school goals and values that had existed between teachers and academics was broken' (p.280).

The general atmosphere of defeatism and gloom was not dispelled by the publication in America in 1972 of the *Jencks Report* on the effect of family and schooling in America which also challenged the liberal doctrine that equalizing opportunities through schooling would inevitably produce equality of outcomes among individuals. The Jencks thesis was certainly influential in Britain and elsewhere: according to Bernbaum (1979) 'the work of Jencks and his associates is amongst the most important in symbolizing the recent changes which have characterized the standing of educational systems' (p.13). At the same time, in their study of class inequality in Britain, first published in 1975, Westergaard and Resler came to the conclusion that the educational changes of the 1960s and early 1970s had not resulted in any major redistribution of educational opportunities between children of different social classes. For example: in the early 1970s, manual workers' children were still less likely to enter a university than were children of 'professional and technical' fathers by a factor of nearly nine times. Indeed, the authors wryly observed that one of the ironical consequences of comprehensive reorganization which was introduced to increase opportunity and reduce class barriers was that 'the effects of those barriers become obscured from view' (Westergaard and Resler, 1975, p.322).

Disillusionment with the education system, particularly at the secondary level, was not confined to right-wing critics or academic sociologists. A group of influential 'de-schoolers' owing much to the ideas outlined by Ivan Illich in his *Deschooling Society*, first published in America in 1970, made the case against universal compulsory schooling and argued for a consideration of viable alternatives in education: alternative content, organization and finance. Illich himself rejected all the basic tenets of progressive liberalism, particularly the idea that education constituted the great equalizer and the path to personal liberation. As far as Illich was concerned, schools should be seen as examplary models of harsh bureaucracies geared primarily towards the indoctrination of docile and manipulable consumers. Since nothing could be done to change this, they should simply be eliminated.

At a political level, 1970 had seen the return of a Conservative government under Edward Heath pledged to withdraw *Circular 10/65* (Rubinstein and Simon, 1973, p.117)[5]. Yet, curiously, it was, in fact, during Margaret Thatcher's four-year period as Secretary of State for Education (1970–74) that more schools became comprehensive than either before or since[6]. Plans made under the previous Labour government, by both Conservative and Labour councils, were in the process of being implemented, and many others were waiting to be approved. Despite her personal hostility towards the comprehensive reform and repeated attempts to save existing grammar schools, the Education Secretary was not able to overturn the prevailing orthodoxy that reorganization was almost inevitable. Indeed, it has been argued (Gow, 1988; Simon, 1988, p.23) that a lingering resentment over this helps to account for her long-standing contempt for independent local authorities, officials of the DES, members of HMI and the educational 'establishment' in general. In an interview with the editor of *The Daily Mail* in May 1987, Mrs. Thatcher herself admitted that she had in effect been defeated over the comprehensive issue in the early 1970s:

> This universal comprehensive thing started with Tony Crosland's
> Circular and all education authorities were asked to submit plans
> in which schools were to go totally comprehensive. When I was
> Minister for Education in the Heath government . . . this great

rollercoaster of an idea was moving, and I found it difficult, if not impossible, to stop. (*The Daily Mail*, 13 May 1987)

The number of comprehensive schools more than doubled in the period of the Heath government, and by the return of a Labour administration in 1974, these schools catered for more than 50 per cent of children of secondary school age. It really did seem as if the comprehensive reform had acquired a momentum of its own which it would be impossible to reverse.

At the same time, there were other factors which seemed to point to the survival of the consensus forged in the mid-1960s. 1972 saw the publication of the DES White Paper *Education: A Framework for Expansion* which promised a great increase in nursery education and a systematic programme of in-service opportunities for teachers; the school leaving age was raised to 16 in 1972/73; and in 1972 and 1973 expenditure on education actually exceeded that on defence: £3,559m compared with £3,493m in 1972 and £4,068m compared with £4,004m in 1973 (*Social Trends*, 1975, p.198, table 13.4)[7]. As David (1988) has pointed out:

> ...no government, whether Labour or Tory, is in office long before the Treasury begins to complain that education spending is too high and is getting out of hand. Ironically, the one period since 1970 when there appeared, in retrospect at least, to be some genuine buoyancy was during the Thatcher years at education. (p.29)

Mrs. Thatcher was the last Education Secretary who could issue a White Paper with the word 'Expansion' in the title. As Saran has observed (1988, p.147), the preoccupations of the late 1970s and 1980s are reflected in such titles as *Falling Rolls in Secondary Schools* (Briault and Smith, 1980) and *Education in Jeopardy: Problems and Possibilities of Contraction* (Dennison, 1981).

The Origins of the Great Debate

Although, as we have seen, there was evidence of disillusionment with the education system in general and the comprehensive reform in particular as early as 1969/70, it can be argued that the real turning-point came in the period 1974–76. To quote Hunter (1984) again: 'paradoxically, the comprehensive system came under greater pressure from the Labour administration of 1974–79 than from the previous Conservative government' (p.278). It was the economic crisis that Britain faced after 1973 that enabled critics of the education service from right across the political spectrum to put forward their remedies for its shortcomings. Morris and Griggs have described December 1973 as 'the end of an era' (1988, p.1). As far as government initiatives were concerned, the key year was 1976, since it saw the compilation of the confidential Yellow Book, the delivery of the Ruskin College speech and the inauguration of the so-called Great Debate. The events of that year can be seen as the response of the Callaghan government to pressures and criticisms that had been mounting since at least 1974. According to Stuart Maclure, editor of *The Times Educational Supplement* since 1969, the Ruskin speech and the Great Debate 'changed the whole context in which the education debate is set'. In breaking the taboo on government intervention in the curriculum, the Callaghan initiative was designed to accomplish a considerable overhaul of the education system, its aims, the content of study, the balance between the various components, and the relationship between education and training (Maclure, 1987a, p.10).

The factors which account for the launching of the Great Debate in 1976 can be collected together under a number of separate headings:

(i) the economic crisis of 1973–75;
(ii) the employers' critique of secondary schooling;
(iii) the media campaign against comprehensives;
(iv) political considerations;
(v) the personality of Callaghan himself.

Each of these deserves to be analyzed in turn, with particular emphasis on the economic factors since these exerted a powerful influence on the Callaghan government's policies in the areas of education and welfare.[8]

The Economic Crisis

As far as the economy was concerned, both in Britain and indeed throughout the Western world, the crucial years were 1973–75. The major world recession that erupted in 1974/75 marked the decisive end of what has been described as 'the longest and most rapid period of continuous expansion world capitalism has ever enjoyed' (Gamble, 1985, p.6). The period 1971–73 had seen a sharp boom in each of the major advanced capitalist countries and a generally rising rate of inflation. Some downturn, it could be argued, was likely to occur in 1974 or 1975, simply as part of the usual rhythm of the business cycle. As an economic system, capitalism has always been marked by instability arising largely from its own internal compulsion to expand. It is, therefore, in the very nature of capitalist development never to proceed smoothly but always unevenly, with great uncontrollable spurts followed by equally uncontrollable periods of slump and stagnation. However, in the case of 1974/75, the generality and depth of the recession were unprecedented in the post-war period and can now be seen as marking the end of the long expansionary phase of post-war accumulation (Currie, 1983, p.89). While it would be wrong to see the recession as having a single cause, its onset was clearly marked by a quadrupling of oil prices by OPEC (Organization of Petroleum Exporting Countries) in 1973.

In the view of both David Marquand, a Labour Member of Parliament from 1966 to 1977, and Tony Benn, Secretary of State for first Industry then Energy in the 1974–79 Labour administration, the economic recession fundamentally altered the map of British politics in the mid-1970s. Marquand has argued (1988a) that from the mid-1940s until the mid-1970s, most of Britain's political class shared a tacit governing philosophy which might be called 'Keynesian social democracy'. It did not cover the whole spectrum of political opinion; nor did it prevent vigorous party conflict. The Conservative and Labour parties often differed fiercely about specific details of policy; on a deeper level, their conceptions of political authority and social justice differed even more. They differed, however, within a structure of generally-accepted values and assumptions. Both front benches in the House of Commons accepted a three-fold commitment to full employment, to the Welfare State and to the coexistence of large public and private sectors in the economy — in short, to the settlement which had brought the conflicts of the 1930s to an end. This post-war consensus disintegrated because it simply could not cope with the economic shocks and adjustment problems of the 1970s:

> The post-war consensus collapsed under the Wilson-Callaghan Government of 1974–79 amid mounting inflation, swelling balance of payments deficits, unprecedented currency depreciation, rising unemployment, bitter industrial conflicts and what seemed to many to be ebbing governability. The Conservative leadership turned towards a new version of the classical market liberalism of the nineteenth century. Though the Labour leadership stuck to the tacit 'revisionism' of the 1950s and 1960s, large sections of the rank and file turned towards a more inchoate mixture of neo-Marxism and the 'fundamentalist' socialism of the 1920s and 1930s. (*ibid.*, p.3)

Similarly, Benn has argued (1987) that what he calls the 'welfare capitalist consensus', which began life in the mid-1940s, finally collapsed in the mid-1970s when the OPEC oil crisis exposed all the underlying weaknesses of the economic system and capitalism could not be revived:

> It became clear that the economic base on which the 'welfare consensus' depended had finally collapsed, actually ending half-way through Labour's term of office in 1976, when the IMF (International Monetary Fund) demanded, and received, assurances that public expenditure would be cut, supposedly to restore business confidence. At the end of its thirty-one-year life span, it was clear that the 'welfare consensus' had neither revitalized British industry nor had retained public support with the electorate, which successively defeated Wilson, Heath and Callaghan, who had all tried to make it work, thus paving the way for the election of a very different kind of Conservative government. (*ibid.*, pp.303–4)

According to this view of events, it would be another ten years before a Conservative government would feel strong enough to implement the ultimate right-wing response to the fundamental contradictions inherent in the 'welfare capitalist consensus'. This would involve attempts to dismantle the Welfare State and to make considerable inroads into the state education system. In the meantime, the Labour leadership from 1976 onwards was desperately seeking to stem the tide of Conservative advance by the adoption of right-wing rhetoric and policies. It could, in fact, be argued that it was actually preparing the way for the arrival of a right-wing Thatcher government.

It was unfortunate for education that the economic difficulties of Western societies in the years that followed 1973 served to challenge the liberal and expansionist beliefs of the 1960s. As Bernbaum (1979) has pointed out: 'if economies are no longer characterized by high rates of growth, then the assumptions that growth is closely related to the benefits obtained through large-scale educational enterprises are more readily challenged' (p.12). With the failure of schools to fulfil the promise of the 1960s that investment in education would produce rapid economic benefits, it was easy to argue that henceforth schooling and its social purposes would have to be politically subordinated to the perceived needs of a capitalist economy undergoing a period of crisis.

The economic recession happened to coincide with a declining demographic trend which also had profound consequences for the education system. Apart from the post-war 'bulge' in births, which peaked in 1947, it was 1964 that produced the highest number of births (876,000 in England and Wales); thereafter each year the numbers fell, to a trough in 1976 (584,000) (see Saran, 1988, p.147). A declining birth-rate was one of the factors which militated against the expansion of the education system and explained the cut-back in the demand for teachers at all levels. It meant that the numbers admitted to initial teacher training could be severely reduced: these had risen in England and Wales from nearly 70,000 in 1964 to nearly 120,000 in 1972; by 1980, however, there were fewer than 36,000 (Thomas, 1985, p.78). The total number of teachers continued to rise until 1978 when the figure was 441,000, but by 1982/83, this had fallen to 414,600 (Walsh *et al.*, 1985, pp.262–3).

The economic difficulties and declining birth-rate meant that at one level the Ruskin speech and the Great Debate could be seen as an attempt by the government to encourage efficient use of limited resources. The need to take contraction seriously had already been stressed by James Hamilton, the new Permanent Secretary at the DES, in a speech at the annual conference of the Association of Education Committees meeting in Scarborough in the early summer of 1976. Mr. Hamilton had argued that local authorities should take full advantage of the decline in the school population:

> It is essential to plan the run-down of the education service no less systematically and deliberately than has been done during the long period of growth which is now ending. (Reported in *The Times Educational Supplement*, 2 July 1976)[9]

In the Ruskin speech itself, the Prime Minister was anxious to stress that the days of expansion were over:

> There has been a massive injection of resources into education, mainly to meet increased numbers and partly to raise standards. But in present circumstances, there can be little expectation of further increased resources being made available, at any rate for the time being. I fear that those whose only answer to our problems is to call for more money will be disappointed. But that surely cannot be the end of the matter. There is a challenge to us all in these days and the challenge in education is to examine its priorities and to secure as high efficiency as possible by the skilful use of the £6 billion of existing resources.[10]

According to Bernard Donoughue, the Prime Minister's chief political adviser, the basic principle of the Ruskin Speech was 'improving the quality as opposed to the quantity of education at a time when resources were constrained' (Donoughue, 1987, p.111)[11].

The Employers' Critique

It was in the straitened economic circumstances described above that the government was prepared to listen to criticisms of the education system from leading employers and industrialists. As well as reiterating many of the concerns of the Black Papers, particularly the need for greater teacher accountability, the employers were anxious to emphasize a particular theme of their own: the failure of schools to prepare their pupils for entry into the world of work. Taken together, the employers' criticisms painted a picture of unaccountable teachers, teaching an increasingly irrelevant curriculum to bored teenagers who were poorly motivated, illiterate and innumerate. To this extent, the schools could actually be held responsible, at least in part, for the rising rate of youth unemployment[12].

A major survey of employers' reactions to young workers was carried out by the National Youth Employment Council (NYEC) in 1974. Drawing on evidence from a variety of sources, including the Institute of Careers Officers, the NYEC Report showed that large numbers of employers were becoming increasingly disillusioned with the output from the schools. They complained of a marked deterioration in the attitudes of young people who were now 'more questioning', 'less likely to respect authority' and more likely to 'resent guidance about their appearance' (NYEC, 1974, p.74). What was clearly lacking was motivation, and this was therefore a key factor in helping to explain the rising levels of youth unemployment:

> ... a large minority of unemployed young people seem to have attitudes which, whatever their cause of justification, are not acceptable to employers and act as a hindrance to young people in securing jobs. (*ibid.*, p.29)

Interestingly, this view was apparently shared by many members of the Trades Union Congress (TUC).

Other commentators argued that because of recent developments within schooling, the pattern of educational control and the habits and characteristics it created were actually developing in opposition to the patterns of behaviour required in the workplace. In a discussion paper which outlined the objectives of vocational preparation for young people, prepared by the Training Services Agency (TSA) at the request of the Manpower Services Commission (MSC) and published in May 1975, the dichotomy was clearly outlined:

> It is becoming increasingly important to help young people to develop an awareness of the world of work and of the way in which wealth is produced and used by society. In recent years, the

social environment in a number of schools, with more emphasis on personal development and less on formal instruction, has been diverging from that still encountered in most work situations, where the need to achieve results in conformity with defined standards and to do so within fixed time-limits calls for different patterns of behaviour. The contrast is more marked where changes in industrial processes have reduced the scope for individual reaction and initiative. (MSC/TSA, 1975, p.15)

In January 1976, *The Times Educational Supplement* published an important article by Sir Arnold Weinstock, Managing Director of the General Electric Company. Entitled 'I blame the teachers', it argued that the shortage of skilled workers, particularly in engineering, could be attributed to the failings of the education system:

Last year, in more than one of our major industrial cities, the engineering employers failed to recruit as many apprentices as they wanted because not enough school leavers achieved adequate educational standards. This is a remarkable indictment of our educational system and one which raises disturbing questions.

According to Weinstock, one of the questions raised was the whole issue of the accountability of teachers and educationists to the community. Could not ways be found of removing teachers who were not thought to be doing a successful job?

Experience indicates that tightly administered organizations, in which you get on if you are good and get out if you are bad, have higher morale and provide more job satisfaction — as well as fulfilling their tasks more efficiently — than their opposites. So perhaps a re-look at this side of the education system would be in the best interests of teachers, as well as of the community.

But the malaise in British education lay far deeper than mere questions of administration and hiring and firing. In Weinstock's view, teachers usually lacked any direct experience of industry and in some cases were overtly hostile to the capitalist ethic and anxious to prepare children to fight against it:

Teachers fulfil an essential function in the community but, having themselves chosen not to go into industry, they often deliberately or more usually unconsciously instil in their pupils a similar bias. In so doing, they are not serving the democratic will. And this is quite apart from the strong though unquantifiable impression an outsider receives that the teaching profession has more than its fair share of people who are actively politically committed to the overthrow of liberal institutions, democratic will or no democratic will ... Educationists in schools, and in the teacher-training colleges, should recognize that they do no service to our children if they prepare them for life in a society which does not exist and which economic reality will never allow to come into existence, unless at a terrible price in individual liberty and freedom of choice. (*The Times Educational Supplement*, 23 January 1976)

Many of the same concerns were expressed by John Methven, Director General of the CBI, in an article published in *The Times Educational Supplement* in October 1976. Entitled 'What industry needs', this was based on a talk Methven had given on 'Secondary education and employ-ment' at a DES course held in Oxford in September on the secondary curriculum and the needs of society[13]. Here Methven argued that educational standards were so low that many pupils left school ill-equipped for almost any kind of employment and dreadfully ignorant about the workings of the capitalist system:

The question of standards dominates much thinking about education today, particularly at the schools level. Employers have contributed to this debate because there has, over recent years, been growing dissatisfaction among them at the standards of achievement in the basic skills reached by many school leavers, particularly those leaving at the official age ... Employers appreciate that advances in education have changed the character of the residual pool of ability in the schools and for this they have been prepared. However, the fact remains that, after one of the longest periods of compulsory education in Europe, many young people seem ill-equipped for almost any kind of employment and woefully ignorant about the basic economic facts.

It was now time for employers to help schools with the planning of their vocational programmes:

Not until recently has industry been admitted even to peer into what has been called 'the secret garden' of the curriculum. Although it understands and respects the reason for this, it does now call for a rather new dimension in employers' thinking and, in our decentralist education system, something of an excursion into unknown territory. Employers generally have supported longer periods of schooling in their own and young people's interests. But they are now convinced that further advances in mass education must be concentrated on improving its quality; and they are ready and willing to help the schools in whatever ways seem appropriate and practicable.

Methven was very anxious to stress a line of demarcation between the responsibilities of schools and those of employers:

Employers are firmly of the view that shortcomings in the vocational preparation of young people are basically an educational problem which cannot be passed on to employers under the guise of training and induction. It is for this reason that employers welcome the development of vocationally biased or relevant studies which has taken place in some schools, and would now wish to see this extended. (*The Times Educational Supplement*, 29 October 1976)

James Callaghan claims to have been very much influenced by the criticisms voiced by Weinstock, Methven and others in the course of 1976. Interviewed by Professor Ted Wragg for the BBC Radio 4 programme *Education Matters*, broadcast on 6 December 1987, he made it clear that in forming his views on education and training, he owed a special debt to Lionel (Len) Murray, General Secretary of the TUC, and John Greenborough, a leading figure in the CBI[14].

The Media Campaign

Both Labour politicians and the civil servants of the DES were keenly aware of the widespread nature and potency of media criticism of the comprehensive system. Bernard Donoughue has claimed that the trenchant media campaign was one of the main reasons why he urged James Callaghan to make an important speech outlining his government's commitment to educational standards[15]. The DES Yellow Book acknowledged that 'the greatest reorganization of schools in our educational history' had met with a generally hostile reception in the media:

The press and the media, reflecting a measure of genuine public concern, as well as some misgivings within the teaching profession itself, are full of complaints about the performance of the schools. (DES, p.5)

The 1977 Green Paper also referred to the general climate of opinion within which the Ruskin speech was delivered:

> The speech was made against a background of strongly critical comment in the press and elsewhere on education and educational standards. Children's standards of performance in their school work were said to have declined. The curriculum, it was argued, paid too little attention to the basic skills of reading, writing and arithmetic, and was overloaded with fringe subjects. Teachers lacked adequate professional skills, and did not know how to discipline children or to instil in them concern for hard work or good manners. Underlying all this was the feeling that the educational system was out of touch with the fundamental need for Britain to survive economically in a highly competitive world through the efficiency of its industry and commerce. (DES, 1977a, p.2)

According to Ball (1984), 'by the early 1970s, fuelled by press and television "horror stories", the level of "public concern" about the state of the nation's schooling had reached the level of a moral panic' (p.6). In fact, the press campaign against modern educational practices in primary and secondary schools reached something of a climax with the publication of a remarkable series of articles and reports in both 'serious' and 'popular' newspapers in the years 1975 and 1976[16]. Regardless of the political sympathies of the newspapers in question, these reports underlined the major themes of what has been described as 'the Conservative education offensive' (Centre for Contemporary Cultural Studies, CCCS, 1981, p.191): standards, discipline in schools and the political motivations of teachers.

In 1972, research had been published by the National Foundation for Educational Research (NFER) which seemed to indicate that in the late 1960s, reading standards had declined among certain groups of children (Start and Wells, 1972). The ensuing furore had led Mrs. Thatcher to set up an enquiry into the whole question of reading and its assessment, to be chaired by Sir Alan Bullock. When the findings of the Bullock Committee, *A Language for Life*, were published in February 1975 (DES, 1975), they were treated with varying degrees of scorn and derision in sections of the popular press. 'W-H-I-T-E-W-A-S-H spells whitewash', said *The Daily Mail*. 'Sir Alan Bullock's report on the teaching of English shrouds the reality in trendy pieties' (19 February 1975).

1976 saw the publication of *Teaching Styles and Pupil Progress*, the report of the research findings of the controversial Lancaster study into primary school teaching methods undertaken by Neville Bennett. The main conclusion of this research was that pupils taught by so-called 'formal' methods (class taught, in silence, with regular testing and a good deal of healthy competition) were, on average, four months ahead of those taught by 'informal' methods according to tests in the basic skills in English and mathematics. There were other groups of teachers who employed so-called 'mixed' styles, but their characteristics were generally too difficult to interpret from the available data (Bennett, 1976). Although this study was heavily criticized for defects in research design and the use of over-simplified categorizations to represent teaching methods (see, for example, Gray and Satterly, 1976; Wragg, 1976; Galton, Simon and Croll, 1980), it was represented in the media as a full-scale scientific study of 'progressive' teaching methods which proved that they simply did not work (CCCS, 1981, pp.200 and 213–4). In fact, the book achieved unprecedented national publicity; and the objections of the critics were largely ignored[17].

Also in 1976, the *Auld Report* on the William Tyndale Junior and Infant Schools was published, showing that a group of primary school teachers had been allowed to continue far too long in what appeared to be gross mismanagement of the curriculum (Auld, 1976)[18]. In the eyes of the media, the William Tyndale case was conclusive proof that enormous harm could be done by 'progressive' teachers in a state school when parents were kept out of school decisions and managers and inspectors were clearly guilty of failing to fulfil their statutory duties. What was true of one primary school in London might well apply to large numbers of primary and secondary schools throughout the country. Newspaper accounts offered the spectacle of unaccountable teachers who were at best 'sincere but misuided' and at worst 'dangerous' and 'politically motivated' (CCCS, 1981, p.195). In October 1976, a leading article in *The Times* went so far as to equate 'the wild men of the classroom' with trade union disruptors and argued that 'they must be brought to heel' (quoted in Simon, 1981, p.7). In the view of *The Guardian*, some rearrangement in the patterns of control was now clearly necessary:

> Only the naive believe teachers can be left to teach, adminis-
> trators to administer and managers to manage. Anyone who
> believes this should be led gently to the report of the William
> Tyndale enquiry, which demonstrates the difficulties of drawing
> clear boundaries of accountability in education. (*The Guardian*,
> 13 October 1976)

Between 1975 and 1977, newspapers were instrumental in creating the idea that schooling in Britain was undergoing some sort of crisis, with teachers unable or unwilling to uphold standards and governors and inspectors incapable of curing the malaise. There were confident assertions that 'parents throughout the country are becoming increasingly frustrated by the lack of discipline and the low standards of state schools' (*The Daily Mail*, 18 January 1975); that 'literacy in Britain is marching backwards' (*The Daily Mirror*, 7 February 1975); that 'millions of parents are desperately worried about the education their children are receiving' (*The Daily Mail*, 27 April 1976). Children were said to blame progressive teachers and child-centred pedagogy for the rising rate of youth unemployment. Parents wanted a greater control of schooling by non-teachers and the return of the traditional grammar school. 'The reforms of the 1960s, especially the introduction of progressive methods and of comprehensives, were held responsible for an alleged decline in general standards and basic skills, for a lack of social discipline and the incongruence between the worlds of school and of work' (CCCS, 1981, p.212).

Hostile treatment of comprehensive schools and of so-called 'progressive' teaching methods was not restricted to the national press. A series of controversial television reports in the mid-1970s[19] culminated in the decision to depict life in a large West London comprehensive in a BBC *Panorama* programme broadcast in March 1977[20]. This programme was severely criticized for concentrating on the problems faced by inexperienced classroom teachers in their probationary year and for depicting playground 'incidents' which had, in fact, been set up in advance by members of the production team. It was argued that the presentation was so unbalanced and biased as to give the programme little or no credibility as a portrayal of a school at work (Chitty, 1979, p.160).

Political Considerations

It was said of Sir Robert Peel by Benjamin Disraeli during a famous speech in the House of Commons in February 1845 attacking the government's apparent change of attitude towards the Corn Laws that the Right Hon. Gentleman had 'caught the Whigs bathing and walked away with their clothes'. Much the same image has been used by many commentators writing about James Callaghan's appropriation of the Conservative Party agenda in making the Ruskin College speech (see, for example, an editorial in *The Times*, 14 October 1976; Cox and Boyson, 1977, p.5; Dale, 1983, p.243; Ball, 1984, p.7; Finn, 1987, p.105; Coe, 1988, p.61). The phrase certainly has a fair degree of validity. The Ruskin speech was designed, in part, to secure short-term political advantage; and the Prime Minister's political advisers were well aware that they were trying to wrest the populist mantle from the Conservatives.

Bernard Donoughue has admitted that in recommending the Great Debate as a government initiative, he was largely influenced by considerations of a party political nature. He was very much aware of the media campaign against progressive developments in education and thought that unless something could be done very quickly, the failings of the system would work to the Conservative Party's electoral advantage:

> I've always been interested in education generally. I went to secondary modern school and then through grammar school to university, so I've seen several sides of the state education system. I am a supporter of comprehensive education. And always have been. But I felt that some of the dogmatists around in the 1970s were really discrediting comprehensive education. I also felt that the permissiveness was meaning that people were simply not working hard enough in the education system. I mean: liberalism was becoming a fig-leaf for idleness. It made it so easy for teachers to do very little on the basis that it was unfair to make the students do very much. And so, although I was a complete supporter of the comprehensive system, I was, in fact, very unhappy. My political finger-tips told me that unless we did something very soon, the whole state and comprehensive system would be discredited by its own failures. And that we had to pull it together pretty sharp. And I wanted to give a lead that would make it possible for the Inspectorate to take a more prominent role. What had clearly become one of the great weaknesses of our system was its non-accountability. The secret garden had become a great weed patch. There had been a tragic transformation from a relatively small group of dedicated teachers in a small profession to a mass industry of teachers, many of whom viewed teaching as just one job like any other. And when you lost the selective dedicated input, which used to be the case, you needed more general accountability. You could no longer rely on the total dedication of the teaching force; it therefore needed more accountability. And the Inspectorate seemed to me to be the only force that could increase the amount of general accountability. I didn't want to have central control of education — I still don't — but for political reasons I wanted greater accountability[21].

The references here to the role of the Inspectorate are interesting, although in 1976, members of HMI were anxious to stress that their educational proposals should *not* be interpreted as advocating greater teacher accountability or any kind of centralized control (see, for example, DES, 1977d, p.1)[22].

The Personality of James Callaghan

Lastly, it is important to say something about the personality of the Prime Minister who launched the Great Debate in 1976/77. While it would surely be naive to accept the view put forward by Fowler (1981, p.23) and echoed by others that education became a political issue in 1976 largely because the Prime Minister's daughter was dissatisfied with her own daughter's maintained primary school, it is nevertheless true that key passages in the Ruskin speech were influenced by Callaghan's own beliefs and experiences.

It is interesting to note that James Callaghan remains the only British politician to have held the four great posts of Chancellor of the Exchequer (1964–67, Home Secretary (1967–70), Foreign Secretary (1974–76) and Prime Minister (1976–79). He was also the only British Prime Minister born in the twentieth century not to have attended university. According to Donoughue (1987), 'this mattered only because he apparently felt it did' (p.10). He was always very conscious of having been brought up by his widowed mother in a very poor home in Portsmouth and of having been forced to leave school at the age of 14 (Morgan, 1987, p.267). He had a suspicion of overtly 'clever' people and suffered from an inferiority complex. His resentment at being consistently underestimated for much of his career was revealed in the answer he gave in a BBC Radio 4 interview broadcast in October 1987 when he was asked if he regretted not having had a university education:

> A lot of people say I'm not clever at all. I'm quite prepared to accept that, except that I got to be Prime Minister, and they didn't[23].

As a result of his own early struggles, he believed passionately in the value of education and in the need for rigorous educational standards to enable working class youngsters to rise above their circumstances (Donoughue, 1987, p.111)[24].

At the same time, his thoughts and actions were very much governed by a profound and old-fashioned sense of moral values. When he took over the Home Office in 1967, he was anxious to reverse the trend towards 'permissive' legislation which he felt had been so evident under his predecessor, Roy Jenkins. As Morgan has pointed out (1987), 'his working-class origins and early Baptist faith combined to make Callaghan notably conservative at the Home Office. He did not like permissiveness, and spoke out against excesses in drug-taking, sexual experiment, gambling and much else besides' (p.270). He believed that schools and ministers of religion should uphold the values of family life and teach young people to be honest and upright citizens. Politicians, too, had a duty to set a good example to the young and defend the moral fabric of the nation. In his autobiography *Time and Chance*, published in 1987, Callaghan writes: 'I had never accepted the dictum of one of my predecessors as Prime Minister who was reputed to have said, "If it's morality you want, you must go to the Archbishop" ' (Callaghan, 1987, p.395).

It is clear that Callaghan did not see himself as a man of radical socialist opinions. To quote Morgan (1987) at some length:

> He was not, by instinct, a man for sustained change. He had too much commitment, both to a basic Victorian ethic and to a solid kind of old-fashioned patriotism, to deflect the nation's energies into significant new channels ... His personal life-style, the substantial farm in Sussex, the friendship with the millionaire Julian Hodge, and directorship of the distinctly controversial Bank of Wales, also did not suggest a tendency towards iconoclasm. (p.274)

Morgan's general view is echoed by Tony Benn who describes Callaghan as 'an absolutely authentic right-winger'. Benn goes on to say:

> Now Callaghan, and in a way it's why I respected him, admitted that he was a right-winger. He was somebody who adhered, in quite a principled way, to a clutch of ideas that were associated with what you might call the Trade Union Establishment, that is to say he was class conscious in the sense that he felt that he represented labour, but not in any way socialist in understanding, inspiration, ideology or analysis. And when he took over as Prime Minister in 1976, he began a whole series of policy changes which culminated in his defeat in 1979. The Great Debate was highly significant because it brought to an end a period of development in comprehensive education where the Party was trying to make progress in the face of governments that were reluctant. But it also began the period when Callaghan went for the billion pound expenditure on the Chevaline Project which expanded the Polaris Programme; when he went for the monetarism which culminated

in the IMF cuts, the pay policy which culminated in the 1978/79 'Winter of Discontent', and so on. You could honestly trace the retreat or re-direction of the Labour Party in a number of key areas quite specifically to Callaghan's election as leader. So that is the general background against which his intervention in the educational field has to be seen, and it would be based, in part, upon his loosely 'old-fashioned' ideas that politics was all about the family, that education was about the three Rs, and that permissiveness and progressivism could be associated with left-wing ideas that had come up through the Labour Party[25].

This, then, was the man who in 1976 decided to make educational reform a key theme of his new administration. It is to the events of 1976 and 1977 that we must now turn.

Notes

1 At a general level, the publicity accorded the first Black Paper can be seen as a re-flection of a changed climate of opinion in the late 1960s. According to Labour MP Jack Straw, Shadow Education Minister and a former President of the National Union of Students, being interviewed for the programme *Talking Politics* broadcast on BBC Radio 4 (27 August 1988), the idea that Britain was on the brink of a socialist revolution in 1968 was something of a myth. There is, indeed, much evidence to suggest that, far from looking forward to some kind of left-wing coup, and contrary to the impression created by two massive demonstrations against American atrocities in Vietnam, public opinion was, in fact, moving decisively to the Right. Following Enoch Powell's notorious speech in April, with its rhetorical reference to 'the River Tiber foaming with much blood', the country's latent racism emerged, ugly and abusive. The public opinion polls in May 1968 established a record for British politics that still stands today: the highest share of public support for any political party. The figure was 56 per cent, and the party was the Conservatives. Labour lagged 28 points behind: another post-war record. Nor was this merely a freak of polling. Between March and June 1968, Labour defended six seats in Parliamentary by-elections and lost five of them, all to the Conservatives. For further discussion of this, see Kellner (1988).

2 The replacement of A. E. Dyson by Dr. Rhodes Boyson as joint-editor for the last two Papers (1975 and 1977) is the only change normally referred to, though there is some reference to the formulation of a 'New Right' policy agenda in 1975 in CCCS (1981) pp.205–7 and Ball (1984) p.7.

3 This is discussed in greater detail in chapter 7.

4 These are discussed in greater detail in chapter 8.

5 The 'withdrawal' took the form of the publication of another circular (10/70) which announced no specific policy. Instead, it stated that local authorities would 'now be freer to determine the shape of secondary provision in their areas', and that proposals would be judged on 'educational considerations in general, local needs and wishes in particular, and the wise use of resources' (DES, 1970a).

6 For figures showing the remarkable increase in the number of comprehensive schools during the period of the Heath government, see Benn and Simon (1972)

p.102; Rubinstein and Simon (1973) p.109. By the beginning of 1975, the percentage of the secondary school population attending comprehensive schools was 70 per cent compared with 31 per cent in 1970 (DES, 1976a, p.5).

7 In 1974, the situation reverted to the norm: £4,864m on education compared with £4,889m on defence.

8 Looked at from another point of view, it could be argued that educational reform represented a welcome diversion from the inevitable preoccupation with economic problems. Mr. (now Lord) Callaghan has himself admitted in his 1987 book of memoirs, *Time and Chance*, that he had very good reasons for wanting to stress his and the Labour Party's commitment to social issues at a time when the centre of the stage was being commandeered by economic disasters and the demise of the government was being forecast with frightening regularity (Callaghan, 1987, pp.397–8 and 408–12).

9 A longer analysis of this important speech will be found in chapter 5.

10 The full text of the Ruskin College speech is reprinted under the title 'Towards a national debate' in *Education*, 22 October 1976, pp.332–3.

11 Donoughue's role in the drafting of the Ruskin speech is discussed in chapter 3.

12 The employers' critique is discussed further in chapter 6.

13 For further discussion of the papers presented at this seminal DES course, see chapter 4.

14 Sir John Greenborough was Chairman of UK Oil Pipelines Ltd from 1971–77 and went on to become President of the Confederation of British Industry (CBI) from 1978–80. He was also a member of the National Economic Development Council (NEDC) from 1977–80.

15 Interview with Bernard Donoughue, 16 January 1986.

16 For an analysis of the treatment of education in two newspapers, *The Daily Mail* and *The Daily Mirror*, between 1975 and 1977, see CCCS (1981) pp.210–15.

17 So powerful was the criticism of Bennett's statistical methods that he was later obliged to rework his data. For a discussion of this development, see Coe (1988) pp.55–71.

18 Between late 1973 and the autumn of 1975, William Tyndale Junior School in Islington in North London was beset with troubles and conflicts which had a devastating effect on its standing in the local community. A group of teachers (including the Head) found themselves in conflict with the managers and eventually the Inner London Education Authority. For differing accounts of the dispute, see Ellis *et al.* (1976); Gretton and Jackson (1976); Dale (1979); Dale (1981).

19 For a discussion of the BBC Television *Horizon* programme devoted in its entirety to the Bennett research, see Cole (1988) p.62.

20 The programme called *The Best Days?* was made by Angela Pope and featured Faraday School in Ealing in West London.

21 Interview with Bernard Donoughue, 16 January 1986.

22 For a further discussion of this point, see chapter 4.

23 Lord Callaghan was being interviewed by Michael Parkinson for the BBC Radio 4 programme *Desert Island Discs* broadcast on 18 October 1987.

24 It is important to note that Callaghan did not suddenly develop an interest in education in 1976. In his autobiography he reveals that on resigning from the Treasury in 1967, he had asked Harold Wilson to be allowed to become Secretary of State for Education — 'an office to which I had always been attracted'. In the event, he was forced to make a straight exchange with Roy Jenkins at the Home Office (Callaghan, 1987, pp.222 and 231).

25 Interview with Tony Benn, 3 July 1986.

Chapter 3

The Yellow Book, The Ruskin Speech and the Great Debate

On 16 March 1976, Harold Wilson announced his resignation as Prime Minister, for reasons that at present still remain obscure, despite the efforts of numerous journalists to uncover the secret of this sudden departure[1]. On 5 April, James Callaghan, who had been Foreign Secretary since February 1974, was duly elected the Leader of the Labour Party and became, therefore, the new Prime Minister. This was followed shortly by the Easter break during which Bernard Donoughue, whom Callaghan inherited as his Senior Policy Adviser, drafted an important memorandum suggesting, among other things, that it would be appropriate, given the widespread interest in the subject, for the Prime Minister to make educational standards an important feature of his new administration. In Donoughue's view, this was an area where the Prime Minister might well reveal his personal concern and commitment:

> I suggested that although it was undesirable for a Prime Minister to meddle in every department's affairs, it would be no bad thing if he were to identify a few areas of policy of genuine interest to himself where he could try to make an impact, and I put foward education as a leading candidate. (Donoughue, 1987, p. 111)

When Callaghan became Prime Minister, Bernard (now Lord) Donoughue was Head of the Downing Street Policy Unit, one of three main bodies (the others being the DES and HMI) anxious and able to play an important role in educational policy-making in 1976[2]. Indeed, the conflict between these three bodies constitutes one of the recurring themes of the period of the Great Debate. It was the Policy Unit which took the initiative in making education an issue of major government concern. According to Callaghan himself (1987) 'its thinking was unorthodox and refreshing, and it had considerable influence when I launched the so-called Great Debate on education' (p. 405).

The Prime Minister's response to Donoughue's paper was certainly positive, and he clearly welcomed the chance to make an important speech on education at the earliest opportunity. In the event, this proved to be a foundation stone-laying ceremony at Ruskin College, Oxford in the middle of October. Donoughue spent part of the summer working on the speech with Elizabeth Arnott, the education specialist in the Policy Unit, and the first draft was ready in the early autumn. Donoughue and Arnott also wrote the section on education which the Prime Minister included in his speech to the 1976 Labour Party Conference at the end of September and which served as a curtain-raiser to the speech delivered at Ruskin College three weeks later[3]. Both speeches were seen by members of the Policy Unit as opportunities to undermine what they saw as DES complacency about the shortcomings of the education system (Donoughue, 1987, pp. 111–13).

In the meantime, the Prime Minister decided to interview leading members of his government using briefing papers drafted by Donoughue:

> It had been my experience that ministers usually asked to see the Prime Minister only when they had a personal problem or had run into a difficulty, and I decided to reverse this. So during the early months after I took office, and in pursuit of my intention not to become over-immersed in the Chancellor's economic problems, I invited other Ministers to come to see me individually and without their officials, to tell me about their work. We sat informally in the study at No. 10 and I put to all of them two basic questions. What were they aiming to do in the Department? What was stopping them? I prepared for these chats by asking Bernard Donoughue and his Policy Unit, in conjunction with my Private Office, to prepare an overview of each Department's activities before I saw the Minister, and Bernard would also suggest certain areas for me to probe. (Callaghan, 1987, p. 408)

One of the first to be interviewed was Fred Mulley, the Secretary of State for Education and Science[4], and when the meeting took place on 21 May, Callaghan raised with him four areas of concern. Was he satisfied with the basic teaching of the three Rs; was the curriculum sufficiently relevant and penetrating for older children in comprehensive schools, especially in the teaching of science and mathematics; how did the examination system shape up as a test of achievement; and what was available for the further education of 16–19-year-olds?[5] Mulley was surprised to learn that the Policy Unit was drafting a major speech on education for the Prime Minister to deliver later in the year. Yet he undertook to prepare a lengthy memorandum on the matters that Callaghan had raised; and the resulting Yellow Book reached the Prime Minister in early July[6].

The Yellow Book

The Yellow Book was a sixty-three-page confidential document compiled by DES civil servants and addressing the issues which concerned the Prime Minister and his political advisers. It began by acknowledging the widespread nature of press and media criticism of the performance of the schools. In the view of its authors, this was particularly perplexing in the light of the remarkable list of post-war achievements:

> On paper . . . the achievements of the education service since 1944 look impressive. We have, despite economic difficulties, coped with an 80 per cent increase in school population; raised the school leaving age twice. For these purposes, massive building programmes have been carried through and the teaching force greatly expanded. For the first time, over the last generation, we have set out to provide a genuinely universal free secondary education, and to that end have put in hand, and largely carried out, the greatest reorganization of schools in our educational history. Yet the press and the media, reflecting a measure of genuine public concern, as well as some misgivings within the teaching profession itself, are full of complaints about the performance of the schools. Why is this? Has something gone wrong? If so, how is it to be put right? (DES, 1976a, p. 5)

The Yellow Book proceeded to analyze the various strands of this criticism relating to both primary and secondary schools and the extent to which the media campaign represented the legitimate concerns and misgivings of parents and employers.

As far as the primary schools were concerned, the criticisms commonly heard were said to fall into a recognizable and fairly consistent pattern. Schools were being blamed for a lack of discipline and application and for a failure to achieve satisfactory results in formal subjects, particularly in reading and arithmetic. In the view of the Yellow Book, much of this was due to parental suspicion of those new approaches to primary teaching which had been endorsed by the Plowden Report of 1967:

> Although the primary schools have not been subjected to the organizational changes to which the secondary schools were exposed, many of them did undergo important changes of character during the post-war years. These changes were the expression of an approach to primary teaching which gained the adherence of many leading practitioners in the schools and colleges of education and were endorsed by the influential

Plowden Report which appeared in 1967. This 'child-centred' approach had as its underlying aims: to deal with children's individual differences, to develop their understanding rather than to feed them with information, and to use their enthusiasms. It was fully developed in only a minority of schools, but its general influence on teaching methods was widespread. From the point of view of internal organization, it normally manifested itself in the abandonment of streaming, in a departure from the class as the normal teaching unit in favour of flexible groups of various sizes, sometimes constituted vertically through age-groups, and sometimes in team teaching. In terms of teaching methods, it invariably involved a move away from rote learning. In addition, to a greater or lesser degree, formal subjects gave way to varied progress of individual or group work, sometimes on a project basis. Aesthetic subjects and 'free expression' were given greater prominence. (*ibid.*, para. 11)

The new approach could have positive results, but it could also be applied uncritically, with a consequent undermining of standards of performance in the three Rs:

> In the right hands, this approach is capable of producing admirable results. Under favourable circumstances, children could be relaxed, confident and happy; schools run on such lines excited widespread international interest and admiration. Able teachers secured these results without sacrificing standards of performance in the three Rs and in other accomplishments; indeed there were steady improvements. Unfortunately, these newer and freer methods could prove a trap to less able and experienced teachers who failed to recognize that they required a careful and systematic monitoring of the progress of individual children in specific skills, as well as a careful planning of the opportunities offered to them. Nor are they always understood and appreciated by parents even when successfully applied . . . As a result, while primary teachers in general still recognize the importance of formal skills, some have allowed performance in them to suffer as a result of the uncritical application of informal methods; and the time is almost certainly ripe for a corrective shift of emphasis. (*ibid.*, paras. 12–13)

Criticisms of the secondary schools were said to be more diverse, but in part they followed the same lines as the criticism of the primary schools:

> ... [they] are based on the feeling that the schools have become
> too easy-going and demand too little work and inadequate
> standards of performance in formal subjects from their pupils. As
> in the case of the primary schools, proficiency in the use of English
> and in mathematical skills are the commonest targets. Some
> employers — some probably recruiting from lower levels of
> ability than was formerly the case — complain that school leavers
> cannot express themselves clearly and lack the basic mathematical
> skills of manipulation and calculation and hence the basic know-
> ledge to benefit from technical training. (*ibid.*, para. 14)

Yet the general feeling of disquiet also embraced other elements which
applied specifically to secondary schooling:

> Some stem from the resentment of middle-class parents at the dis-
> appearance of the grammar schools, and reflect the fear that the
> comprehensive schools will offer a less rigorous education and,
> ultimately, worse career opportunities to their sons and
> daughters. Some arise from the more participatory style of schools
> which may permit 13- to 14-year-old pupils to choose unbalanced
> or not particularly profitable curricula or to opt in numbers insuf-
> ficient for the country's needs for scientific and technological
> subjects. In addition, there are pressures from a variety of
> specialized lobbies for the secondary curriculum to embrace their
> particular aims, and there are complaints if the response to these
> pressures is judged to be inadequate. These pressures are not only
> diverse, but in some cases directly conflicting. (*ibid.*, para. 15)[7]

All this having been conceded, it was clear that secondary schools
were subject to a number of inevitable constraints:

> First, the schools inevitably and rightly seek to enshrine and trans-
> mit the values of the society that they serve. But our society is
> undergoing almost continuous, quite rapid change, with un-
> certainties about its own values which undermine the assurance
> with which the teachers and the schools can approach their task.
> Second, and linked with this, society is pluralist — in many as-
> pects, for example in its attitudes to sex education and religious
> education. It is quite simply impossible to satisfy all sections of a
> pluralist society. Third, the schools are but one influence on
> children and not always the most significant. The schools can seek
> to extend pupils' sources of information and capacity to make
> critical judgements, but in many socially sensitive areas, the

climate outside school of their homes and peer groups is likely to be more influential. Fourth, there is a shortage of time in which to pursue all the relevant objectives, about 1,000 days, in fact, for a whole five-year secondary school course.

There has also been a fifth difficulty of short-term character, associated with the raising of the school-leaving age in 1972. This, like the earlier rising to 15 in 1947, generated some short-term problems which are now receding. On the one hand, the first cohorts of pupils had not expected to be kept at school to 16 and included some who were the more recalcitrant on that account; on the other, despite considerable national and local efforts, many teachers had not worked out the full implications of a five-year course for all pupils. It now appears that the great majority of the age-group are integrated into courses designed to take pupils through to 16. There remain, however, considerable problems about the proper shape of these five-year courses for all pupils. (*ibid.*, paras. 18–19)

According to the Yellow Book, it was classroom control, or rather the lack of it, that was a particular source of anxiety in the light of the trends and developments already outlined. Many teachers apparently felt that their disciplinary problems had been accentuated by comprehensive reorganization and the 1972/73 raising of the school-leaving age. Some of them had lowered their expectations accordingly:

> In an almost desperate attempt to modify styles of teaching and learning so as to capture the imagination and enlist the cooperation of their more difficult pupils some of them have possibly been too ready to drop their sights in setting standards of performance... (*ibid.*, para. 23).

Two further weaknesses and sources of concern were then outlined, both of which were to exert a powerful influence on government thinking, regardless of the political complexion of the party in power. The first of these concerned the alleged failure of some schools to adequately prepare their pupils to enter the world of work:

> ... some teachers and some schools may have over-emphasized the importance of preparing boys and girls for their roles in society compared with the need to prepare them for their economic roles. It would be anachronistic and unfair to blame the schools for this, because, to the extent that they exhibited this bias, they were responding to the mood of the country and indeed to

the priorities displayed by the wider policies of successive governments; but . . . the time may now be ripe for a change (as the
national mood and government policies have changed in the face
of hard and irreducible economic facts). (*ibid.*, para. 24).

The second weakness concerned 'the variation in the curriculum
followed by pupils in different schools or parts of the country or in different
ability bands'. This was particularly pronounced in years four and five
when pupils could choose from a long list of subject options. This had at one
time been seen as one of the great strengths of the comprehensive school;
now it was a 'source of worry' which could be remedied only by 'the
creation of a suitable core curriculum'. (*ibid.*, para. 25)

What, then, could be done to restore public confidence in the state
education system? Of the many themes taken up by the Yellow Book, three
are of special significance for the purposes of this study and will be discussed at some length both in this and in later chapters: the need to establish
generally accepted principles for the composition of a 'core curriculum' for
the secondary school; the need to make suitable provision for vocational
elements within school education 'for those who will benefit from this'; and
the realization that an essential prerequisite for effective curriculum
change along lines approved of by the government was an assault on the
principle that 'no one except teachers has any right to any say in what goes
on in schools' (*ibid.*, paras. 25, 35 and 58). The Department did not seek
'enhanced opportunity to exercise influence over curriculum and teaching
methods' (*ibid.*, para. 58) for its own sake; it needed control in order to
promote changes in schools, at both the primary and secondary levels,
which would restore public confidence in the system. The civil servants of
the Department felt they had a legitimate right to be concerned about
standards and the efficiency of the system because they were accountable to
politicians and parents who would always demand value for money. A core
curriculum and vocational courses would do much to allay the misgivings
of parents and employers.

In addition to these major themes, three subjects of immediate
concern were each accorded lengthy treatment in the pages of the Yellow
Book: the work of the Schools Council; the role of the Assessment of
Performance Unit (APU); and examination reform.

The Schools Council had been in existence for twelve years, but its
output was felt to be disappointing, and it had not shown itself capable of
developing whole-school curriculum strategies. Here the role of teachers
was said to be of crucial importance since their representation on the
Schools Council, given its existing constitution, could effectively block the
discussion of genuine curriculum innovation. Clearly, it was open to

question whether the constitution of the Council was appropriate to the tasks before it:

> The Schools Council has performed moderately in commissioning development work in particular curricula areas; it has had little success in tackling examination problems, despite the availability of resources which its predecessor (the Secondary Schools Examination Council) never had; and it has scarcely begun to tackle the problems of the curriculum as a whole. Despite some good quality staff work, the overall performance of the Schools Council has, in fact, both on curriculum and on examinations, been generally mediocre. Because of this, and because the influence of the teachers' unions has led to an increasingly political flavour — in the worst sense of the word — in its deliberations, the general reputation of the Schools Council has suffered a considerable decline over the last few years. In the light of this recent experience, it is open to question whether the constitution of the Schools Council strikes the right balance of responsibility for the matters with which it deals. (*ibid.*, para. 50)

No such doubts were evident in the Yellow Book's consideration of the role, actual and potential, of the Assessment of Performance Unit. The APU had been formally announced in 1974 in a DES White Paper *Educational Disadvantage and the Educational Needs of Immigrants* (DES, 1974) and had come to the attention of educationists in 1975 with the publication of a paper 'Monitoring pupils' performance' by Brian Kay (1975), the author being the first Head of the Unit[8]. The Yellow Book reminded its readers that the terms of reference of the APU, as set out in the 1974 White Paper, were:

> To promote the development of methods of assessing and monitoring the achievement of children at school, and to seek to identify the incidence of under-achievement. (DES, 1974, p. 16)

The tasks of the Unit were then reported as being:

1 To identify and appraise existing instruments and methods of assessment which may be relevant for these purposes.
2 To sponsor the creation of new instruments and techniques for assessment, having due regard to statistical and sampling methods.
3 To promote the conduct of assessments in cooperation with local education authorities and teachers.

4   To identify significant differences related to the circumstances in which children learn, including the incidence of under-achievement, and to make the findings available to all those concerned with resource allocation within the Department, local education authorities and schools. (*ibid.*)

If the Unit's start had been slow and inauspicious, this was blamed by the Yellow Book partly on the hostility and resentment shown in some quarters of the teaching profession, notably by members of the National Union of Teachers (NUT), and partly on the delay in finding a suitable chairman for its consultative committee. Now, however, the Unit was busily engaged in the first of its four tasks by following up the recommendations of the Bullock Report about the testing of reading and the use of language, by setting up a monitoring system in mathematics (following on from development work at the NFER), and by making a start in considering the assessment of science. It should then be encouraged to turn its attention to other significant areas of the curriculum:

> The work of the Assessment of Performance Unit should be increased and its programme accelerated, so far as the intrinsic disciplines of its work and the availability of competent research and development workers permit. Here the major problem is to persuade the teaching profession that this is all to their advantage; we shall need also to staff the Unit appropriately. (*ibid.*, para. 58)

In matters relating to examination reform, and particularly to the introduction of the Certificate of Extended Education (CEE) for 17-year-old students and the replacement of GCE 'O' level and CSE by a new common system of examination at 16 + , the Yellow Book was exceedingly cautious.

The CEE was designed to provide an examination target for boys and girls of about 17 who wished to continue their education at school after the age of 16 but did not have the ability to tackle GCE 'A' level courses. It had strong support within the various teachers' organizations and had already secured the backing of the Schools Council, but this enthusiasm was clearly not shared by the DES and the Inspectorate:

> This new examination is strongly advocated by the National Union of Teachers and by other groups which, in the main, support the government's secondary education policies to which they regard it as complementary. Nevertheless, the Department and Inspectorate have misgivings about its merit. The demand for it has almost cetainly been overstated, and the educational

programmes followed by some pupils in the target group are of doubtful relevance to their needs. The new examination would not be useful as a stepping-stone to further education courses (nearly all of which are geared to entry at either 16 or 18). On general grounds, the onus should be on the proposers to show it is worthwhile to add to the financial and other burdens of external examining in schools. (*ibid.*, para. 31)

In the event, a decision on the new examination was postponed many times, until the uncertainty was ended in May 1982 with the publication by the Conservative government of its proposals for a new and very different 17+ qualification to be called the Certificate of Pre-Vocational Education (CPVE) (see Mortimore, Mortimore and Chitty, 1986, pp. 60–5).

The Yellow Book was hardly more enthusiastic about a single system of examining at 16+ which had been suggested by the Schools Council as early as 1970 (only five years after the introduction of the CSE). The work undertaken by the Council had not convinced the DES that the very real practical difficulties had been solved:

> In principle, the creation of a common system of examination at 16+ might eliminate some of the difficulties associated with the present double system. But the Schools Council have not succeeded in demonstrating that the considerable technical and educational difficulties of examining over a very wide spectrum of ability have been solved, and they have not offered an agreed and workable plan for the administration of the proposed new examination by the existing examining bodies. The Department's reservations are shared by important sectors of the education world. (*ibid.*, para. 32)

Again it was left to the Conservative government to take the final decision on a common system of examining, this time as late as June 1984[9].

The Leaking of the Yellow Book

The Yellow Book is dated July 1976, but sections of it were not leaked to the press until the middle of October, a few days before the Prime Minister was scheduled to give his important speech on education at Ruskin College, Oxford. *The Guardian* carried a front-page article on the Book on October 13 under the headline 'State must step into schools'; and this was followed two days later by a major three-page report on the document in *The Times Educational Supplement*.

Although the Yellow Book does not actually talk in terms of introducing a *national* curriculum for all secondary schools, this was the theme highlighted by *The Guardian* in its front-page article:

> A plan to introduce a basic national curriculum for Britain's secondary schools has been put to the Prime Minister in a memorandum from the Department of Education and Science.
>
> This proposal, which at a stroke would end 100 years of non-interference in state education, is made in a confidential document specially commissioned by Mr. Callaghan. Its sixty-three pages constitute a severe indictment of the failure of secondary schools to produce enough scientists and engineers, and the memorandum calls for drastic measures to change the attitude of children entering schools, and for much tighter control by Inspectors of the education system . . .
>
> Extracts from the document, a copy of which is in *The Guardian's* possession, warn that 'in the face of hard and irreducible economic facts', the time may be ripe for major changes in the curriculum of all secondary schools, ending the traditional rights of teachers to control the curriculum . . .
>
> The central theme of the memorandum is to argue for a return to an agreed 'core curriculum' in secondary schools which, after agreement from local education authorities and teachers, should be introduced to ensure improved standards and a return to the study of mathematics and science. (*The Guardian*, 13 October 1976)

The same issue of *The Guardian* carried an editorial generally welcoming the DES initiative and looking forward to a reduction in the professional independence of teachers:

> Shudders will be seismically recorded in many teachers' common rooms today in response to our exclusive report . . . of a confidential government plan to introduce a national curriculum for schools. Is nothing sacred? No principle has been more hallowed by British governments than the rule that they should not interfere in the curriculum of state schools. Prompted initially by the fear of governments attempting to preach their own particular ideology or doctrine, the rule has been reinforced in recent times by the desire of the teaching unions to keep control of the classroom. Like doctors, teachers too have become increasingly committed to professional independence. But just as the clinical independence of doctors is eventually going to have to be

reduced . . . so too is the far more recent professional independence of teachers. (*ibid.*)

The editorial anticipated that 'the loudest protests' would come from the
teachers, but argued that the need for a national curriculum was 'as good
an example as any to point up the demarcation problems'. A core
curriculum laid down by the government would clearly necessitate some
rearrangement in the patterns of control:

> The need is for a better balance. Obviously, this should not take
> the form of Whitehall dictating on what every student does — nor
> does it mean the State must intervene in the selection of textbooks.
> But in a school week of (say) thirty-five periods, there should be a
> requirement that twenty out of the thirty-five periods are reserved
> for 'core' subjects. (*ibid.*)

The Times carried an editorial on the leaked memorandum headed
'The Department's Black Paper' on 14 October. It welcomed 'the beginning
of a government drive to bring back standards into teaching, concentrating
on the basic skills of reading, writing and arithmetic'. Yet this was also
probably the first occasion when reference was made to the Government's
appropriation of the Opposition's clothes. In the view of the editorial:

> That this initiative should come from a Labour Government is
> ironic, since all the groundwork in recent years has been made by
> the Right. Mr. Callaghan is stealing Tory clothing. (*The Times*, 14
> October 1976)

Edited extracts from the Yellow Book and critical reactions to them
took up the first three pages of *The Times Educational Supplement* of 15
October. The front-page report was headlined 'DES report to Prime
Minister sparks off angry protests' and made it clear that large sections of
the educational establishment were deeply suspicious of the government's
intentions. Particularly critical was the National Union of Teachers (NUT)
which argued that turmoil would be created in schools 'if we went from a
Callaghan curriculum one year to the Thatcher theology in the next'[10].
Given the chance to reply, the DES emphasized that the government would
'not be calling for state control over the curriculum'; and a press statement
from 10 Downing Street pointed out that there was nothing unusual or
sinister about a government department preparing a memorandum for the
Prime Minister:

> When the Prime Minister is going to make a major speech, it is
> common practice for him to call for a memorandum from one of

his ministers. This then becomes one of the briefing documents he uses. (Quoted in *The Times Educational Supplement*, 15 October 1976)

The view of *The Times Educational Supplement* itself was that the quality of education was now being embraced as a major political issue and that this being the case, the approach adopted by the Yellow Book might well be considered preferable to the policies advocated by some of the Conservative Party's more right-wing supporters:

> Both parties now believe that there is a political time-bomb ticking away in the schools. The Conservatives think public anxiety must favour them. They strike attitudes in defence of basic standards in the belief that this is the way to exploit the anxiety. Mr. Callaghan and Mrs. Williams may well have reached a not dissimilar political assessment, and believe they must defuse the time-bomb before it has time to go off. This they hope to do by bringing curricular issues into the open. Most people in the education service — including those whose initial reaction to the Yellow Book will be hostile — will prefer this approach to the Black Paper postures which Conservative education spokesmen have begun to assume. (*The Times Educational Supplement*, 15 October, 1976)

It is not clear exactly who leaked the Yellow Book to *The Guardian* and *The Times Educational Supplement* in the middle of October. It may have been, as Morris claims (1987b), a 'public-spirited' act, designed to embarrass the government (p. 211). On the other hand, according to Sheila Browne, at that time Senior Chief Inspector, the feeling inside the Inspectorate was that a decision had been taken 'at the highest level' to leak sections of the memorandum to the press to 'test the water' prior to the delivery of the Ruskin speech[11]. Fowler (1981) claims that the leaks were authorized by No. 10, although Bernard Donoughue has denied that the Policy Unit was in any way responsible (p. 23)[12]. The timing of the leaks would certainly tend to support the view that they were authorized, or at least approved of, by the government. It can surely be no coincidence that sections of the Book first appeared in *The Guardian* five days before the Prime Minister's visit to Oxford. It has been argued (Reid, 1978, p. 8; Hargreaves, 1982, pp. 218–9) that the initiation of the Great Education Debate was a carefully stage-managed exercise. The teachers' unions were deliberately encouraged to believe that teacher autonomy was being directly threatened:

... a series of leaks to the press ... hinted at some draconian move on the part of the government and of the DES against teacher autonomy, through the imposition of some kind of national curriculum. This enabled the initiative to remain with the side of the DES, while the teachers' organizations, in particular, gave vent to their anger in anticipation of the worst. (CCCS, 1981, p. 217)

In the event, the proposals in the Prime Minister's speech could be presented as being moderate and positive in the light of some of the more hysterical predictions of the government's intentions.

The furore caused by reports of the Yellow Book was referred to by the Prime Minister in his Ruskin speech, albeit euphemistically, in a number of half-mocking, half-serious references to his criticis. The Prime Minister was anxious to defend his intervention by presenting himself as the representative of the lay community, daring to question the views of experts:

There have been one or two ripples of interest in the educational world in anticipation of this visit. I hope the publicity will do Ruskin some good, and I don't think it will do the world of education any harm. I must thank all those who have inundated me with advice: some helpful and others telling me less politely to keep off the grass, to watch my language, and that they will be examining my speech with the care usually given by Hong Kong watchers to the China scene. It is almost as though some people would wish that the subject matter and purpose of education should not have public attention focussed on it; nor that profane hands should be allowed to touch it.

I cannot believe that this is a considered reaction. The Labour movement has always cherished education: free education, comprehensive education, adult education. Education for life. There is nothing wrong with non-educationalists, even a Prime Minister, talking about it again. Everyone is allowed to put his oar in on how to overcome our economic problems, how to put the balance of payments right, how to secure more exports, and so on and so on. Very important, too. But, I venture to say, not as important in the long run as preparing future generations for life ...

... where there is legitimate public concern, it will be to the advantage of all involved in the education field if these concerns are aired and shortcomings righted or fears put at rest ...

The debate that I was seeking has got off to a flying start even before I was able to say anything. ... It will be an advantage to the teaching profession to have a wide public understanding and support for what they are doing. And there is room for greater understanding among those not directly concerned of the nature of the job that is being done already.

These comments were very late additions to the speech, their inclusion prompted by the newspaper speculation and union observations of the previous week. As Mr. Callaghan has commented in his book of memoirs:

> ... the Great Debate I had hoped to launch at Ruskin had left the slipway and entered the water even before I had time to crash the bottle of champagne on its bows. (Callaghan, 1987, p. 410)

Misconceptions about the Yellow Book

The interest and controversy surrounding the Yellow Book in the years since lengthy extracts first appeared in *The Guardian* and *The Times Educational Supplement* have given rise to two popular misconceptions about its authorship and influence: firstly, that it represented HMI thinking on the state of education in 1976 (see, for example: Kogan, 1978, p. 65; CCCS, 1981, p. 217; Fowler, 1981, p. 23; Simon, 1981, p. 10; Hunter, 1984, p. 280; Nuttall, 1984, p. 167; Coe, 1988, p. 62); and, secondly, that it was the basic inspiration for the Ruskin speech delivered later in the year (see, for example: Reid, 1978, p. 4; Fowler, 1979, p. 25; CCCS, 1981, p. 217; Hunter, 1984, p. 280; Nuttall, 1984, p. 167; Kirk, 1986, p. 4; Morris, 1987b, p. 211).

These misconceptions were, to a large extent, fostered by contemporary commentators and, particularly, by the important editorial in *The Times Educational Supplement* of 15 October 1976 which credited the Inspectorate with far too much influence in 1976 and at the same time failed to appreciate the seminal role of Bernard Donoughue and his colleagues. All the evidence suggests, and this chapter will seek to show, that the Yellow Book was prepared by DES officials *without* the active involvement of HMI; and that the Ruskin speech was largely the work of the Prime Minister's political advisers in the Downing Street Policy Unit. It can be argued that the Great Debate was not an HMI initiative and that it did not proceed along lines of which HMI approved.

The Myth of HMI Authorship of the Yellow Book

When *The Times Educational Supplement* received its leaked copy of the Yellow Book a few days before Mr. Callaghan's speech, it was immediately assumed that Sheila Browne and her HMI colleagues had played a leading role in its preparation[13]. This was the view put forward in the paper's editorial, which also argued that the DES and the Inspectorate would have to rely on the persuasive quality of their advice in the absence of any legal mechanisms of control:

> ... With the encouragment of Sir William Pile, the former Permanent Secretary at the DES, Miss Browne has for more than a year had a group of HMIs working on curriculum and standards in primary and secondary education, paving the way for a more direct intervention by the Department. Large hints have been dropped ... that the DES believe that the privacy of the secret garden should no longer be sacrosanct. The obvious instrument for any such intervention is the Inspectorate — hence the important part played by the HMIs in preparing a memorandum for the Prime Minister ...
>
> Yet the Inspectorate somehow have to put forward their proposals for a model core of curriculum which should form the basis of the educational experience of all children up to a stipulated level, without arousing so much hostility and alarm that the project is still-born. Much of their initial work has already been done. All that remains is to take off the wraps. The whole operation calls for unlimited tact and delicacy; but nobody needs to point out the pitfalls — the first reaction from the National Union of Teachers and others reveal these only too well. But it won't be sufficient for the teachers to attack this as a breach with long tradition: it is disenchantment with that tradition which has produced both public anxiety and this HMI initiative. Some press reports have spoken of the government taking 'control' of the curriculum. There is, however, no suggestion that there will be any change in the legal mechanisms of control: the DES and the Inspectorate will have to rely on the persuasive quality of their advice. There is no other practical approach for them to adopt at this stage. (*The Times Educational Supplement*, 15 October, 1976)

It is perhaps easy to understand why contemporary observers should have over-estimated the part played by the Inspectorate in the compilation of the Yellow Book. It was known that members of HMI were working on plans for a common curriculum for the secondary school, and it was not sufficiently appreciated that theirs was a very different concept from that of the core curriculum advocated by the DES memorandum[14]. At the same time, the extracts from the memorandum which appeared in the press seemed to envisage a very important role for the Inspectorate in the construction and implementation of the government's plans:

> HM Inspectorate is without doubt the most powerful single agency to influence what goes on in schools, both in kind and standard. The Inspectorate antedates the Department, and remains professionally independent of it; like the Department, it is answerable to the Secretary of State. It is the oldest instrument for monitoring the education system and, from this primary function, it derives a second major role, that of improving the performance of the system. No exercise of power is involved in this search for improvement; the Inspectorate, by tradition and by choice, exerts influence by the presentation of evidence and by advice . . .
>
> Considerable attention has already been devoted by the Inspectorate to the organization of secondary schools. This includes both the advantages and disadvantages of different patterns of comprehensive organization and the implications of different types of internal organization. Courses and conferences have been organized to help headteachers and others with special responsibilities to cope with the novel problems of organization in comprehensive schools. Within the Inspectorate, studies have been made both of the state of education in different geographical areas and of different subjects within the curriculum. Surveys of different aspects of the work of the schools (which extend to their social as well as their educational role) have been written and published (concerning, for example, the needs of immigrants, pupils with learning difficulties, and careers education) . . .
>
> There need be no fear that the DES could not make use of enhanced opportunity to exercise influence over curriculum and teaching methods: the Inspectorate would have a leading role to play in bringing forward ideas in these areas and is ready to fulfil that responsibility. (DES, 1976a, pp. 15, 18 and 25)

Yet Sheila Browne, who figured prominently in contemporary speculation about the true architects of the government's strategy, would wish to deny HMI responsibility for the thinking outlined in the Yellow Book and for the DES initiatives which followed. In Miss Browne's words:

> Although HMI would have been consulted on various aspects of the document, the Yellow Book was essentially the product of the DES. It should *not* be viewed as an HMI statement on standards in education or on the quality of the teaching profession — despite the frequent references to the role and importance of the Inspectorate. It was drafted by DES officials at the behest of the Prime Minister . . . It should therefore be seen as a *confidential* DES document, a *transaction* between the Secretary of State and the Prime Minister[15].

Miss Browne also denies that the Inspectorate was responsible for the memorandum's oft-quoted criticisms of the work of the Schools Council.

In support of her statement, *The Times Educational Supplement* has recently made use of a short editorial marking the publication of James Callaghan's memoirs, *Time and Chance* in April 1987 to modify its original observations:

> The Yellow Book clearly laid the ground-work for most of the centralizing initiatives of the next decade . . . Where *The TES* went wrong in 1976 . . . was in attributing too much of the Great Debate initiative to the Inspectorate instead of to ambitious administrators in the DES, stiffened by Mr. Callaghan's back-room boys. (*The Times Educational Supplement*, 17 April 1987)

Sheila Browne's version of events is also substantiated by a close examination of the style and language of the Yellow Book itself. These had much in common with those of later DES publications and certainly showed little evidence of HMI input. Reid has pointed out, for example (1978, p. 9), that the Yellow Book phrase 'The time has probably come to try to establish generally accepted principles for the composition of the secondary curriculum for all pupils' (DES, 1976a, p. 11) is echoed in 'It is clear that the time has come to try to establish generally accepted principles for the composition of the secondary curriculum for all pupils', to be found in the 1977 Green Paper (DES, 1977b, p. 11). The use of the terms 'common core' and 'core curriculum' (DES, 1976a, pp. 11 and 22; DES, 1977b, p. 11) contrasts sharply with the HMI model of a broad, generally balanced curriculum common to all secondary pupils which specifically rejects the concept of the 'common core' as often comprising, particularly in the forth and fifth years, little more than English, mathematics, religious education and physical activities (DES, 1977d, p. 4). DES authorship of the Yellow

Book also helps to explain the document's criticism of new trends in primary-school teaching which would have been highly hypocritical had it been made by members of an Inspectorate which had done so much to pioneer 'progressive' methods in the wake of the Plowden Report (DES, 1967).

The Myth of DES Responsibility for the Ruskin Speech

The second misconception concerns the relationship between the Yellow Book and the Ruskin College speech. As we have seen, it has generally been assumed that the Ruskin speech was based solely on the DES memorandum; and a number of important themes were certainly common to both. The leaking of the Yellow Book a few days before the Prime Minister's Oxford speech obviously gave credence to the view that the two must be intimately connected. This view has gone largely unchallenged for at least a decade.

When, therefore, Bernard Donoughue claimed in an article in *The Times Educational Supplement* in May 1987 and in *Prime Minister*, his inside account of the premierships of Harold Wilson and James Callaghan, that he had been the instigator and principal author of the Ruskin speech (*The Times Educational Supplement*, 29 May 1987; Donoughue, 1987, p. 111), his involvement in the enterprise came as something of a shock to many commentators[16], and he was bitterly criticized by Max Morris, a former high-profile President of the National Union of Teachers, for distorting the true facts.

Mr. Morris made his feelings clear in a letter to *The Times Educational Supplement* in June 1987:

> It is . . . quite extraordinary to read an account of the provenance of the Ruskin speech which makes no mention whatsoever of the secret Yellow Book prepared for the Prime Minister by the DES and leaked to *The Times Educational Supplement* which public-spiritedly published its tissue of distortions, half-truths and plain whoppers. It was the Yellow Book which was the occasion for the speech, which was hyped to the skies in advance . . . Lord Donoughue claims the credit for drafting the speech. He is welcome to the credit for a very poor effort which was, in fact, drafted by a DES official who will now be grateful to be relieved of the responsibility by such a distinguished writer of fiction. (Letter to *The Times Educational Supplement*, 19 June 1987)

Max Morris reiterated his criticisms in a review of the Donoughue memoirs published in *Education* in September 1987:

> Donoughue's talent as a fiction writer blossoms to full flowering in his account of Callaghan's Ruskin speech and of Shirley William's venture into showbiz, the 'Great Debate'. It was he, we are told, who interested Mr. Callaghan in education, and the Policy Unit is awarded the doubtful credit of drafting the Ruskin speech. This handling of the story would have failed Donoughue his 'O' levels, let alone his Doctorate. The Prime Minister had considerably earlier asked Fred Mulley for a report on the state of education and this had led to the production of the notorious and secret Yellow Book.
>
> This document was so outrageous . . . that it was public-spiritedly leaked to *The Times Educational Supplement* and *The Guardian* to the chagrin of the incompetent civil servants who penned the trash. (Their new master was Sir James Hamilton, whom Donoughue naturally praises.) Of this, there is no inkling in the book, only a brief, cryptic reference to a *discussion* between Callaghan and Mulley in the early summer of 1976.
>
> Donoughue's weakness, typical of boffinism, is to believe that the world is run by advisers who write documents for powerful people. These advisers, Donoughue's colleagues in his Unit, are all described as 'brilliant' or 'excellent' (his range of adjectives is limited), and they always knew the solutions to the most intractable problems. But it was the Yellow Book of the Old Guard, Hamilton's Public School 'heavies' of the DES, that inspired the Ruskin speech, with all its fateful consequences, not the private views of the Policy Unit. (Morris, 1987b, p. 211)

Donoughue's claims were, however, supported by Mr. Callaghan. In his own book of memoirs, *Time and Chance* published in April 1987, the former Prime Minisiter accepted that the main draft for his speech had emanated from the Policy Unit (p. 410). He has since agreed that the original idea for a major speech on education came from Bernard Donoughue[17]. Furthermore, in an interview with Professor Ted Wragg in the *Education Matters* series, broadcast on BBC Radio 4 on 6 December 1987, he claimed not to have actually *seen* the 1976 Yellow Book. He was quite certain it was not the inspiration for the Ruskin speech. Indeed, the only Yellow Book he could ever recall reading was the one produced by Lloyd George at the end of the 1920s![18]

The Donoughue version of events has also been supported by

Christopher Price, Parliamentary Private Secretary to Fred Mulley in 1976:

> The whole educational establishment was coming under siege in 1976. Mr. Callaghan was surreptitiously ordering his Ruskin speech to be prepared — outside the suspect Department of Education — because he felt the education card was rapidly slipping from Labour's hands. (Price, 1985, p. 170)

It would seem obvious that many major political speeches have a number of different authors. We are probably very near the truth if we argue that a number of separate papers were prepared for the Ruskin speech. The most detailed papers came from the Policy Unit, but there was also an input from the DES incorporating presumably some of the ideas put forward in the Yellow Book. Bernard Donoughue then had the task of co-ordinating all the material. This view of events is supported by Mr. Callaghan himself:

> The truth about the Ruskin speech is no different from that of many other speeches, namely that several people had a hand in its preparation. I have no doubt that a draft came from the Department of Education and that the speech was worked on by the Private Office at No. 10. Lord Donoughue had an important part in co-ordinating the papers that were prepared under the general guidance that I would have given, both before a first draft appeared and during the preparation of the subsequent drafts. It would certainly be fair to say that Lord Donoughue was a prime instigator of the idea[19].

According to Donoughue, the speech would have been more hard-hitting if the Policy Unit had been allowed to have its own way:

> We prepared the first complete draft of the Ruskin speech. Then it was amended, as always, as it was put through the machine, and there were definitely attempts from elsewhere in Whitehall to water it down, which we tried to resist, and the Prime Minister himself wrote in his own phrases and his own language. The final version was not as strong as we would have wished[20].

Themes of the Ruskin Speech

Both James Callaghan and Bernard Donoughue had clear ideas about the message they wanted to put across in the Ruskin speech. According to Callaghan:

My general guidance for the speech was that it should begin a debate about existing educational trends and should ask some controversial questions. It should avoid blandness and bring out the criticisms I had heard, whilst explaining the value of the teachers' work and the need for parents to be closely associated with their children's schools. It should ask why industry's status was so low in young people's choice of careers, and the reasons for the shortage of mathematics and science teachers. (Callaghan, 1987, p. 410)

For Donoughue, it was particularly important that the Speech should concern itself with the improvement of standards and the concept of teacher accountability:

... in the speech, I included all the feelings which I shared with the Prime Minister on the need for more rigorous educational standards, for greater monitoring and accountability of teachers, for greater concentration on the basic skills of literacy and numeracy, and for giving greater priority to technical, vocational and practical education... (Donoughue, 1987, p. 111)

The speech itself embraced a number of themes which clearly interested both the Prime Minister and the Policy Unit[21]. First and foremost, there was the need to make effective use of the money — roughly £6 billion a year — that the government was spending on education. In recent years, there had been a massive injection of resources into education, mainly to cope with increased pupil numbers and partly to raise standards. Now the challenge was to raise standards still further by the skilful use of existing resources:

With the increasing complexity of modern life, we cannot be satisfied with maintaining existing standards, let alone observe any decline. We must aim for something better ... But in present circumstances, there can be little expectation of further increased resources being made available, at any rate for the time being ... and a challenge in education is to examine its priorities and to secure as high efficiency as possible by the skilful use of the £6 billion of existing resources.

The Prime Minister reported that in his travels around the country in recent months, he had been made aware of public concern about the state education system. This concern assumed two forms. On the one hand, there were complaints from industry that 'new recruits from the schools sometimes do not have the basic tools to do the job that is required'. On the other, there was the concern felt by parents and others that the new informal methods of teaching 'seem to produce excellent results when they are in well-qualified hands, but are much more dubious when they are not'.

The Prime Minister suggested that a convenient way of tackling both these problems was to see education as having the twin goals of equipping children for 'a lively, constructive place in society' while at the same time fitting them 'to do a job of work'. Certain basic requirements flowed automatically from an acceptance of this analysis:

> Both of the basic purposes of education require the same essential tools. These are basic literacy, basic numeracy, the understanding of how to live and work together; respect for others; respect for the individual. This means acquiring certain basic knowledge and skills and reasoning ability. It means developing lively, inquiring minds and an appetite for further knowledge that will last a life-time. It means mitigating as far as possible the disadvantages that may be suffered through poor home conditions or physical or mental handicap . . .

Above all, teachers had to accept that where educational standards were concerned, theirs was not the only voice with a right to be heard:

> I take it that no one claims exclusive rights in this field. Public interest is strong and legitimate and will be satisfied . . . To the teachers I would say that you must satisfy the parents and industry that what you are doing meets their requirements and the needs of our children. For if the public is not convinced, then the profession will be laying up trouble for itself in the future.

According to the Prime Minister, the areas that needed further study as a matter of priority included: the methods and aims of 'informal instruction'; the case for a so-called 'core curriculum' of basic knowledge; the means by which the use of resources might be monitored in order to maintain a proper national standard of performance; the role of the Inspectorate in relation to national standards; the relationship between industry and education; and the future structure of public examinations. These were all to be regarded as proper subjects for discussion and debate.

The Prime Minister was anxious to deny that he was joining those who paint 'a lurid picture of educational decline'. This was not his view of the situation:

> My remarks are not a clarion call to black paper prejudices. We all know those who claim to defend standards but who in reality are simply seeking to defend old privileges and inequalities.

What he was calling for was a public debate on education in which all the interested parties — 'parents, teachers, learned and professional bodies, representatives of higher education and both sides of industry, together with the government' — should feel able to participate. It should be a rational debate based on the facts. All those concerned should respond positively and with due regard to the achievements of the past thirty years. It was, after all, appropriate that a Labour Prime Minister should launch such an enterprise:

> The traditional concern of the whole Labour movement is for the education of our children and young people on whom the future of the country must depend . . . It would be a betrayal of that concern if I did not draw problems to your attention and put to you specifically some of the challenges which we have to face and some of the responses that will be needed from our educational system.

It was particularly important that teachers should welcome the government's initiative. Mr. Callaghan has commented in his autobiography (1987) that what he was asking for from teachers was 'a positive response' and 'not a defensive posture in the debate which I hoped would begin' (p. 411).

The Ruskin speech has to be viewed on a number of different levels, all of them interrelated. Essentially, it marked at the very highest political level the end of the phase of educational expansion which had been largely promoted by the Labour Party and at the same time it signalled a public re-definition of educational objectives. Its timing was, in part, a response to immediate events: the acute economic crisis, escalating unemployment and a declining birth-rate. The days of expansion were clearly over; there had to be more skilful use of existing resources. It was also an attempt to wrest the populist mantle from the Conservative Opposition and pander to perceived public disquiet at the alleged decline in educational standards. Sections of the popular press had played a major role in undermining public confidence in the comprehensive system; and popular reservations about 'progressive' teaching styles appeared to be justified by the William Tyndale case and by the Bennett study of primary teaching methods. The government was anxious to demonstrate that it shared the concerns of ordinary parents. Then again, the speech marked a clear shift on the part of the Labour leadership towards policies which would facilitate greater government control of the education system. This was obviously necessary if government ideas on the curriculum were to be implemented. For, above all, the speech represented a clear attempt to construct a new educational consensus around a more direct subordination of education to what were perceived to be the needs of the economy.

Mr. Callaghan has claimed in a number of radio and television interviews[22] and in his book of memoirs (1987, p. 410) that there was much media hostility to the idea that a Prime Minister should think himself knowledgeable enough to comment on educational matters. He has always been particularly critical of the treatment his initiative received in the pages of *The Times Educational Supplement*:

> ... I tripped over some appalling educational snobbery — *The Times Educational Supplement* wrote an article that was both scornful and cynical about my intention. It complained that while I was a professional politician, I was no more than an amateur educationalist, and doubted the propriety of my raising questions on what should be taught and how it was to be taught. It said that I was falling a victim of an attempt by the schools inspectors to gain more control. *The Times Educational Supplement* did not object to a debate, but it should be conducted by those who knew what they were talking about, and I should not trespass into this sensitive and professional field. (*ibid.*, p. 410)

In fact, the editorial in *The Times Educational Supplement* of 22 October 1976 was more supportive than Callaghan suggests and generally welcomed the Prime Minister's initiative in confronting the argument that 'the subject matter and purpose of education should not have public attention focussed on it'. The editorial saw the Ruskin address as 'a major speech by a Prime Minister to serve notice on the schools that they are accountable to the public and can reasonably be expected to give an account of their stewardship'. The main point of the editorial was that the speech did not go far enough, and it called for the Government to demand evidence of systematic curriculum planning and evaluation on the part of every school and every local education authority. Teachers must respond positively to the Prime Minister's challenge:

> Now that the Prime Minister has uttered in more or less the terms which had been predicted, the immediate effect is one of anticlimax ... This sense of anticlimax lies in the 'so what?' question at the heart of Mr. Callaghan's homely rhetoric. He has put the Department of Education and Science on the spot. Elizabeth House now has to come up with specifics, where, hitherto, it has been enough to talk generalities. Now we shall see how good have been the preparations inside the DES for this central initiative. But this is not enough ...

Until each school, and each local authority, can produce evidence of systematic curriculum planning and evaluation, with careful attention to basic skills, the public will continue to feel that a gigantic cover-up is going on. The teachers' unions' paranoid reaction to any legitimate public concern about standards simply increases the suspicions, and gives added incentive for politicians, whether national or local, to meddle in teachers' professional concerns.

The public remains to be convinced that teachers know what they are doing. Unless it is convinced, there is the danger of an imposed 'core curriculum' that will distort, rather than underpin, important objectives of schooling. Even if the core is designed to occupy a modest space on the timetable, only the most confident teachers will avoid devoting the lion's share of their (and their pupils') energy to it. In the eyes of many teachers, and almost all pupils, parents and employers, the rest of the curriculum will take on the status of non-examined general studies in an 'A' level course.

Everybody knows . . . that attempts to impose curricula and methods on teachers are at best ineffective and at worst counter-productive . . . If teachers — those in classrooms, not the professional organization men — were to stay sulking in their tents while this battle rages around them, we should be in for a very sterile period in education. (*The Times Educational Supplement*, 22 October 1976)

Right-wing commentators were quick to point out that the Prime Minister had appropriated sizeable portions of their agenda but professed to feel flattered and relieved that their views had been taken so seriously. In the words of Dr. Rhodes Boyson, Conservative MP and former comprehensive school headteacher:

For ten years, I have been advocating a return to standards. There will be a great sigh of relief among parents and Black Paper writers everywhere. Let me say we don't mind which government does this, and I welcome Mr. Callaghan's initiative. (Reported in *The Times Educational Supplement*, 15 October 1976)

A similar view was taken in a letter to Members of Parliament at the beginning of *Black Paper 1977*:

In October 1976, Mr. Callaghan, the Prime Minister, attempted to steal our clothes, which have always been freely available. He repeated our assertions that money is being wasted, standards are too low, and children are not being given the basic tools of literacy and numeracy. (Cox and Boyson, 1977, p.5)

The Opposition Spokesman on Education, Norman St. John-Stevas, also welcomed the government's new and sensible approach to education:

There are signs that in some respects the political parties are moving closer together on educational matters. I welcome the conversion of Mr. Callaghan and Mrs. Williams to much of what the Conservative Party has been saying on standards and parental rights and influence. That is all to the good. (St. John-Stevas, 1977, p.9)

One of the important themes of the Ruskin speech which survived the period of the Great Debate and became a guiding principle of policy, regardless of the political complexion of the government in power, was the need to make effective use of limited financial resources. Shirley Williams, who replaced Fred Mulley as Education Secretary in September 1976, gave early warning of the new emphasis in a speech at the North of England conference in January 1977:

We must find the most effective ways of using a budget, which, though large, is no longer increasing in real terms; and we must redeploy the resources of teachers and buildings released as a result of the declining birthrate.

All this would be a big enough programme of work for the next five years. But it will not suffice. For, perhaps partly as a reaction to the speed of change in education, many voices of criticism have been raised, about standards of achievement in schools, about discipline, about the quality of teaching...

I am convinced we have resources enough to make our next priority an improvement in the *quality* of our education parallel to the remarkable improvement in its *quantity* that I have already outlined...

The juxtaposition in our country of one of the longest periods of compulsory education in the world with a poor record of low productivity, low growth, low investment, and indifferent design and marketing skills must make us all reflect. (Quoted in Hunter, 1981, p.67).

As Bernard Donoughue has pointed out (1987), the policy outlined here was continued without significant alteration under Mark Carlisle and Sir Keith Joseph in the subsequent Conservative administrations (p.113).

The Great Debate

The centrepiece of the Great Debate comprised eight regional one-day conferences held in February and March 1977 for which the DES took firm control of the agenda. As an important part of the preparations, the Ruskin speech was followed by a series of preliminary meetings with a limited number of educational and industrial organizations at which a paper outlining possible issues for consideration was discussed. This paper was given the title *Schools in England and Wales: Current Issues — An Annotated Agenda for Discussion* and was dated November 1976. In order to try and focus the discussion, the main issues were set down under four broad headings: curriculum; monitoring/assessment; teacher training; and school and working life. In one important respect, the 'Annotated Agenda' went further than either the Yellow Book which preceded it or *Educating Our Children*, the final 'background paper' for the regional conferences which was published at the beginning of 1977. In the section headed 'monitoring/assessment', it argued that 'national examination results give some picture of performance of pupils at age 16 upwards, but constitute an imperfect measure of the performance of the educational system'. It then asked: 'Is there a case for tests in English Language and mathematics to be taken by all pupils . . . at certain ages, possibly 8, 11 and 13?' (DES, 1976b, p.4). The corresponding section in *Educating Our Children* spoke in terms of 'assessment by sampling' (DES, 1977b, p.6) rather than of checking on the 'standards' to be reached by individuals or by schools which was the kind of emphasis which the 'Annotated Agenda' seemed to be making. The subtle change may have owed something to the lack of evidence to support claims that standards had actually fallen. In other words, there was no real need to introduce a national system of testing to make schools and teachers more accountable.

As Reid (1978) has pointed out, little thought was given to the format of the Great Debate, in spite of the fact that the rarity of the event made it impossible to claim that there was a well-established tradition of how such things should be managed:

> It seems to have been assumed that the pattern of debate would be of the type commonly associated with legislative assemblies. The gatherings would be large, most participants would be 'representing' someone or something, and contributions would be limited to one or two statements per person. (p.5)

Others have pointed out that while the gatherings were indeed large, they were not on a scale calculated to embrace all shades of opinion:

Initial expectations, that there might be an exercise in some kind of participatory democracy in the discussion of issues, were quickly shattered when it became clear that only 200 invited guests and the press would be invited to the different legs of the debate (CCCS, 1981, p.219).

Likewise the conference agendas were necessarily limited in scope, with an undue concentration on secondary schooling. Indeed, the background paper itself showed some awareness that this kind of debate might not be able to tackle all the major areas of concern:

In a conference lasting one day, only a limited number of issues can be discussed profitably. This means that many of the policy issues of concern to the government . . . must be left for discussion and consultation on other occasions . . . Four main topics have been chosen for debate. These are:

(a) the curriculum;
(b) the assessment of standards;
(c) the education and training of teachers;
(d) school and working life. (DES, 1977b, p.1)

Max Morris has recalled that seven sets of people were invited to each of the eight conferences. They included: representatives of the schoolteachers' unions as well as of those from further and higher education, parents, local authority personnel, employers, trade union representatives, men and women of local significance and DES nominees. After the official speakers had had their say, less than three-quarters of an hour was allowed for 200 articulate people to discuss each of the four main topics on the agenda. Clearly many of those invited had very little opportunity to air their views.

According to Morris:

Even one parent would be very lucky to get five minutes' worth of rostrum time — as would a single trade unionist or employer . . . As a serious educational exchange, the whole operation was farcical . . . How could meetings organized in this way produce anything of value? (Morris, 1987a)

Meeting the NUT leaders at the very end of the consultation exercise, Mrs. Williams argued that there was clearly a 'majority view for the official DES position on the merits of a core curriculum, even though no resolutions had been put at the conferences and no votes taken. She did, however, concede that there had been no support for a centrally organized curriculum (*ibid.*).

The Great Debate culminated in the publication in July 1977 of a Green Paper, *Education in Schools: A Consultative Document*, following up many of the themes which had been identified in the Yellow Book and in the Ruskin speech and at the eight regional conferences. According to Bernard Donoughue, the Policy Unit was highly dissatisfied with all the early DES drafts of this Paper, believing them to say far too little about standards, discipline and teacher accountability. An attempt was therefore made to persuade the Prime Minister to insist on a far more dynamic approach. In Donoughue's words:

> The incident represented Whitehall at its self-satisfied, condescending and unimaginative worst. However, at this time I was contacted by some of the younger officials at the DES who said that they shared our view of their Department's attitude; they too wanted a more positive approach, and they hoped that we in Downing Street would insist on improvements. Shirley Williams also indicated that she was willing to take a more radical line provided that she would rely on continuing political support from the Prime Minister when the unions inevitably kicked up rough. We were encouraged by these responses and briefed the Prime Minister to insist on a more positive and radical approach. This message was accepted internally if not always publicly (little change was made to the Green Paper in its final form), and the Department slowly moved its stance to one more in line with the principles and proposals laid out in Mr. Callaghan's Ruskin speech. (Donoughue, 1987, pp.112–3)

Callaghan's own version of events also suggests that the 1977 Green Paper was the subject of some measure of disagreement between the DES and the Policy Unit:

> Shirley submitted the first draft of a Green Paper giving her Department's views in May... With the active help of Bernard Donoughue and his Think Tank, the Department's rather introverted draft, which addressed itself mainly to educationalists, was broadened to appeal to a wider public. The Liberals, whom we had undertaken to consult, had no major comments, and Shirley personally undertook much of the redrafting and livened up the turgid language of the Green Paper. The Cabinet agreed to publication on 7 July 1977. (Callaghan, 1987, p.411)

Despite Donoughue's reservations, the Green Paper did, in fact, repeat many of the critical observations that had been made in the confidential Yellow Book, and it did so in the knowledge that these judgments had since been endorsed both by the Prime Minister and by participants in the various regional conferences. It accepted that there was legitimate ground for cirticism and concern:

> There is a wide gap between the world of education and the world of work. Boys and girls are not sufficiently aware of the importance of industry to our society, and they are not taught much about it. In some schools, the curriculum has been overloaded, so that the basic skills of literacy and numeracy, the building blocks of education, have been neglected. A small minority of schools has simply failed to provide an adequate education by modern standards. More frequently, schools have been over-ambitious, introducing modern languages without sufficient staff to meet the needs of a much wider range of pupils, or embarking on new methods of teaching mathematics without making sure the teachers understood what they were teaching, or whether it was appropriate to the pupils' capacities or the needs of their future employers. (DES, 1977b, p.2)

The Green Paper went on to argue that there was a need to investigate the part which might be played by a 'protected' or 'core' element of the curriculum common to all schools and that work in secondary schools should be made more relevant to the demands of life in a modern industrial society. At the same time, as Simon pointed out in a critical initial response (Simon, 1977, p.18), the Paper marked a new phase in policy-making in its 'clear assertion of an active (leadership) role for the DES in relation to educational (as apart from administrative) matters'.

The Great Debate in Retrospect

Both Donoughue and Callaghan have claimed to be well pleased with the progress and outcomes of the Great Debate. For Donoughue, it was the Ruskin speech which really caused people to start questioning entrenched attitudes:

> I was very pleased that the Prime Minister's speech had shaken things up. I was disappointed but not surprised by the predictable reaction of many of the more vested interests of the education system, not least by that of the National Union of Teachers. But I was pleased that things got moving; and the reaction in some quarters of hostility and shock definitely proved that there was a

need for something to be done. I was disappointed with the rate of progress — but then I always am. I still believe that we were pointing education in this country in the right direction[23].

Mr. Callaghan is also delighted with the long-term consequences of his initiative:

A decade later, the echoes of the Great Debate can still be heard. It had its impact on the curriculum; it promoted a better understanding between schools and industry; and it affected the teaching of science and mathematics, and led to changes in teachers' training courses. More needs to be done and I regret the slowness of change, but the Ruskin speech was successful in calling attention to a number of doubts and shortcomings in both objectives and practice, and triggered a public interest which has intensified rather than flagged as the years have gone by. (Callaghan, 1987, pp.411–2)

Yet neither the Ruskin speech nor the subsequent Great Debate has received much praise from teachers or educationists. According to Professor Denis Lawton, the Prime Minister's intervention was regarded as 'a great anticlimax'; and the verdict of many of those involved in the public discussion was that 'it was not a debate and it was not very great' (Lawton, 1980, p.39). For Professor Ted Wragg, the Great Debate was 'a bit of a farce' (Wragg, 1986a, p.4). Similarly, Stuart Maclure has described the whole exercise as 'something of a damp squib' (Maclure, 1987a, p.11), while at the same time conceding that it effectively changed the relationship between the DES and the system.

Looking back at the progress of the Great Debate, we can now see that it marked something of a watershed in the post-war history of secondary schooling. The project started off as the brainchild of the Downing Street Policy Unit, but the agenda was gradually appropriated by the DES bureaucracy. Ball has argued that it had the effect of 'giving government legitimation to the media-based campaigns aimed at the comprehensive schools, and it crucially undermined the already waning confidence of parents in their children's teachers' (Ball, 1984, p.8). In the forefront of the Debate was an emphasis on the need to make schools and teachers more accountable. At various levels in the discussion, a prime role was given to industrialists and employers who argued that the new comprehensive schools had signally failed to service the needs of British industry. According to Beck: 'Perhaps the most damaging educational legacy of the Callaghan government's policy of linking education to industrial regeneration was the legitimacy it gave to forms of educational practice which substitute political socialization for evidential education' (Beck, 1983, p.229). The message that both the Policy Unit and the DES were trying to get across is perhaps aptly summarized in a single sentence in the 1977 background paper *Educating Our Children*:

> Whether or not it is found that standards have remained constant, risen or fallen over some past period is less important than whether the standards which are being achieved today correspond as nearly as possible to society's requirements. (DES, 1977a, p.6)

Notes

1 In 1976, just before and just after his resignation as Prime Minister, Harold Wilson made a number of charges about South African activities in British politics, and, furthermore, expressed anxieties about MI5 activity in relation both to the 1974–76 Labour government and to himself personally. These charges have been investigated by Robin Ramsay and Stephen Dorril in *Wilson, MI5 and the Rise of Thatcher: Covert Operations in British Politics, 1974–78*, published as *The Lobster* No. 11, in April 1986. More recently, some of Wilson's allegations have, of course, been substantiated in Peter Wright's banned memoirs *Spycatcher*, published in America by Viking Penguin in 1987. The charges are interesting in that they help to account for the atmosphere of tension, anxiety and crisis which certainly marked the Wilson and Callaghan years from 1974 to 1979.
2 For a discussion of the relationship between these three bodies, see the relevant section in the Introduction.
3 The paragraphs devoted to education in the speech are quoted in the section on the New Vocationalism in chapter 6.
4 Few will have cause to remember Fred (now Lord) Mulley's mercifully brief period at the Department of Education and Science. The fact that he was considered suitable for the post in June 1975 was perhaps an indication of Harold Wilson's own assessment of the importance of educational matters. He left the Department in September 1976; and one might be forgiven for calling to mind H. L. Mencken's famous epitaph for the pathologically inert American President, Calvin Coolidge: 'He had no ideas, and was not a nuisance'.
5 Callaghan's four areas of concern are outlined in his book of memoirs (1987, p.409) and at the beginning of the Yellow Book (DES, 1976a, p.3).
6 It is commonplace to argue that the Yellow Book was compiled *after* the discussion between the Prime Minister and the Secretary of State which took place on 21 May 1976. I learn from Stewart Ranson, however, that in the course of his own research into centre-local relations in education in the 1970s, he was told by a DES official that work had actually begun on the document in 1974.
7 Reid has pointed out (1978, p.4) that little or no attempt is made in the Yellow Book to formulate the criticisms in more specific ways or to review the data that might assist in evaluating them. 'Rather [the discussion] assumes the worries to be well founded and puts up speculative theories about how the problems may have been caused' (*ibid.*, p.5). Reid also argues that, paradoxically, the repeated use of terms like 'possibly' and 'may have' serves to reinforce the indictment by implying that kindness forbids the telling of the plain truth, rather than to soften it by admitting the lack of hard evidence for the points that are being made (*ibid.*).

8 The origins and objectives of the Assessment of Performance Unit (APU) are discussed in the introductory notes by Caroline Gipps and Harvey Goldstein to Harold Rosen's paper *The Language Monitors* (Rosen, 1982, pp.7–14).

9 For a discussion of the perceived shortcomings of the new common system of examining at 16 + , see chapter 6.

10 The NUT was still implacably hostile three months later. Speaking to an NUT conference in January 1977, Mr. Sam Fisher, Chairman of the NUT's Education Committee, described the Yellow Book as 'misinformed, overtly biased and malicious' (reported in *The Times Educational Supplement*, 21 January 1977).

11 Interview with Sheila Browne, 24 July 1986.

12 Interview with Bernard Donoughue, 16 January 1986. The Inspectorate, the DES and the Downing Street Policy Unit all had to endure a 'leak enquiry', which proved fruitless.

13 Sheila Browne had joined the Inspectorate in 1961 and was Senior Chief Inspector from 1974 to 1983. Since 1983, she has been Principal of Newnham College, Cambridge.

14 For a further discussion of this point, see chapter 4.

15 Interview with Sheila Browne, 24 July 1986.

16 He was, in fact, repeating claims he had made in the interview referred to above.

17 Letter to the author, 8 October 1987.

18 The Yellow Book was the popular name given to *Britain's Industrial Future*, a document published in February 1928 and representing the thinking of a small but high-powered group of Liberals (see Simon, 1974, pp.151–2).

19 Letter to the author, 8 October 1987.

20 Interview with Bernard Donoughue, 16 January 1986.

21 Some of these are dealt with in greater detail in later chapters.

22 See, for example, the interview with Brian Walden broadcast on Channel Four Television, 17 April 1987; that with Michael Parkinson broadcast on BBC Radio 4, 18 October 1987; and that with Professor Ted Wragg broadcast on BBC Radio 4, 6 December 1987.

23 Interview with Bernard Donoughue, 16 January 1986.

Chapter 4

Towards a National Curriculum: 1976–87

At a policy-making level, the National Curriculum envisaged for this country over the past fifteen years has assumed at least two major forms: a professional common-curriculum model put forward by a small but influential group of Her Majesty's Inspectorate and a bureacratic core-curriculum model advocated by the civil servants of the Department of Education and Science. The impression has often been created that these both amount to the same thing in practice which is, in fact, very far from the truth.

As has been argued elsewhere (Lawton, 1987a and 1987b; Lawton and Chitty, 1987; Chitty, 1988), the professional common-curriculum approach, as depicted, for example, in the three HMI Red Books published between 1977 and 1983 (DES, 1977d; 1981b and 1983c), reflects a genuine concern with the quality of the teaching process and with the needs of individual children. It seeks to undermine traditional subject boundaries and uses subjects to achieve higher level aims. It requires teachers who are well-motivated, well-trained, and skilled in identifying any specific learning problems for individual pupils. It is wary of any system geared to writing off large sections of the school population as failures.

The bureaucratic core-curriculum approach, on the other hand, is concerned with the 'efficiency' of the whole system and with the need to obtain precise statistical information to demonstrate that efficiency. It is concerned with controlling what is taught in schools and making teachers generally more accountable to the central authority. Whereas the professional approach focusses on the quality of input and the skills, knowledge and awareness of the teachers, the bureaucratic approach concentrates on output and testing. Whereas the professional approach is based on individual differences and the learning process, the bureaucratic approach is associated with norms or benchmarks, norm-related criteria and judgments based on the expectations of how a statistically-normal child should perform. Whereas the professional curriculum is concerned with areas of learning and experience, the bureaucratic curriculum is based on traditional subjects.

The HMI Model

Red Book 3, *Curriculum 11–16: Towards a Statement of Entitlement*, tells us that it was in April 1975 that a group of HMI was convened 'to develop ideas within the Inspectorate about the nature and purposes of the curriculum for pupils aged eleven to sixteen' (DES, 1983c, p. 1). In fact, HMI had taken on a planning role with regard to the secondary curriculum the year before, when Sheila Browne became Senior Chief Inspector, and it had shown an interest in whole-school curriculum policies since at least 1969.

Schools Council Working Paper 33, *Choosing a Curriculum for the Young school Leaver*, provides an interesting account of the Scarborough conference of June 1969 where at least one of the discussion groups (which included an HMI representative) was beginning to question the Schools Council's piecemeal approach to curriculum planning:

> [A] major problem to be faced was whether we were giving so much freedom to each individual school that continuity for our pupils in a mobile society was ignored. In fact, do we not have so many *general* curricular questions to answer that there ought to be a project on the curriculum *as a whole*? Are we right to be jiggling with the pieces in order to find new ways of putting them together? Is there a need to look at the whole conception of secondary education, and would this help heads to make their choices? . . . .One group, in defining the curriculum, was moving towards considerations of this kind, while an HMI representative pointed out that there was a group in the Inspectorate already giving it serious thought. He defined the essentials of a good curriculum as giving importance to personal development, aesthetic experience, experience of the material world and of society, and 'transcendentalism' — ideals and inspiration. (Schools Council, 1971, p.26)

The timing here is significant. The late 1960s marked the end of a period of ten or more years which has been described by Lawton and Gordon (1987a) as 'probably . . . the lowest period of HMI influence and morale' (p. 24). For one thing, there was the continuing problem of overlap between HMI and local authority inspectors; and it was also felt within the Inspectorate that its professional expertise was not making itself felt. In an interview with Maurice Kogan published in 1971, Edward Boyle, who had served at the Ministry of Education in 1957–59 and in 1962–64, conceded that the civil servants had not always made effective use of the professional knowledge of HMI:

> Looking back over the period we're thinking of, about fifteen years, the Inspectorate has played less of a part in policy-making than I for one would have liked to see. I think this was certainly true over the whole question of secondary reorganization . . . I don't think there was a sufficiently strong tradition that when you had a major discussion, the Senior Chief Inspector should normally be invited in . . . I think there may have been personal reasons over the years why this tended not to happen. But, for whatever reason, he didn't play a big enough part in policy making in the Department, whoever he was. (Boyle and Crosland, 1971, pp. 130–1)

The findings of the 1967/68 Parliamentary Select Committee which scrutinized the work of HMI made it clear that there was a desperate need for HMI to find a new role and one, moreover, which did not duplicate the work of LEA advisory services. The document *HMI Today and Tomorrow*, published in 1970, could therefore be seen as an attempt by the Inspectorate to justify its very existence — an attempt, so to speak, at self-promotion:

> . . . the Inspectorate acts in the confidence that a long tradition of independence has given it the right to speak its mind on educational issues. It recognizes the right of its employer not to listen to its words, not to publish its writings, but would insist on the established privilege that what it does say or write should reflect the independent free judgment of an individual or of a professional group. Everything seems to indicate that this particular privilege of the Inspectorate is the significant one in the eyes of others who work in the field of education.
> . . . An increasing amount of [the Inspectorate's] time is spent in working together with others who serve in education and play their part in innovation, reform and future planning. Many, but not all of these, are practising teachers. The Inspectorate takes part in the public debate on education and has to establish contacts, to acquire and to share information, not only with teachers, but with many other parties to the educational process. It is increasingly called on to advise those who are working on the

social, industrial and technological problems which now impinge on education.

Neither teachers nor inspectors can assume the right to determine educational ends. These are issues which ultimately society itself has to decide. They can, however, acquire some expert knowledge of the means and of how to apply them. But to do so effectively requires them, besides cultivating habits of observation and study, to participate in discussion and to open channels of communication within the profession to which they belong and beyond it. The Inspectorate together with many others, employed by LEAs, universities and colleges or linked in membership of associations and societies, helps to accumulate and to sift the evidence and so to provide those who need it with the foundations on which to make reasonable decisions. (DES, 1970b, pp.3–4)

In its search for a *raison d'etre* in the early 1970s, it was seen by HMI to be one of its main tasks to address what SCI Sheila Browne was to refer to as 'the paradox that the age of the common school is the age of the non-common and sometimes distinctly uncommon curriculum' (Browne, 1977, p. 39). In a speech to the Council of Local Education Authorities' (CLEA) annual conference in July 1977, she outlined some of the important questions concerning the whole secondary curriculum which members of HMI had been attempting to answer:

To take the whole curriculum, can it be right that the experience of pupils in our secondary schools and even in the same school is so diverse? Should there be such a difference of shape between the curriculum for the academic and that for the less academic? Is there really no such thing as a secondary curriculum proper for all pupils? Can one claim that the present curriculum is built positively rather than negatively (and somewhat competitively) by the crowding out of this or that? Do all these individual curricula give and ask enough? Perhaps particularly for the most able, is the traditional curriculum sufficiently forward and outward looking? For all pupils, does it sufficiently foster the knowledge, skills and qualities of mind and feeling that would serve — and here one takes off into the rather grandiose world of educational aims — society, the country's interest, and our very small world? (*ibid.*, p. 42)

Although Sheila Browne claimed elsewhere in her talk that HMI had a critical rather than an initiating role to play in curriculum planning, addressing the issues which she outlined actually led to the pursuit of a number of new strategies, foremost among them being the planning of a common-culture curriculum. It is also true that while the Yellow Book of 1976 saw the reduced activity of the Inspectorate in the 1960s as largely 'a result of over-reaction to the emergence of the Schools Council' (DES, 1976a, p. 17), it was, in fact, the experience of working with the Council that led members of the Inspectorate to see that there were important curriculum issues that were not being properly addressed. As Lawton and Gordon have pointed out (1987a):

> The Schools Council was . . . extremely reluctant to deal with curriculum on a national basis: they were concentrating on curriculum development rather than curriculum planning, dedicated to a programme of alternative curricular offerings from which teachers could freely choose. (p. 108)

But there was also a need for national planning in terms of a common curriculum; and it was this gap which the Inspectorate sought to fill.

By the mid-1970s, HMI planning was taking place alongside DES attempts to formulate a viable core curriculum of its own. Yet it is important to emphasize that the two groups were engaged on separate exercises and that HMI thinking on the curriculum was not represented in the 1976 Yellow Book, which was prepared without the active involvement of HMI.

Within eighteen months, the group of HMI convened in April 1975 to develop ideas on the secondary curriculum (known within the Inspectorate as the Curriculum Publications Group or CPG) had produced a series of draft papers which were then offered as an HMI contribution to a DES conference on 'The Secondary Curriculum', held at the University of Oxford in September 1976. These papers were also to form the nucleus of Red Book 1, *Curriculum 11–16*, which, though dated December 1977, was not, in fact, published — owing to a printers' strike — until March 1978.

In one of his introductory papers for the Oxford conference, R. A. Wake of the CPG conceded that there was still a basic need in this country to arrive at some sort of agreement about the aims and objectives of the secondary curriculum. At the same time, it was important to stress that any worthwhile curriculum must involve more than the accumulation of facts and the acquisition of skills:

> A major element in a 'national debate' on secondary education is that there is no easily discernible consensus within schools, let alone outside them, about the purposes of the curriculum. From this never-ending world of argument — much of it under-

standably low level — comes demands for 'a survival kit curriculum'. This infers that we should arrive at a national consensus about the essentials that should be in all secondary curricula: essential knowledge; essential skills.

It is necessary to realize that basic curriculum involves far more than the achievement of particular levels in stated skills at specific ages, or of some generally accepted body of knowledge (and in any case, how is agreement on this to be reached?).

Current anxiety about 'standards' means that the achievement of particular levels in stated skills at specific ages must be taken seriously, and incorporated into all curricula; but there will nevertheless be continuous discussion as to how 'education according to aptitude and ability' will best be *achieved*: that is, method as well as essential content and skills must be discussed in the light of all available evidence.[1]

Following on from this, it was emphasized that the Curriculum Publications Group preferred a common 11–16 curriculum to be followed, for at least two-thirds of the week, by *all* pupils. Moreover, traditional subjects would be considered useful only to the extent that they contributed to the education of each individual pupil in the light of a checklist of areas of personal development or experience to be used as the basis of curriculum construction. Such a checklist would obviously be cross-disciplinary by definition, and close analysis of the worth and relevance of each individual subject was to be seen as the essential prelude to the planning of work of an inter-disciplinary nature. According to Wake:

It is imperative that teachers should be asked to look through their subjects/areas to the disciplines inherent in them. Only when one is clear about a discipline can one plan effectively to undertake interdisciplinary work.[2]

As a result of the Oxford conference, a decision was taken to establish an exercise on curricular enquiry in which a small number of schools would join LEA advisers and HMI in reviewing their own curricula using the checklist drawn up by the Curriculum Publications Group. Five local authorities, Cheshire, Hampshire, Lancashire, Nottinghamshire and Wigan, agreed to join HMI in this exercise, involving teachers from forty-one schools. Work began in 1977, with participants using the draft HMI papers, then unpublished, as an initial stimulus to their thinking and work (DES, 1983c, p. 1).

Curriculum 11–16, or Red Book 1, published in March 1978, made the ideas debated at the Oxford conference available to a wider audience. Yet by that time, the very concept of a common or common-core curriculum had become associated with the suspicion that the Callaghan government was primarily concerned to bring about greater control of education. Accordingly, the authors of Red Book 1 felt it necessary to assert right at the outset that their ideas should be judged on their merits as *curriculum* proposals:

> These papers have been overtaken by events, and it is important that neither their content nor their purpose should be misunderstood... There is no intention anywhere in the papers which follow of advocating a centrally controlled or dictated curriculum... The group of HM Inspectors who wrote these papers felt that the case for a common curriculum, as it is presented here, deserves careful attention and that such a curriculum, worked out in the ways suggested, would help to ameliorate the inconsistencies and irrationalities which at present exist, *without entailing any kind of centralized control*. (DES, 1977d, p. 1, my emphasis)

It seems clear from this statement that the attitude of HMI was already markedly different from that of the civil servants of the DES.

As foreshadowed in the draft papers for the Oxford conference, Red Book 1 put forward a checklist of eight 'areas of experience', to be used as the basis of curriculum construction or of reshaping and redefining existing curricula:

- The aesthetic and creative
- The ethical
- The linguistic
- The mathematical
- The physical
- The scientific
- The social and political
- The spiritual (*ibid.*, p. 6)[3]

This checklist could then be translated into a timetable for the older pupils in a comprehensive school in the following way:

subject	periods
English	5
Mathematics	5
A modern language	4
A science	5
Religious education and a social study	4

Art/craft/music	4
Careers education	2
Physical activities	3 (*ibid.*, p. 7)

Based on a forty-period week, it would correspond to the HMI estimate that the common curriculum should occupy at least two-thirds of the total time available. The eight remaining periods could then be used for the provision of two further option blocks, allowing pupils to choose additional subjects (for example: a second foreign language or a classical study or another science) or to devote more time to subjects already being studied.

Yet the authors of the Red Book made it clear that, in its crude form, this model fell far short of what they wanted to see in practice. Such curriculum construction in terms of subjects was acceptable when, but only when, everyone was clear what was to be achieved through them:

> It is . . . important to emphasize the fact that subject or 'course' labels often tell us surprisingly little about the objectives to be pursued or the activities to be introduced, still less about the likely or expected levels of achievement. An individual subject may make valid, although varied, contributions in different schools; or to different pupils in the same school; or to the same pupils at different ages or stages of individual development. Any framework to be constructed for the curriculum must be able to accommodate shifts of purpose, content and method in subjects, and of emphasis between subjects. In other words, it is not proposed that schools should plan and construct a common curriculum in terms of subject labels only: that would be to risk becoming trapped in discussions about the relative importance of this subject or that. Rather, it is necessary to look through the subject or discipline to the areas of experience and knowledge to which it may provide access, and to the skills and attitudes which it may assist to develop. (*ibid.*, p. 6)

Here we find clear echoes of the sentiments expressed in R. A. Wake's introductory papers for the Oxford conference.

At the same time, the authors of Red Book 1 were anxious to point out that there was no one model of good practice, and that the curriculum should *not* be viewed as some sort of straitjacket. There must be flexibility to allow for differing needs and abilities. The essential point to grasp was that any curriculum provided for pupils up to the age of 16 should be capable of demonstrating that it offered properly thought out and progressive experience in all the eight areas of experience included in the HMI checklist:

> Whatever the model, all pupils of whatever ability do not normally follow identical courses: within each 'subject', there are possibilities of shaping detailed content, pace and method to suit differing needs and capacities, and different pupils choose different subjects to serve the same curricular aim. What are of prime importance are the intentions and learning objectives to be realised, and the coherence and balance of the total programme for each pupil. (*ibid.*, p. 7)

The authors were, of course, aware that in years four and five, the education of many pupils was strongly orientated towards external examinations, but they did not see this as an insurmountable obstacle to the implementation of their proposals:

> It is important that the framework provided by the external examinations system should not hinder schools from implementing programmes that they acknowledge to be necessary for the development of individuals and of whole groups of pupils. There is, however, as is widely demonstrable in the work of many schools, no reason why education should stop as soon as an examination syllabus is embarked upon; indeed, a clearer and widely agreed definition of curricular objectives could assist the development of improved instruments of assessment, including public examinations. Examination boards have shown themselves in recent years encouragingly willing to develop new approaches in response to changing perceptions of needs and fresh curricular thinking. (*ibid.*, p. 7)

By 1983, the thinking outlined in the first Red Book had developed to the point where members of HMI were talking in terms of an 'entitlement curriculum' — a broad framework representing a synthesis of the vocational, the technical and the academic. Red Book 3, *Curriculum 11–16: Towards a Statement of Entitlement*, was the final report of the partnership between five local authorities and a group of HMI, and it outlined the general conclusions of those participating in the project:

> It seemed essential that *all* pupils should be guaranteed a curriculum of a distinctive breadth and depth to which they should be *entitled*, irrespective of the type of school they attended or their level of ability or their social circumstances, and that failure to provide such a curriculum is unacceptable... The conviction has grown that all pupils are entitled to a broad compulsory common curriculum to the age of 16 which introduces

them to a range of experiences, makes them aware of the kind of society in which they are going to live and gives them the skills necessary to live in it. Any curriculum which fails to provide this balance and is overweighted in any particular direction, whether vocational, technical or academic, is to be seriously questioned. Any measures which restrict the access of all pupils to a wide-ranging curriculum or which focus too narrowly on specific skills are in direct conflict with the entitlement curriculum envisaged here. (DES, 1983c, pp. 25 and 26)

The three Red Books, together with the 1980 pamphlet *A View of the Curriculum*, represented the significant contribution from HMI to the continuing education debate after 1976. Whatever one's view of their principal recommendations, it can at least be argued that small groups of HMI were genuinely trying to tackle some of the broad questions listed by Sheila Browne in her 1977 address. Yet in one sense, it could all be described as a pointless exercise. By 1987, no one in the government was interested in the answers.

The DES Model

The concept of a core curriculum developed by the DES in the 1970s differed from the common curriculum model advocated by HMI in a number of important respects: it still allowed a considerable degree of pupil choice, being little more in years four and five than a variation of the 'core-plus-options' syndrome; and it was conceived of primarily in terms of traditional subjects.

The idea of a core curriculum was not itself new. In the inter-war years, the curriculum in all secondary schools was tightly controlled, not only by the Secondary Regulations but also by the fact that most pupils were expected to take the School Certificate examination. The School Certificate was a group examination requiring at least five passes including English. In effect, all secondary schools worked with a core curriculum which, though established by the Regulations, was, in fact, implemented by the structure of a group examination. This ended only because the Secondary Regulations were made obsolete by the 1944 Education Act and the School Certificate was replaced, in 1951, by the new single-subject GCE Ordinary level examination. By the early 1950s, most grammar schools had abandoned any idea of a core or common-core curriculum.

Many of the secondary modern schools which grew up in the 1940s and 1950s experimented with basing their curriculum on social studies as the dominating core to which everything else then had to be subservient. As Cannon has argued, such schemes failed for a number of reasons, not least the need for schools to be seen to be achieving good examination results in a variety of subjects:

> Most important probably were the social and economic pressures which led to an increasing concern for standards, and, in particular, to their expression in examination qualifications. (Cannon, 1964, p. 22)

In their search for respectability, many of the new secondary moderns became pale reflections of the grammar schools. This naturally entailed adhering to a curriculum which observed traditional subject boundaries.

The concept of a core curriculum was attractive to those who drafted the confidential Yellow Book in 1976, presumably being seen as a convenient device for ensuring greater uniformity and accountability within the education system. However, it was not considered necessary to define the concept in detail or to provide any intellectual justification for its adoption. Clearly, the DES would have an important role to play in defining the core and securing its introduction, and it may well be that the *fact* of control was simply more important than the *form* of control. Whatever the reason, the paragraph on the curriculum in the Yellow Book was remarkable for its lack of both clarity and precision:

> A source of worry is the variation in the curriculum followed by pupils in different schools or parts of the country or in different ability bands . . . An analysis of the courses followed by individual pupils in school, particularly perhaps the most and least able, would reveal further causes for dissatisfaction in terms of the general balance of their studies. The time has probably come to try to establish generally accepted principles for the composition of the secondary curriculum for all pupils, that is to say a 'core curriculum' . . . The creation of a suitable core curriculum will not, however, be easy. Pupils in their later years of secondary schooling (up to and beyond the age of compulsory attendance) have a wide range of interests and expectations, and suitable provision will have to be made for vocational elements within school education for those who will benefit from this. Extensive consideration and consultation would be needed before a core curriculum could be introduced. (DES, 1976a, pp. 10–11)

The 'core curriculum' idea was taken up by Prime Minister in his Ruskin College speech where the curriculum was listed as one of the fields that 'need study because they cause concern':

They are the methods and aims of informal instruction; *the strong case for the so-called 'core curriculum' of basic knowledge*; next, what is the proper way of monitoring the use of resources in order to maintain a proper national standard of performance; then there is the role of the Inspectorate in relation to national standards; and there is the need to improve relations between industry and education (Reprinted in *Education*, 22 October 1976, pp. 332–3, my emphasis).

As promised in the speech, a number of these issues were taken up by Secretary of State Shirley Williams and placed on the agenda of the Great Debate of 1976/77. They were then discussed in the Green Paper *Education in Schools: A Consultative Document*, presented to Parliament in July 1977. Here it was argued that the secondary curriculum had been under great pressure from the constantly growing demands upon it. It had become overcrowded, with too much variation between schools and 'essential educational objectives' being 'put at risk'. The proposed remedy was the creation of a suitable core curriculum:

The balance and breadth of each child's course is crucial at all school levels, and this is especially so during the later years of compulsory education . . . It is clear that the time has come to try to establish generally accepted principles for the composition of the secondary curriculum for all pupils. This does not presuppose uniform answers: schools, pupils, and their teachers are different, and the curriculum should be flexible enough to reflect these differences. But there is a need to investigate the part which might be played by a 'protected' or 'core' element of the curriculum common to all schools. There are various ways this may be defined. Properly worked out, it can offer reassurances to employers, parents and the teachers themselves, as well as a very real equality of opportunity for pupils. (DES, 1977b, pp. 10–11)

Clearly, little agreement had yet been reached on the actual composition of the core, but reference was made in the Green Paper to five subjects that had an incontestable right to be included:

English and religious education are in most schools a standard part of the curriculum for all pupils up to the age of 16, and it is not true that many pupils drop mathematics at an early stage . . . Few, inside or outside the schools would contest that alongside English and mathematics, science should find a secure place for all pupils at least to the age of sixteen, and that a modern language should do so for as high a proportion as practicable. (*ibid.*, p. 11)

The 'core curriculum' concept was developed further in two DES documents: *A Framework for the School Curriculum*, published in January 1980, and *The School Curriculum*, published in March 1981. The first of these documents went so far as to specify what proportion of time should be spent on some subjects but this idea was widely criticized. A year later, *The School Curriculum* argued that minimum time allocations should be left to the discretion of local authorities and teachers:

> English, mathematics, science and modern languages are generally treated as separate items in school timetables . . . It is important that every school should ensure that each pupil's programme includes a substantial and well-distributed time allocation for English, mathematics and science up to age sixteen, and that those pupils who do take a modern language should devote sufficient time to it to make the study worthwhile. The Secretaries of State do not suggest minimum times which should be devoted to these subjects. Any suggested minima might too easily become norms, or be interpreted too rigidly. It is for the local education authorities to consider, in consultation with the teachers in their areas, whether to suggest minimum time allocations in these subjects, as broad guidance for schools. (DES, 1981a, p. 14)

The School Curriculum clarified the right and responsibility of the Secretary of State to have a concern for 'the content and quality of education', but it was decidedly schizophrenic in its whole approach to curriculum design. In the circumstances, it was perhaps inevitable that it should reflect a lack of consensus within the DES itself between the bureaucratic and the professional standpoints. A year before, *A Framework for the School Curriculum* (DES, 1980a) had specified a limited core of required subjects, justified largely in utilitarian terms. Immediately afterwards, the HMI consultation paper *A View of the Curriculum* (DES, 1980b) had advocated a strongly liberal-humanist rationale for a broadly common curriculum and had argued against 'an excessively instrumental view of the compulsory period of education' (p. 15). The 1981 discussion document made no attempt to resolve the issue, talking in terms both of subjects and of 'areas of experience'. As Maw has argued (1985), '*The School Curriculum* could be seen to *incorporate* two views of a national curriculum framework without *reconciling* them' (p. 97). In one particular paragraph, it was conveniently suggested that each school could simply sidestep the problem by developing more than one kind of curriculum analysis:

> The Secretaries of State recognize that the curriculum can be described and analyzed in several ways, each of which has its advantages and limitations. They have thought it most helpful to express much of their guidance in terms of subjects, because secondary school timetables are almost always devised in subject terms, they are readily recognized by parents and employers, and most secondary school teachers are trained in subjects. But a subject title hardly indicates the content or level of study, or the extent to which teaching and learning meet particular objectives. Moreover, many important elements of the curriculum are to be found 'across the curriculum', rather than exclusively within any one subject. A subject title is a kind of shorthand, whose real educational meaning depends on the school's definition of what it expects children will learn and be able to do as a result of their studies in the subject in question. Some subjects contribute to more than one aim of the curriculum; some aims need a contribution from more than one subject. In analyzing the curriculum, therefore, other frames of reference are also required. These may be in terms of the skills required at particular stages of a pupil's career; or of areas of experience such as the eight used in HM Inspectors' working papers on the 11–16 curriculum . . . In translating general principles into practice, schools need to develop more than one kind of analysis as working tools of curriculum planning. (DES, 1981a, p. 6)

This was a masterly example of the art of pandering to all bodies of opinion without attempting to arbitrate on their worth.

Developments Since 1981

There is evidence to suggest that in the years following the publication of *The School Curriculum*, the DES and HMI were coming closer together in their attitudes towards curriculum planning. This convergence may have been short-lived, but its significance can be judged from a close study of the 1985 DES document *Better Schools*. Here four pages were devoted to 'A professional judgment', where the comments made were entirely based on HMI evidence, particularly on evidence of weaknesses in primary, middle and secondary schools (DES, 1985c, pp. 4–8). In a later section, it was argued that the government's task in reaching a 'broad agreement about the objectives and content of the school curriculum' (which it was acknowledged would take 'several years to accomplish') would be carried out through policy statements, such as the recently published *Science 5–16: A Statement of Policy* (DES, 1985b), and through HMI publications. These HMI publications would be designed both to inform and to stimulate discussion:

> ... In particular, publications in the recently-inaugurated Curriculum Matters series will build up a general description of the objectives of the curriculum as a whole for all children of compulsory school age, and the contribution which individual areas and subjects can make towards those objectives. They will examine individual subjects and curricular elements in more detail, considering, where appropriate, such matters as teaching approaches, and proposing objectives to be attained at the ages of (in particular) 11 and 16. (DES, 1985c, pp. 9–10)

A later paragraph reiterated that HMI publications would have the task of giving a complete account of the contribution which each subject or curricular element could make to the 5–16 curriculum as a whole (*ibid.*, p. 18).

The Curriculum from 5 to 16 was the second paper to be published in the new Curriculum Matters series and appeared, like *Better Schools*, in March 1985. HMI once again argued that there were limitations in a curriculum which was no more than a list of subjects. The overall curricular framework was viewed from *two* essential and complementary perspectives: first, *areas of learning and experience*; and second, *elements of learning*, that is, the knowledge, concepts, skills and attitudes to be developed. The 1977 checklist had now been expanded to *nine* areas of learning and experience:

- The aesthetic and creative
- The human and social
- The linguistic and literary
- The mathematical
- The moral
- The physical
- The scientific
- The spiritual
- The technological (DES, 1985a, p. 16)

The ethical had become the moral; the linguistic had become the linguistic and literary; the social and political had become (significantly) the human and social; and the additional area was the technological. Once again it was emphasized that schools needed to examine existing practice to establish the extent to which particular topics, aspects and subjects were already contributing to these areas and to the development of knowledge, concepts, skills and attitudes:

> Schools should ensure that, however the work of pupils is organized, each of the above areas of learning and experience is represented sufficiently for it to make its unique contribution, part of which is to assist in the development of knowledge, concepts, skills and attitudes which can be learnt, practised and applied in many parts of the curriculum. (*ibid.*)

This document was not seen to be at variance with DES strategies. As late as November 1985, the DES held a conference on evaluation and appraisal, as a follow-up to *Better Schools*, at which Sir Keith Joseph paid tribute to the work of HMI in helping to reach national agreement on curricular objectives while, at the same time, providing valuable information about standards in schools:

> The White Paper *Better Schools* set out the government's views, and described the way in which we proposed to carry matters forward through the twin channels of government policy statements and HMI's 'Curriculum Matters' papers, which would offer a professional elaboration of the issues raised by various areas and subjects within the curriculum. I want to make it clear that the government takes a wide view of the curriculum, and therefore of assessment. Both are concerned not only with knowledge, skills and understanding, but also with values and attitudes, including behaviour and the preparation of pupils for adult life and employment.
>
> ... HMI inspect and assess quality and standards of both teaching and learning. This work is undertaken not just to inform the government about the health of the education system as a whole; nor simply to provide those directly concerned with the institutions inspected with a basis for assessing and improving their current practice. HMI's work is also undertaken to inform the education system and the public at large about current standards, and to promote improvements throughout the system at all levels.
>
> That is why HMI now publish and disseminate a range of documents, on broad and narrow topics, aimed at a wide reader-ship. They are, I know, always looking for fresh ways of

presenting their findings so as to enhance their important contribution to our understanding of the way the quality and achievements of the system change over time. (DES, 1986a, pp. 182 and
184)

Yet ministerial approval of the work of HMI was short-lived; and the
Curriculum Matters series has been virtually ignored by both civil servants
and politicians. In the same month that the DES held its conference on
evaluation and appraisal, an editorial appeared in *The Times Educational
Supplement* pointing out that with the arrival of the new General
Certificate of Secondary Education (GCSE), any notion of a core curriculum for years four and five of the secondary school would have to be found
in the form of a spread of GCSE entries:

It is now clear that all the Inspectorate's efforts to steer
curriculum planning towards an exploration of a full range of
areas of experience have failed to lift the secondary school
programme out of its entrenched subject-defined tradition. (*The
Times Educational Supplement*, 29 November 1985)

In Maw's view (1988, p. 57), the Inspectorate itself can, to some
extent, be blamed for this. As Maw sees it, the authors of the main HMI
discussion documents have 'never provided any philosophical rationale for
their "areas of experience", and have altered and added to them over time
without explanation'. At the same time, she argues, 'the subject-specific
"Curriculum Matters" bulletins largely ignore the areas of experience'. This
is indeed curious and points to a certain lack of conviction within HMI
itself. Areas of experience are mentioned briefly only in the pamphlets on
geography (DES, 1986b, pp. 2–3) and on modern foreign languages (DES,
1987b, pp. 2–3); and in neither case is there any attempt to explain precisely
how the subject in question makes its special contribution to the areas of
experience. The DES is now firmly committed to a national curriculum
based on subjects; and areas of experience have been dismissed by Kenneth
Baker as 'Education-speak' (DES, 1987a, para. 11).
    It can also be argued that, through no fault of its own, the Inspectorate
has been unable to provide an effective counter-balance to the formidable
pressure exerted on the DES since 1986 by the Downing Street Policy Unit
and advisers close to the Prime Minister. It certainly seems clear that as the
1987 election drew near, members of HMI were taken by surprise at the
speed with which government plans were being produced. In a lecture
delivered at the University of Durham in 1986 and published in 1987, Eric
Bolton, who had been Senior Chief Inspector since 1983, was still talking

confidently of the excellent working relationship that now existed between the DES and HMI:

> Following *Better Schools*, the front runners in the push towards reform and national agreement about the school curriculum are the Government and the DES in terms of executive action and policy development, and HM Inspectorate in respect of the professional debate and advice. (Bolton, 1987a, p. 8)

As late as April 1987, when the government's intentions were clear, the Chief Inspector was still arguing that HMI and teachers could make their voice heard on the precise form of the National Curriculum. Speaking to the Mathematical Association, he said that politicians must not be allowed to take control of the National Curriculum and dictate what was taught in schools. Some kind of national framework was inevitable, since all political parties had expressed a desire to see it. But whatever 'the frights and horrors' it might cause the profession:

> It will be a better curriculum coming from people who know what they are talking about than if it is left to be decided by politicians and administrators.

The debate was going ahead, but nothing was cut and dried beyond a general outline:

> Don't wait to be asked to make your views known ... It is silly politicians indeed who fly totally in the face of the best professional advice they can get. (Reported in *The Times Educational Supplement*, 17 April 1987)

If Kenneth Barker read this speech, it certainly did nothing to persuade him to seek professional approval for his policies.

The 1987 National Curriculum

The philosophy of the National Curriculum outlined in the 1987 consultation document (DES, 1987c) had much in common with the narrow, subject-based instrumental approach of earlier DES attempts to construct a core curriculum[4]. With its ten foundation subjects, three of them (English, maths and science) forming the 'core' of the curriculum, it seemed to many to represent a crude extension of the 1980 *Framework*. This being so, it could hardly be expected to appeal to those who had supported the HMI case for a common culture curriculum which was not based on subjects as ends in themselves. As Lawton has pointed out (1987b):

There is nothing wrong with subjects provided they are treated as means and not as ends. Virtually all the enlightened views on curriculum planning are now agreed that subjects should be regarded as important only if they help to reach other objectives which, in turn, have to be justified . . . All this is ignored in the consultation document: no justification is put forward for the selection of the foundation subjects; no argument put forward to give priority to the core subjects; no attempt made to relate subjects to wider objectives.

Similarly, the whole notion of an arbitrary list of ten subjects has been characterized as both 'vague and mechanistic' in a letter to *The Independent* from a group of academics at the University of Sussex (Abbs *et al.*, 1987):

The subjects listed seem to be no more than lumps extracted from the curriculum *status quo* which the government happens to approve of. What we need . . . is some appreciation of the broad unifying categories (humanities, arts, sciences) which, when placed properly together, might come to represent some kind of balance.

With its emphasis on assessable outcomes and its complete lack of a philosophical rationale (see White, 1988), the 1987 consultation document appeared to bring the whole concept of a national curriculum into disrepute. It meant that a great opportunity had been lost. In the words of Peter Cornall, Senior County Inspector for Cornwall, speaking at the School Curriculum Development Committee's National Conference in Leeds in September 1987:

Many of us have no quarrel with a largely common curriculum: on the contrary, we have been trying for years to convert others by example. What we could not have foreseen is the manner in which all this is happening, a manner so ill-matched to an issue of such fundamental national importance. Surely the foundations of no lasting monument are laid in obscurity, by artificers whose credentials cannot be scrutinized? A forum much nearer in character to a Royal Commission, consisting of known persons, presenting a Report beyond all suspicion of partisan influence or short-term considerations, could have commanded support and goodwill, far beyond what even the most thorough and competent of Civil Service papers can expect to do. Instead, we have the gravely-flawed product of amateurs, a hasty, shallow, simplistic sketch of a curriculum, reductionist in one direction, marginalizing in another, paying only a dismissive lip-service to the professional enterprise and initiative on which all progress depends. (O'Connor, 1987a, p. 34)

Here again, we have the view, expressed earlier by Eric Bolton, that, to command widespread support, a national curriculum must be based, at least in part, on professional opinion and experience.

There is, then, clearly no indication of HMI being actively involved in the final preparation of the 1987 consultation document.[5] Not only is this apparent in its rejection of the HMI concept of 'areas of experience'; it is also clear from the statement that 'attainment targets ... will establish what children should normally be expected to know, understand and be able to do at around the ages of 7, 11, 14 and 16, and will enable the progress of each child to be measured against established national standards' (DES, 1987c, pp. 9–10). Apart from any other considerations, crude notions of 'pass' and 'fail', implicit in many models of benchmark testing, could hardly be said to reflect HMI views on assessment. SCI Eric Bolton, writing in the spring of 1987 *before* the National Curriculum consultation document was published, warned against the use of any system of evaluation and testing that could result in an 'undue narrowness' of teaching and learning. Clearly, he argued, 'evaluation and accountability go hand-in-glove with any concern with quality', and ways must therefore be sought of assessing standards in schools and colleges (Bolton, 1987b, p. 8). Yet while accepting that an education service costing around £16 billion annually had to be subject to review, evaluation and assessment, 'if for no other reason than the fact that any government must be able to assure itself and the electorate that it is getting value for the money it spends', Eric Bolton also pointed out that it was far from easy to arrive at accurate objective assessments both of schools and of pupils:

Standards may apply to fairly straightforward matters such as mastery of a particular process, or of decoding letters and words on the printed page so as to begin to be able to read. But it becomes a much more difficult matter to set and assess standards and expectations when the issues are those of understanding and applying a mathematical process to problem-solving, or understanding what is read and extrapolating from it. Even more difficult to assess and to encourage are such matters as standards of behaviour and decent relationships with others, yet they are matters that much concern schools and society at large. Even where there are some output measures available nationally such as external examination results, they have to be handled with care when attempting to make comparisons between schools, LEAs, or components of the system, such as grammar and comprehensive schools. What has to be done in such circumstances is to: show how the results stand considering where the pupils started from (the value-added concept); and show how the results stand for any particular school or group of schools in relation to results gained by schools nationally. Neither of these is a straightforward process, and the first of them is fiendishly difficult, demanding as it does that account is taken of pupil background and ability. There are no agreed or easy ways of doing either of these . . . Not everything that is worthwhile, or required, is measurable in any precise, objective way. (*ibid.*, p. 12)

The curriculum proposals in the Baker Education Bill, together with the itemized requirements for attainment targets, programmes of study and assessment arrangements, have also been criticized by former SCI Sheila Browne. Speaking to the North of England Education Conference in Nottingham in January 1988, and anxious not to condone blind opposition to the Bill, she could not disguise her feeling that the national curriculum framework was both shallow and hastily-conceived:

We know perfectly well that each pupil gets one basic education and only gets it once, whatever the later opportunities. We know the choices of what is included or excluded are vital in a very real sense. We may not like the current definition of the National Curriculum or the means proposed for achieving it. But this new educational baby should neither be thrown out with the rather murky bath water nor disowned on cheap grounds of disreputable parentage. And that must be the wrong image, since the National Curriculum is in most respects barely conceived. It has a great deal of growing to do and it will, for a very long time, need the nurture of practically everyone represented at this conference. (Reported in *The Times Educational Supplement*, 8 January 1988)

In the light of recent statements by Eric Bolton and Sheila Browne, and of its unique position as an independent member of the educational establishment, it is perhaps hardly surprising that HMI should have incurred the hostility of a number of right-wing pressure groups anxious to undermine the influence of professional educationists. In December 1986, for example, the Hillgate Group[6] published their pamphlet *Whose Schools?*

A *Radical Manifesto* in which they argued the case for a full-scale investigation into the activities of the Inspectorate:

> ... we believe the time has come for a full and independent survey of the Inspectors, whose role has undergone considerable unsupervised change since the institution was first established in 1839. The only recent official survey is entirely bland, and seems to permit and to condone a far wider range of activities on the part of HMI than has ever been expressly authorized by Parliament[7]. We believe the time has come to define the procedures, criteria and accountability of the Inspectors, who are as likely as any other section of the educational establishment to be subverted by bureaucratic self-interest and fashionable ideology. (Hillgate Group, 1986, p. 14)

In a later pamphlet, *The Reform of British Education*, published in September 1987, the ranks of those who were said to have worked hard to undermine traditional values in education and frustrate the pursuit of excellence were extended to embrace the civil servants of the DES. HMI advisers and DES civil servants must not, it was argued, be allowed to take control of the new statutory bodies set up as a result of the National Curriculum proposals in the Education Reform Bill:

> If so many bodies are really necessary, then we hope that several members of each of them will be appointed from *outside* the educational establishment, whose collective failure over the past decades has virtually forced the Government to put forward its current reforms. And it is important that the proceedings of these bodies should not be dominated by the Secretariat provided by the DES, or by their HMI advisers. In the subject of English, for example, it has been persuasively argued that HMIs have done nothing to arrest the decline in the teaching of grammar and true literacy, and indeed have often actively encouraged it[8]. We repeat that we have no confidence in the educational establishment, which has acted as an ideological interest group, and which is unlikely to further the Government's aim of providing real education for all. It would be worth insisting that the new bodies should be enabled to function wholly independently of the DES, and with HMI present in an advisory capacity only. (Hillgate Group, 1987, pp. 9–10)

Not only has HMI curriculum expertise been virtually ignored by Kenneth Baker and his advisers; it now seems that the very existence of the

Inspectorate is bitterly resented by the ideologues of the New Right. It remains to be seen how HMI will be used in the implementation of the National Curriculum. If the New Right has its way, the HMI role will be strictly limited, since members of the Inspectorate are held to be at least partly responsible for the sorry state of the education service.

Notes

1 These observations appeared in R. A. Wake's unpublished general introductory paper 'The 11–16 curriculum' prepared for those invited to attend DES Short Course N605 on 'The secondary curriculum' held in Oxford, 6–11 September 1976.
2 This extract is also taken from the papers prepared by R. A. Wake for the Oxford conference.
3 These 'areas of experience' were listed in the Red Book in alphabetical order so that no other order of importance could be inferred: in the view of HMI, they were equally important.
4 The actual composition of the National Curriculum is discussed in depth in the final chapter.
5 When asked at a reception held at the University of London Institute of Education on 16 June 1987 to launch the book *HMI* (by Denis Lawton and Peter Gordon) whether HMI were in any way involved in the shaping of the new National Curriculum, SCI Eric Bolton found it expedient to evade the question and talk instead about the various curriculum documents produced by the Inspectorate since the 1976/77 Great Debate.
6 The writings of the Hillgate Group (Caroline Cox, Jessica Douglas-Home, John Marks, Lawrence Norcross and Roger Scruton) are discussed in detail in the final chapter.
7 Lawton and Gordon have pointed out (1987b) that this is an inaccurate statement. The 'bland survey' here referred to is included in the notes and references of the Hillgate pamphlet as *The Work of HM Inspectors in England and Wales*, DES, 1983, but this was *not* the survey: it was merely a follow-up to the survey and its full title should read *The Work of HM Inspectorate in England and Wales: A Policy Statement by the Secretary of State for Education and Science and the Secretary of State for Wales* (1983b). The full survey was *Study of HM Inspectorate in England and Wales* (1983a), which was the Report of the scrutiny of HMI coordinated by Sir Derek (now Lord) Rayner appointed by the Prime Minister. The Rayner Report, published in March 1983, was extremely searching and far from 'bland' in its style.
8 This presumably refers to the Centre for Policy Studies pamphlet by John Marenbon, *English our English: The New Orthodoxy Examined*, published in 1987.

Chapter 5

The 'Secret Garden' Invaded:
Central Control of the Curriculum,
1976–87

The ten years that elapsed after the Ruskin College speech and the so-called Great Debate were notable for a number of trends and developments, in addition to the search for an agreement on a common or core curriculum, which give the period a peculiar unity and can be collected together under four main headings: centralization; differentiation; vocationalization and privatization. This chapter examines the movement towards central control of the curriculum after 1976, beginning with a brief discussion of the relationship between central government, local authorities and teachers in the period 1944 to 1976. Later chapters will be devoted to the related issues of differentiation and vocationalization and to early attempts at privatizing the system.

Background to the Debate over Central Control

The period from 1944 to the beginning of the 1960s has been described (Lawton, 1980) as 'the Golden Age of teacher control (or non-control) of the curriculum' (p. 22). Since the Elementary Regulations had been abolished in 1926, and the Secondary Regulations were allowed to lapse in 1944, primary and secondary teachers in the post-war period were able to enjoy a considerable degree of autonomy in curriculum matters — even if they failed to take full advantage of it.

Under Section 23 of the 1944 Act, dates of terms, length of the school day, and secular instruction, in all except voluntary-aided secondary schools, were to become the responsibility of the local education authority, unless otherwise provided for in the school articles of government:

> In every county school and, subject to the provisions hereinafter contained as to religious education, in every voluntary school except an aided secondary school, the secular instruction to be given to the pupils shall, save in so far as may be otherwise provided by the rules of management or articles of government for the school, be under the control of the local education authority. (Education Act, 1944, p. 19)

In most schools, however, the actual decisions about curriculum content and teaching methods were to be taken by the headteacher and his/her staff, under the general, if somewhat perfunctory, oversight of the school governing body.[1] Not that this was an entirely autonomous process. As Aldrich and Leighton have pointed out, such decisions were invariably influenced by a number of factors, notably: 'examination syllabuses, university and other entrance requirements, the availability of teachers and teaching materials, the advice of local and government inspectors, the subject choices of pupils and parents (p. 55). What was lacking was specific guidance from the central authority, hence the justification for Lawton's evocative description.[2]

The post-war years have also been described as the years of optimism and consensus in education (Kogan, 1978) and as the partnership years (Hall, 1985). The main political parties were committed to educational expansion, and, by the early 1960s, there was even a fair degree of consensus about the necessity for the comprehensive reform. In this benign political climate, it was comparatively easy to operate the partnership model and assume that it would remain an enduring feature of the education service. Looking back over the early post-war years in his influential book *Education: An Introductory Survey*, first published in 1957, W. O. Lester Smith could write with pride of the virtues of a national system locally administered:

> This tradition of partnership is the outstanding feature of our educational administration . . . The partnership has had its ups and downs, and there are often sharp differences of opinion; but they are mainly differences about means and methods, for there is a remarkable unity of aim and purpose. (pp. 139–40)

In Smith's view, the distribution of power was closely associated with issues of freedom and democracy:

> No freedom that teachers in this country possess is so important as that of determining the curriculum and methods of teaching. Neither the Minister nor the local education authority exercises

authority over the curriculum of any school beyond that of agreeing the general educational character of the school and its place in the local educational system (*ibid.*, p. 161)

The post-war Ministry was happy to boast of its policy of non-intervention with regard to curriculum matters — arguing that consensus was preferable to control. In 1950, the Ministry celebrated its Jubilee: there had been a unified central department for half a century as a consequence of the Board of Education Act of 1899. George Tomlinson (Minister in 1947–51) and the Permanent Secretary, Sir John Maud, crystallized the story in their joint introduction to the Ministry's Report for 1950:

This is the story of a progressive partnership between the central department, the local education authorities and the teachers. To build a single, but not uniform, system out of many diverse elements; to widen educational opportunity and at the same time to raise standards; to knit the educational system more closely into the life of an increasingly democratic and industrialized community: these are among the main ideas which, despite two major wars, have moved legislators and administrators alike. (Ministry of Education, 1951, p. 1)

They went on to emphasize the absence from the Report of any reference to the school curriculum:

If this Report comes into the hands of readers from overseas, as we hope it will, they may be expected to look first for a substantial chapter on educational method and the curriculum of the schools. They will not find it. This does not, of course, mean that the schools have made no response to the new knowledge about the nature and needs of children or to the changing conceptions of the function of education in a democratic community. The reason is that the Department has traditionally valued the life of institutions more highly than systems and has been jealous for the freedom of schools and teachers. In all matters, therefore, affecting the curriculum and methods of teaching, it has been content to offer guidance by means of 'Suggestions'[3] and in the main to rely on Your Majesty's Inspectorate. (*ibid.*)

From 1944 until at least the early 1960s, this was the attitude maintained by ministers when pressed to intervene on some aspect of the school curriculum. It was a key area where Britain's education system could be compared favourably with that operating in other countries in Europe.

In 1951, a party of teachers from Britain visited the Soviet Union to study its education system first hand. Sir Ronald Gould, the General Secretary of the National Union of Teachers, was a member of the party; on his return, he gave a talk on the radio to explain the contrast, as he saw it, between the Russian and the British system of education. After remarking on the generous staffing there, the cleanliness of the schools, the well-stocked school libraries and the ample equipment, he spoke of the uniform and rigid pattern of the curriculum. What, he had asked his hosts, were the supposed advantages of such rigidity? 'I was given only one answer', Gould told his listeners, 'that when a child moves from place to place, it is easy to pick up the work in his new school. No doubt that is so, but is it sufficient — or even the main — reason for the enforcement of uniformity?'[4]. He then gave as his main reasons for preferring the British system its flexibility and diversity. 'I make no bones about it,' he concluded. 'Give me the English approach'. (Quoted in Smith, 1957, pp. 164–5)

In 1960, there were some indications that the cosy era of partnership and teacher autonomy was coming to a premature end. Debating the 1959 Crowther Report in the House of Commons, Sir David Eccles (Conservative Minister of Education in 1959–62) made it clear that there was a desire at the Centre to gain more control over the school curriculum:

> I regret that so many of our education debates have had to be devoted almost entirely to bricks and mortar and to the organization of the system. We hardly ever discuss what is taught to the seven million boys and girls in the maintained schools. We treat the curriculum as though it were a subject, like 'the other place', about which it is 'not done' for us to make remarks. I should like the House to say that this reticence has been overdone. Of course, Parliament would never attempt to dictate the curriculum, but, from time to time, we could, with advantage, express views on what is taught in schools and in training colleges. As for the Ministry of Education itself, my Department has the unique advantage of the countrywide experience of Her Majesty's Inspectorate. Nowhere in the kingdom is there such a rich source of information or such a constant exchange of ideas on all that goes on in the schools. I shall, therefore, try in the future to make the Ministry's own voice heard rather more often, more positively, and, no doubt, sometimes more controversially. For this purpose, we shall need to undertake inside the Department more educational research and to strengthen our statistical services. Crowther . . . prodded us to do this, and action is now in hand. In the meantime, the section in the Report on the Sixth

Form is an irresistible invitation for a sally into the secret garden of the curriculum. (*Hansard*, H. of C., Vol. 620, Cols. 51–2, 21 March 1960)

Here in March 1960 was the earliest suggestion of a venture by the central authority into what was thought to be forbidden territory.

Two years later, in 1962, the Curriculum Study Group was established, without prior consultation with organized educational interests. The Group was to comprise HMIs, administrators and experts coopted from the outside. It would provide a nucleus of full-time staff to organize and coordinate research studies. Its work would be linked, however loosely, with that of the universities, practising teachers, local authorities, research organizations, professional institutes and others concerned with the content of education and examinations. According to Manzer (1970) 'Eccles envisaged the Group as a relatively small, "commando-like unit", making raids into the curriculum' (p. 91). Yet the hostility of professional educators was such that in 1963 the new Minister of Education, Sir Edward Boyle, decided that the Group should be replaced by a more acceptable organization. The Lockwood Committee was set up and recommended that there should be a Schools Council for the Curriculum and Examinations.

The new Council, which met for the first time in October 1964 with Sir John Maud as its Chairman, was not at all the sort of group which Sir David Eccles had had in mind. It was an independent body with a majority of teacher members. Its declared purpose was to undertake research and development work in curricula, teaching methods and examinations in schools. In all its work, it aimed to adhere to the general principle, expressed in its constitution, that each school should have the fullest possible measure of responsibility for its own curriculum and teaching methods based on the needs of its own pupils and evolved by its own staff.[5] In, for example, Working Paper 53 *The Whole Curriculum 13–16*, published in 1975, it was suggested that the aims of a school should be stated in a 'covenant' to which parents, pupils, teachers and society at large could subscribe. Yet the Paper was also anxious to uphold the principle of teacher autonomy in curriculum matters:

> British schools have for long been jealous of their independence in curricular matters. However much they may turn to outside bodies for resources, information and advice, they insist that the curriculum must be of their own making. We strongly affirm our support for this position for . . . we believe the surest hope for the improvement of the secondary-school curriculum lies in the

·· continuing professional growth of the teacher, which, in turn, implies that teachers take even greater responsibility for the development of schools' curriculum policies. Moreover, we have stressed the distinctive nature of the curriculum policies appropriate to particular schools and it would be a denial of this to attempt to prescribe the sort of policies they should adopt. (Schools Council, 1975, p. 30)

In the light of such statements, it has been argued (Barnes, 1977) that 'both the constitution and the workings of the Council underlined the twin principles of school autonomy and teacher control' (p. 21).

Lawton (1980) and Kogan (1978) have both argued that by the early 1960s the end of the period of educational harmony and consensus was in sight with a swing back to central control. Yet, despite the declared wishes of Sir David Eccles, there is much evidence for concluding that teacher autonomy and educational harmony were not really under serious threat in the 1960s.[6] According to Hunter (1984) it was in the mid-1960s that 'Crosland and Boyle presided over the benign consensus which was the basis of the organizational implementation of the comprehensive system' (p. 274).[7] The Schools Council, as we have seen, posed no threat to the concept of teacher autonomy: as Lawton himself has pointed out (1980), 'its influence in curriculum development was considerable, yet it could never have been said to have possessed control, or even much power, in curriculum matters' (p. 67). Then again, the power and influence of HMI actually declined in the 1960s when it was not clear what the role of the Inspectorate should be.[8] For one thing, there was the continuing problem of overlap between the work of HMI and that of local authority inspectors; and members of the Inspectorate clearly regretted that their professional expertise was not making itself felt (Lawton and Gordon, 1987a, p. 25). After 1968 their influence appeared to diminish still further when the emphasis was on advice and support with a much reduced role for the formal inspection of schools; and the DES Yellow Book of 1976 made reference to the reduced influence of the Inspectorate in the immediate past, attributing it largely to its uneasy relationship with the Schools Council (DES, 1976a, p. 17). The Assessment of Performance Unit (APU) may be seen as an example of the DES clearly trying to exert some central influence on the curriculum, but it was not established until August 1974. In the Yellow Book, the period immediately prior to 1976 was described as 'the era of assertive "teacher power"' (*ibid.*). This may well be considered something of an over-statement; but it is arguable that in the early 1970s, Lawton's 'Golden Age' was still a reality for most schools and for most teachers.

According to Ranson (1980), the power of teachers and of local authorities had actually *increased* by the early 1970s, with central government unable to arrest the decline in its influence:

> The balance of power between the partners in education had at the end of the sixties and early seventies swung very much towards the local authorities and to heads and teachers in schools (for whom the Schools Council, the influential Plowden Report and the CSE exam had enhanced professional control of curriculum and assessment) . . . The Centre, bereft of funds and the necessary statutory instruments, had become manifestly unable to secure policy implementation through persuasion alone. (p. 10)

None of this mattered particularly so long as everybody was moving in the same general direction. In the mid-1970s, it was still fashionable in some circles to talk in terms of harmony and consensus. For example, Timothy Raison of the Centre for Studies in Social Policy was arguing in a pamphlet published in 1976 that 'to a considerable extent, the Secretary of State acts as the guardian of the educational system, rather than as its administrative head' enjoying the benefits of 'a substantial degree of consensus about what should be taught and how' (Raison, 1976, pp. 15 and 42). As late as 1979, Sir William Pile, formerly Permanent Secretary at the DES, was still talking in terms of partnership and arguing that teachers still enjoyed considerable autonomy in curriculum planning:

> The biggest single virtue of the Education Act 1944, it can be argued, was that it determined that no one interest group should have a monopoly of power, and the distribution of power that it enacted has proved over thirty years to have been stable, effective and appropriate. It produced . . . an all-embracing network of dispersed responsibility . . . The immense freedoms that rest in professional rather than political or bureaucratic hands have undoubtedly produced over the years much of the richness and flexibility that are characteristic of the British education process. (Pile, 1979, pp. 236–7)

1976 as a Turning Point

Despite the tendency of some contemporaries to adhere to the rhetoric of a dying consensus, it was clear to many by 1976 that the partnership years were coming to an end, or, perhaps more accurately, that the *terms* of the partnership were about to change significantly. For reasons already discussed, it was in 1976 that the political viewpoint and the bureaucratic viewpoint coincided. With the deepening economic crisis associated with balance of payments difficulties and spiralling domestic inflation, the central authority was increasingly preoccupied with re-examining the bases of centre-local relationships in order to clarify and redefine points of control. In the view of both politicians and civil servants, there had to be greater control of education in general, and of the secondary curriculum in particular, in order to ensure a marked improvement in standards and wide acceptance of the view that a major task of schooling was to equip pupils to meet the needs of society. It was after 1976 that partnership was replaced by accountability as the dominant metaphor in discussions about the distribution of power in the education system.

The new emphasis on quality, standards and accountability in education certainly marked a departure from the accepted order of things. As Eric Bolton, the present HMI Senior Chief Inspector, has observed:

> Throughout the 1950s, 1960s and early 1970s, the main concerns of central government and LEAs in respect of education appear to have been about teacher numbers and supply, school buildings and the organizational form of maintained secondary education. Issues relating to quality, standards and accountability were left to the schools and the advisers and the examination boards: national and local government played little part in these matters. Almost nowhere in government documents of the period are there references to standards of learning, examinations, or the curriculum. (Bolton, 1987b, p. 10)

According to Bolton, the post-oil-crisis shock and the very high inflation that were features of the mid-1970s caused governments in all the developed world to look again at public spending: in this respect, Britain was no exception. This was the main reason why quality and standards of achievement in education began to move to centre stage. The consequences were to prove far-reaching. Again to quote Bolton:

> Within education itself the questioning . . . began to reveal to a wider public the wide variation in standard achieved, curricula offered and resources provided for education across the country: matters which the Inspectorate had been complaining about for some time, but which had gained little acknowledgment or active attention . . . The concerns about education, like the demographic decline in students, began to include further and higher

education. These were added to by increasing evidence from international comparisons that Britain was not doing as well as other more-or-less analagous countries, particularly in producing engineers, mathematicians and scientists adept in the new technologies that had become so intrinsically linked with economic health and well-being. Our education system began to be seen as critical both in having contributed to the worrying state of affairs and in bringing about desired improvements. In short, good in parts as our education service is, it became firmly established that it was not as good as it could be, in that more of it ought to be as good as the best, nor as good as it should be to equip the nation with the skilled and talented people required to maintain and even enhance our standing in the world. Consequently, the search was on to find out how to set about raising standards. (*ibid.*)

The solutions advocated in the DES Yellow Book were moves towards curriculum standardization and greater acceptance by the government of responsibility for the general direction of the education service. The time had apparently come to formulate generally accepted principles for the composition of a 'core curriculum' (DES, 1976a, p. 11), although it was accepted that there had to be extensive consideration and consultation before such a curriculum could be introduced. At the same time, there was a need for more positive initiatives from the Centre:

It will also be good to get on record from ministers, and in particular, the Prime Minister, an authoritative pronouncement on the division of responsibility for what goes on in school, suggesting that the Department should give a firmer lead. Such a pronouncement would have to respect legitimate claims made by the teachers as to the exercise of their professional judgment, but should firmly refute any argument — and this is what they have sought to establish — that no one except teachers has any right to any say in what goes on in schools. The climate for a declaration on these lines may, in fact, now be relatively favourable. Nor need there be any inhibition for fear that the Department could not make use of enhanced opportunity to exercise influence over curriculum and teaching methods: the Inspectorate would have a leading role to play in bringing forward ideas in these areas and is ready to fulfil that responsibility. (*ibid.*, p. 25)

The Yellow Book represented the bureaucratic view of affairs in 1976. Yet while there is evidence throughout the document of a keen desire to exert greater influence over the school curriculum, the emphasis was still at this stage on exhortation, persuasion and encouragement.

Significantly, 1976 was also the year when James Hamilton took over from Sir William Pile as Permanent Secretary at the DES[9]. The new Secretary shared the civil servants' concern for a stronger voice in curriculum matters and was to be described by Stuart Maclure in *The Times Educational Supplement* (24 April 1983) as an 'unrepentant centralist'. In the same month that the Yellow Book was completed, he made an important speech at the annual conference of the Association of Education Committees in Scarborough in which he warned that, in future, his department would be taking 'a much closer interest' in what was taught in schools. Talking about Section 1 of the 1944 Education Act, he said:

> This must mean more than seeing that teachers, buildings and other resources are available on whatever scale the country can afford. It must mean, I believe, a much closer interest by the Department in the curriculum in its widest sense, the assessment of performance, and even the relationship of teaching method to performance.

According to Hamilton, teachers had traditionally reserved the right to decide what was taught in schools, but now the key to the 'secret garden of the curriculum' had to be found and turned. For too long, the views expressed by the professionals had ignored the wishes of parents and pupils. It was the task of government to discover the views of the customers:

> I wonder whether all of us in the education service should not be prepared to admit that we shelter too often behind so-called expertise and take too little notice of the views expressed by our millions of customers — parents and their children. (Reported in *The Times Educational Supplement*, 2 July 1976)

As far as the Permanent Secretary was concerned, the Department now had two major tasks: to secure agreement on a new framework for the school curriculum; and to plan the run-down of the education service at a time of economic contraction and limited resources.

Contributors to a conference of the British Educational Administration Society (BEAS) with the title 'Educational administration and the curriculum: Issues and trends in Britain and some other European countries', held in London in September 1976, were agreed that while attempts were being made in Continental systems to loosen controls over the curriculum, in this country the trend was towards a tightening of controls and the establishment of some common guidelines. It was generally accepted that there were areas of concern in British schools and that methods would have to be devised of ensuring that lay voices be heard on curricular issues and that schools falling short of reasonable expectations be encouraged to seek improvement. The government might well have to intervene to ensure that minimum standards were being met, although it would be preferable if this could be achieved through the effective functioning of governing bodies. Whatever the solution adopted, all this seemed to be at variance with what was happening, for example, in France. In the words of one contributor:

> Our two apparently different systems appear to be moving closer towards the middle of the spectrum. The French attempt decon-centration... Recent statements from the DES suggest moves to more centralized curricular control in England. (Glatter, 1977, p. 113)

Also in September 1976, the Education, Arts and Home Office Sub-committee of the House of Commons Expenditure Committee published its report on policy-making in the DES, which contained a section on 'The DES and the curriculum' (*Tenth Report from the Expenditure Committee*, 1976, paragraphs 57–65). In this, the Sub-committee urged the Secretary of State to take a greater interest in the curriculum and educational standards, while also maintaining that this was not to be taken to imply the advocacy of a deliberate move towards centralized control. It was also anxious that its proposals should not be construed as a desire for political interference in the classroom, although it was not clear what the term 'political' actually meant in this context.

The campaign to establish the government's legitimate right to a say in the composition of the school curriculum was taken a stage further with the delivery of the Ruskin College speech in October 1976. The Prime Minister was anxious to repudiate the suggestion that education policy in general, and curriculum policy in particular, could be said to be the exclusive concern of any one group:

> If everything is reduced to such phrases as 'educational freedom versus state control', we shall get nowhere... Parents, teachers, learned and professional bodies, representatives of higher education and both sides of industry, together with the govern-ment, all have an important part to play in formulating and expressing the purpose of education and the standards that we need.

With its thinly-veiled attack on teacher autonomy, the Ruskin speech was a key manifestation of what Hall (1985) has described as 'the centralist tendency'. As a *Times* leader writer pointed out eight months later (27 June 1977), the speech gave the DES the initiative to develop a policy of change from the centre. As we have already seen, this was clearly necessary if government ideas on the school curriculum were to be implemented. For both politicians and civil servants, central control was not simply a good thing *in itself*. It was the essential prerequisite for moving the education system in certain directions. Without it, strategies for differentiation and vocationalization could not be implemented.[10]

The Prime Minister's sentiments were clearly shared by his new Secretary of State for Education and Science, Shirley Williams, and given similar expression in a speech she delivered at Rockingham College of Further Education on 22 October 1976:

> Among the splendours of the English [education] system are its flexibility, its imagination, and the freedom of the teacher in the classroom. No one wishes to jeopardize that. But the curriculum is a matter in which many people have a stake: parents, teachers, employers, trade unions, Parliament and, of course, the government itself. We have, through discussion and debate, to produce the most satisfactory curricula we can. (Quoted in NUT, 1977, p. 4)

Yet, despite the assurances of the Prime Minister and of his Secretary of State, a clear recognition of the perceived need to curtail 'teacher power' was inscribed in the very format of the Great Debate which followed the Ruskin College speech. As Bates (1984) has pointed out:

> The 'Great Debate' reflected a trend towards defining and limiting the boundaries of teacher autonomy. The very initiation of a public debate on education, involving the unprecedented consultation of industrial organizations, served as an explicit reminder to the teaching profession . . . that the curriculum was not solely their responsibility to determine . . . Thus the 'Great Debate', irrespective of its content, simply as a *means* of intervening in education, helped to change the political context in which educational issues were discussed. (p. 199)

In a sense, the partnership model was still intact, but one of the partners was certainly trying to assert its authority while, at the same time, challenging some of the basic assumptions which had underpinned the old consensus.

From the Ruskin Speech to the National Curriculum

With regard to the movement towards centralized control of the curriculum, the years following 1976 can usefully be divided into three main periods: the first of these, from 1976 to 1981, was one of attempted central control through curriculum documents emanating from the DES and HMI; this was followed, in the years from 1981 to 1986, by a period of attempted control through the introduction of new examinations and curriculum initiatives; and finally, in 1986/87, came the start of a period of more direct intervention and control through the National Curriculum and many of the other provisions of the Baker Education Act.

1976-81

Documents issued by the DES after 1976 emphasized the general accountability of the education service to society at large; the new leadership role of the Secretary of State in educational matters of public concern; and the need to seek agreement with other interested parties on a framework for the school curriculum. The first of these documents, the eagerly-awaited Green Paper of July 1977, *Education in Schools: A Consultative Document*, summarized the position succinctly as a justification for future action:

> Education, like any other public service, is answerable to the society which it serves and which pays for it . . . It would not be compatible with the duty of the Secretaries of State to 'promote the education of the people of England and Wales', or with their accountability to Parliament, to abdicate from leadership on educational issues which have become a matter of lively public concern. The Secretaries of State will therefore seek to establish a broad agreement with their partners in the education service on a framework for the curriculum, and, particularly, on whether, because there are aims common to all schools and to all pupils at certain stages, there should be a 'core' or 'protected part'. (DES, 1977b, pp. 212)[11]

The Green Paper went on to outline the role of the local education authorities in coordinating the curriculum and its development in their own areas, taking account of local circumstances, consulting local interests and drawing on the work of various curricular research and development agencies. The next step in the process to improve the planning and development of the curriculum would be for the Secretaries of State to invite the local authority and teachers' associations to take part in early consultations about the conduct of a review of curricular arrangements in each local authority area. This review would be heralded by the issuing of a circular:

> The intention of the Secretaries of State is that . . . they should issue a circular asking all local education authorities to carry out the review in their own areas in consultation with their teachers and to report the results within about twelve months. The Department would then analyze the replies as a preliminary to consultations on the outcome of the review and on the nature of any advice which the Secretaries of State might then issue on curricular matters. (*ibid.*, p. 13)

Circular 14/77 was duly published in November 1977, inviting local authorities to 'assemble relevant information and to report the results to the Secretaries of State by 30 June 1978' (DES, 1977c, p. 1). By the time the Report on the review was published, in November 1979, a general election had taken place and the Labour government had been removed from office. Yet it is indicative of the consistency of intentions in the DES at this time, regardless of the political complexion of the government of the day, that the assumptions of a review initiated by a Labour Secretary (Shirley Williams) should be warmly endorsed in a subsequent report by a Conservative Secretary (Mark Carlisle).

The document published in 1979 revealed that many local authorities were insufficiently informed about what went on in their schools. *Local Authority Arrangements for the School Curriculum* began with a commentary on the responses to *Circular 14/77* which argued that in too many cases, local authorities were not aware of the curricular policies and objectives of the schools in their areas (DES, 1979a, pp. 2–7). According to Holt (1983), this was hardly a surprising revelation, but it served a useful purpose:

> It was a foregone conclusion that the Report would establish what everyone knew: that LEAs had not troubled to acquire a detailed knowledge of school curriculum policies, least of all attempted the forlorn task of evaluating schools. The Circular was a device which managed to make the LEAs look as if they were failing in their duties, and thus allowed the DES to take the initiative. (pp. 20–1)

Yet there was no question of the DES actually discarding the partnership model at this stage. The 1979 *Report* envisaged a leadership role for the Secretaries of State within a context of shared responsibilities:

> [The Secretaries of State] believe they should seek to give a lead in the process of reaching a national consensus on a desirable frame-work for the curriculum and consider the development of such a framework a priority for the education service . . . The Secretaries of State do not seek to determine in detail what the schools should teach or how it should be taught; but they have an inescapable duty to satisfy themselves that the work of the schools matches national needs. This task cannot be undertaken from the centre alone. The Government must bring together the partners in the education service and the interests of the community at large; and with them seek an agreed view of the school curriculum which would take account of the range of local needs and allow for local developments, drawing upon the varied skills and experience which all those concerned with the service can contribute. (DES, 1979a, pp. 2–3 and 6–7)

There might be some infringement of teacher autonomy; but individual teachers would always be looked to for 'subject expertise and professional experience, and the fullest knowledge of opportunities and contraints, and of individual pupils' capabilities and expectations' (*ibid.*, pp. 3–4).

The Inspectorate also accepted in their 1980 discussion document, *A View of the Curriculum*, that a nationally agreed framework for the curriculum would, inevitably, limit somewhat the freedom of individual schools and teachers; but the emphasis was still on mutual confidence and shared responsibilities:

> A common policy for the curriculum . . . cannot be a prescription for uniformity. Enabling all pupils to achieve a comparable quality of adult life is a more subtle and skilled task than taking them all through identical syllabuses or teaching them all by the same methods. It requires careful assessment of children's capabilities and continuing progress, and selection of those experiences and activities which will best enable them to acquire the skills and knowledge they need in common and to develop to the full their own potential. There is need for mutual confidence between schools and the wider public in agreement about aims and in identification of the means to their realization. In practice, that means that the broad definition of the purposes of school education is a shared responsibility, whereas the detailed means by which they may best be realized in individual schools and for

individual children are a matter for professional judgment. (DES, 1980b, pp. 2–3)

The partnership model was clarified further in the 1981 DES document *The School Curriculum*. Having argued that the 5–16 curriculum must respond to the changing demands made by the world outside the school, the paper pointed out that recent evidence from HMI national surveys of primary and secondary schools[12] revealed that too many pupils were not being prepared for the realities of the adult world. Yet this did not require a fundamental rethink of the balance of power within the system:

> This calls, not for a change in the statutory framework of the education service, but for a reappraisal of how each partner in the service should now discharge those responsibilities assigned to him by law. The Secretaries of State consider that curriculum policies should be developed and implemented on the basis of the existing statutory relationship between the partners and that this process must be based upon a clear understanding of, and must pay proper regard to, the responsibilities and interests of each partner and the contribution that each can make. (DES, 1981a, p. 2)

The government had no wish to undermine the crucial role of schools and teachers in curriculum planning:

> It is the individual schools that shape the curriculum for each pupil. Neither the government nor the local authorities should specify in detail what the schools should teach. This is for the schools themselves to determine ... What schools teach and achieve is largely a measure of the dedication and competence of the head teacher and the whole staff and of the interest and support of the governing body. (*ibid.*, p. 3)

Although *The School Curriculum* was criticized in the educational press and elsewhere for its interventionist stance on the curriculum, it was, in fact, in direct descent from preceeding DES and HMI policy documents. In retrospect, the DES desire for greater influence in 1981 seems tame in comparison with the many sweeping new powers assumed by the Secretary of State under the terms of the 1988 Education Reform Act. Moreover, there was no guarantee in the early 1980s that DES or HMI curriculum proposals were actually being translated into practice at the level of the individual school or college. Evidence reaching the Department, both from HMI and in response to *Circular 14/77* pointed to a disconcerting inertia on the part of many local authorities and schools.

The stream of DES and HMI documents on the curriculum stopped in 1981. It seemed that the DES bureaucrats had tired of the politics of persuasion. It has been argued (Nuttall, 1984; Maw, 1985) that, having failed in their attempt to determine what was taught in schools through documents like *A Framework for the School Curriculum* (DES, 1980a) and *The School Curriculum* (DES, 1981a), they simply decided to try to achieve their aims by other means, notably the instigation of examination reforms. It is, therefore, significant that the new CPVE (Certificate of Pre-Vocational Education) and the proposed AS (Advanced Supplementary) levels emanated from the Department and that criteria for the new GCSE (General Certificate of Secondary Education) have been vetted there. This argument has certainly been endorsed by Sir James Hamilton who was DES Permanent Secretary until 1983. Looking back over his seven years at the Department at a conference organized by the Association for Science Education in June 1983, he argued that the government had generally shown too much 'delicacy' about making its presence felt in the classroom:

> I believe we erred on the side of safety. I believe that we could, with benefit, have produced a more pungent, a more purposive analysis... There is an argument for the DES acting more directly in certain limited areas of the curriculum. Otherwise, other agencies will move in to fill the gaps they perceive, possibly to deleterious effect... The present exercise of reforming examinations at 16+ should be seen as part of this process of establishing greater central control. (Reported in *The Times Educational Supplement*, 1 July 1983)

Other important examples of the centralizing process between 1981 and 1986 would include: the announcement in 1982 that the Schools Council would be abolished in 1984 (despite a rigorous programme of committee streamlining and a favourable report from the Trenaman Committee); the control of teacher education through the introduction of the Council for the Accreditation of Teacher Education (CATE); the control of in-service training for teachers by means of a specific grant, as outlined in the 1985 DES document *Better Schools* (DES, 1985c, p. 54); the introduction and development of the Technical and Vocational Education Initiative (TVEI) funded by the Manpower Services Commission (MSC); the introduction of a 'rate-capping' policy for local authorities in 1983; and the use of education support grants under the terms of the 1984 Education (Grants and Awards) Act as part of a shift towards categorical funding. Of these, the introduction of TVEI and the new financial measures introduced by the government were of particular significance for the centralizing process in education.

The (New) Technical and Vocational Education Initiative is an interesting example of the power and influence of the Manpower Services Commission in the period when David (now Lord) Young was its Chairman from 1982 to 1984 (see Chitty and Worgan, 1987; Low, 1988). It started life with fourteen pilot projects in the autumn of 1983. By 1986, it involved 65,000 students in 600 institutions working on four-year programmes designed to stimulate work-related education, make the curriculum more relevant to post-school life and enable students to aim for nationally-recognized qualifications in a wide range of technical and vocational subject areas. For the purposes of this chapter, this curriculum innovation will be looked at from the point of view of its implications for the centralizing process in curriculum planning. [13]

The Initiative was announced in a House of Commons statement by Margaret Thatcher on 12 November 1982. Replying to a question from Sir William van Straubenzee, the Prime Minister said:

> Growing concern about the existing arrangement (for technical and vocational education for young people) has been expressed over many years, not least by the National Economic Development Council. I have asked the Chairman of the Man-power Services Commission, together with . . . the Secretaries of State for Education and Science, for Employment, and for Wales, to develop a pilot scheme to start by September 1983, for new institutional arrangements for technical and vocational education for 14–18-year-olds, within existing financial resources, and, where possible, in association with local education authorities. (*Hansard*, H. of C., Sixth Series — Vol. 31, Cols. 271–2, written answers to questions, 12 November 1982)

The fact that it was the Prime Minister, rather than David Young, the Chairman of the MSC, or Sir Keith Joseph, the then Secretary of State for Education and Science, who announced that a pilot scheme was to start in the following September, may be indicative of the importance attached to this Initiative or symptomatic of a developing rivalry between the DES and the MSC for control of education and training. According to Dale (1985), all the main bodies concerned with education were taken completely by surprise:

> The announcement came like a bolt from the blue to all the most directly interested parties. Neither the DES, the local education

authority associations, the teacher professional organizations, nor even the MSC had been consulted before the announcement was made. (p. 41)

If Dale is correct, this was indeed a mould-breaking development, not least in the mode of its conception. He suggests that the original plan for the Initiative was jointly conceived by a triumvirate of David Young, Sir Keith Joseph and Norman Tebbit (at that time Secretary of State for Employment). This theory is backed up by Young himself who conceded in an interview published in *Education*, (19 November 1982, pp. 385–6) that there had been 'a few ruffled feathers' about the way the decision had been taken. The Prime Minister had apparently decided to 'set the ball rolling' after a meeting of the National Economic Development Council in early November when the relationship of education to industry had been the main topic of discussion. But, according to Young, preparations had been taking place 'for some time' between Sir Keith Joseph and Norman Tebbit, and he himself had been closely involved. Accepting his version of events, it is possible to argue that while the introduction of the (N)TVEI was not the only innovation of the 1980s to be promulgated directly from the Centre, it was surely unique at that time in that the Civil Service apparently played no part in its gestation.

Both David Young and Norman Tebbit issued press releases on 12 November 1982 welcoming the Initiative, the MSC statement claiming that:

This is an invitation to the local education authorities to work in partnership with us to further advance vocational education for young people. (MSC, 1982)

Yet it was the precise nature of that 'partnership' that was to cause alarm and confusion in the weeks that followed. The reference by the Prime Minister in her Commons statement to 'new institutional arrangements' and to collaboration with local authorities 'where possible' gave rise to considerable fears that a new kind of institution was envisaged — or, rather, that something like the old technical school was to be revived. Yet *within a week*, it had been decided that local education authorities should, in fact, be involved in the implementation of the new scheme, even though the debate continued as to whether the schools selected for participation should be 'transformed' into technical high schools or whether instead (as eventually happened) the scheme would simply involve support for additional technical and vocational options *within* existing comprehensive schools. As *Education* pointed out at the time (26 November 1982, p. 410), the civil servants at the DES found themselves in a very difficult position:

The Department of Education and Science [had been] caught in a rather ambivalent position by the rapid turn of events. On the one hand, they were urging the local authorities to take part in the Initiative; on the other, they let it be known that they entirely understood and sympathized with the doubts the LEAs expressed about the constitutional propriety of the MSC administering and funding part of the service for which local authorities are responsible under the 1944 Act.

It seemed to many commentators in 1982 that TVEI represented a powerful challenge not only to the power of the local education authorities but also to that of the DES itself. In its first edition after the Prime Minister's House of Commons announcement, *The Times Educational Supplement* carried an editorial headlined 'Bring back the DES' which was remarkably hostile to an initiative which had been in the public domain for only a week and for which there was virtually no available documentation:

> Mrs Thatcher's bombshell last Friday has given yet another hefty jolt to the kaleidoscope of relationships which determine educational policy and curriculum development. The new Chairman of the Manpower Services Commission, Mr. David Young, has only had to wait a matter of six months before initiating a new imperialistic drive downwards into the secondary school. The Prime Minister and Mr. Norman Tebbit have brushed the Department of Education and Science aside . . . entrusting the planning, the direction and the finance of this major attempt to offer a new set of vocational options at around the age of 14 to Mr. Young and his colleagues . . .
>
> The Prime Minister's statement referred to 'new institutional arrangements for technical and vocational education for 14–18-year-olds within existing financial resources', and 'where possible, in association with local education authorities'. The inclusion of the words 'where possible' has sent a *frisson* of alarm through the local education authorities . . . This alarm signal seems to have been fully intended . . .
>
> It seems that Mr. David Young . . . was quite prepared to consider the creation of a number of new, free-standing technical and vocational education centres under MSC control . . .
>
> This formula would be too much for Sir Keith Joseph . . . who has apparently convinced his colleagues that, given the existence of a large pot of gold, a lot of education authorities would be prepared to set up schemes of their own which would meet the MSC requirements . . .

There must be acute dissatisfaction and anxiety about the way in which the scheme has been launched...

It must not be allowed to pass without serious debate. For the doubtful benefit of a quick response, the government is risking the further debilitation of the DES and the indefinite postponement of any serious attempt in Elizabeth House to make real education policy and build up the consensus needed to sustain it. (*The Times Educational Supplement*, 19 November 1982)

This forthright editorial could be said to capture the sense of insecurity and exclusion which was consequent on the clandestine nature of the TVEI launch. It also illustrated clearly the tension between the MSC and the DES. If the editorial is correct in its interpretation of events, then Keith Joseph is cast in the somewhat unaccustomed role of a calm, moderating influence. In the event, the more radical aspects of the original proposal were quickly shelved, and this was probably because the government simply did not feel strong enough in 1982 to alienate both the civil servants of the DES and the local education authorities. Whatever the reason, William Shelton, Parliamentary Under-Secretary for Education, felt able to state in a speech on 23 November:

There has been no *putsch* at Elizabeth House. Education in this country is still under the control of the Department in partnership with the LEAs. (Quoted in *Education*, 26 November 1982, p. 40)

There may well have been tensions between DES civil servants and MSC officials, but it seems clear that Sir Keith himself saw the Commission as a useful tool in the process, dear to his heart, of vocationalizing the curriculum for a significant proportion of the ability range.[14]

Alongside the use of the Manpower Services Commission to fund the TVEI, the Thatcher government — and particularly in its second term (1983–87) — adopted a number of financial measures which enhanced its control of education. In 1983, for example, the government sought control over local government expenditure by legislation giving it the power to limit the rates in any authority where it considered the existing level of expenditure to be too high. Being a major item of local government expenditure, education inevitably suffered as a result of this 'rate-capping' policy. From 1984 onwards, local authorities had less control over educational spending and more final decisions were now in the hands of central government. Many local authorities complained that at the very time when the DES was asking for improved curriculum planning, central government was limiting their spending in such a way as to make that planning almost impossible.

At the same time, the 1985/86 financial year saw the introduction of education support grants under the terms of the 1984 Education (Grants and Awards) Act. This Act enabled the government to pay education support grants to local education authorities for specific 'innovations and improvements' that it wished to encourage. It was not, of course, *extra* money earmarked for education, but money *withheld* from the Rate Support Grant. It was reported in *The Guardian* (22 January 1986) that the government had plans to extend this practice in order to exert more central control over education. At that time, the government was limited by statute to giving 0.5 per cent of spending (£50 million) through direct grants tied to specific purposes. But this was later increased to 1 per cent, so that the government could offer local authorities specific grants to finance their lunch-time supervision schemes in schools. In a provocative speech at Cardiff in April 1986 to the annual assembly of the Assistant Masters and Mistresses Association (AMMA), Chris Patten, at that time Minister of State for Education, gave a clear warning that the government was quite prepared to use direct funding to increase its control over education. If that control were not achieved in this way, other means would have to be found of operating the education system:

> The recent introduction of education support grants marked an extremely modest move towards making at least some of the grant specifically payable for identified educational purposes. No doubt the tension between general and specific funding of local authorities will continue. We shall need to consider whether a change in the balance may be necessary as the partnership evolves. We must make this partnership work, or else we shall need to find some other way of organizing and running the nation's schools. (Reported in *The Guardian*, 5 April 1986)

It is not clear exactly what this particular threat entailed in 1986; and, in the event, Chris Patten himself did not survive into the Baker era at the DES.

The period from 1981 to 1986 was also notable for increasing central influence on the curriculum of a frankly party political nature. Statements were made by ministers and others which would have been considered quite improper in earlier periods. In March 1982, for example, Sir Keith Joseph, in a speech at the annual convention of the Institute of Directors, stated that:

> ... I think we would all agree — and it is sad — that there is too little understanding in this free society of how the free society works — too little understanding in this country's economy, so

dependent upon the effectiveness of free enterprise, of how free enterprise works — and that is a weakness that is sad and damaging . . .

I welcome the efforts of businessmen in all sorts of ways to open the eyes of schoolchildren and schoolteachers to the realities of business life, but I believe it has to be done in a campaign to come within a moral education. It is not good enough to explain the management of business. A child's imagination has to be seized by explaining the role of business in the moral world, as well as in the physical world.

. . . I do not know how many businessmen would be happy to be confronted by a microphone and asked the question: 'what is the moral justification for profit?' Unless a person can answer that question, and answer all the questions that flow from the answer to that question, I do not believe that he or she is able effectively to teach business-education links in schools; and the answer we all know is that 'profit is only morally justified when it is earned within the law and harnessed to competition'. It is competition that harnesses the self-interest of the businessman to the interests of the consumer, and once that is appreciated, I believe it puts a totally different complexion upon business.

I do not know that many businessmen understand sufficiently clearly in the front of their minds the moral role of business. You can have free enterprise without having freedom — and there are such countries, that have free enterprise and do not have what we understand as freedom. But . . . you cannot have freedom without having free enterprise — and that is the case that has to be put in schools.[15]

This was a curious speech, coming as it did from a politician who claimed to condemn all forms of political indoctrination in schools. It appeared to suggest that children should be taught that belief in the capitalist ethic was a moral imperative. According to the report of the speech in *The Times Educational Supplement* (26 March 1982), Sir Keith had argued that 'schools should preach the moral virtue of free enterprise and the pursuit of profit'.[16]

The government was also worried at this time about the growing popularity of the Campaign for Nuclear Disarmament and the growth of peace studies in secondary schools. On 22 June 1982, in the House of Commons, the Education Minister, Dr. Rhodes Boyson, was asked by Harry Greenway for his views on 'a new subject that is creeping into schools under the guise of political education called "peace studies", which is causing immense concern to parents because in some areas it is unadulterated unilateralism and pacifism'. The Minister replied by echoing his colleague's concern:

> I share my Honourable Friend's . . . concern about the growth of peace — or, rather, appeasement — studies because that is basically what they are. (*Hansard*, H. of C., Sixth Series — Vol. 26, Col. 146, oral answers, 22 June 1982)

Schools were to be encouraged to make use of the Central Office of Information pamphlet *A Balanced View*, which outlined the government's case for retaining nuclear weapons.

Sir Keith Joseph took up the issue at a conference organized by the National Council of Women of Great Britain in March 1984. He deplored the teaching of 'peace studies' as a blatant attempt at indoctrination:

> I must say . . . that I regret the label 'peace studies'. I do not question integrity. But I deplore attempts to exploit the emotional connotations of the word 'peace', so as to beg intensely serious and intensely difficult questions . . . I deplore attempts to trivialize the substance of the issue of peace and war, to cloud it with inappropriate appeals to emotion, and to present it so one-sidedly that the teacher is guilty of indoctrination. Such attempts are an insult to the teaching profession and a disservice to the cause of education in an open society . . . I deplore attempts to preach one-sided disarmament to primary pupils ('babes against the bomb') under the guise of teaching them, as they must be taught, to be kind and considerate to others; or to offer to older pupils only one of the many views about national defence. (DES, 1984)

Yet despite evidence of a clear desire on the part of the government to influence the teaching of certain 'controversial' school subjects, Sir Keith Joseph's period as Secretary of State (1981–86) was not marked by any attempt from the centre to specify precisely the composition of the school curriculum, either in terms of areas of study or of syllabuses. As late as March 1985, the government was disclaiming any intention of introducing legislation to control the curriculum in an important section in the document *Better Schools*:

> . . . it would not in the view of the government be right for the Secretaries of State's policy for the range and pattern of the 5–16 curriculum to amount to the determination of national syllabuses for that period. It would, however, be appropriate for the curricular policy of the LEA, on the basis of broadly agreed

principles about range and pattern, to be more precise about, for example, the balance between curricular elements and the age and pace at which pupils are introduced to particular subject areas (e.g. a foreign language) . . . The government does not propose to introduce legislation affecting the powers of the Secretaries of State in relation to the curriculum. (DES, 1985c, pp. 11–12)

Developments Since 1986: The End of Partnership

The passing of the 1988 Education Reform Act is a clear indication that the 'partnership years' are now truly over. This would appear to be obvious to a number of contemporary commentators, and it is clearly a source of much regret. Speaking at the North of England Education Conference in January 1988, former SCI Sheila Browne reflected on the changes that had taken place since her departure from the Inspectorate in 1983:

> . . . one is left wondering what it is that has changed or not changed in the four years since I was translated to Cambridge, that means a legislative sledgehammer is now thought necessary . . . Apart from a growing impatience with the slowness of developments, what has changed most is the sad decline of working trust between and among the partners and, at times, the substitution of a mode of public confrontation which seems sometimes so blind that it is ready to deny the self-evident right, if it emanates from any source except oneself . . . Whether this can be corrected now that the Bill with all its depressing implications is on the table, and with the teachers' professional position unresolved, is doubtful. But corrected it has to be, if education is to become anything like as good as it could be or, indeed, if it is to be seen to be as good as it is . . . . (Reported in *The Times Educational Supplement*, 8 January 1988)

According to Morris and Griggs (1988), the outstanding feature of the period since the mid-1970s has been 'the destruction of the partnership between government, local authorities and teachers which had been the foundation of our education system for many years' (p. 24). They point out that 'it is ironical that the partnership has ended at the same time as the increase in public expectation of education should have greatly strengthened it'. For Tim Brighouse, the then Chief Education Officer for Oxfordshire, writing in *Education* in April 1988, the situation was so depressing it induced in people a feeling of helplessness that could threaten democracy itself:

Fundamentally, the Education Reform Bill, like other parts of current legislation, is an attack on the distribution of power between central and local government in favour of the former. It may be that as the twenty-first century approaches and in a country of 55 million people with a proud history in defence of human rights and in the peaceful practice of democracy, it is proper that we should rely on a simple crude vote of the population every five years to give democratic control over *all* the major aspects of our life. On the other hand, it may induce in an ever-increasingly educated people such a sense of powerlessness which will threaten the last vestiges of democracy. (*Education*, 15 April 1988, p. 307)

Finally, according to Jackson Hall, formerly Director of Education for Sunderland, the end of partnership also marks the passing of the constitutional settlement drawn up in 1944: 'the Bill is not about the development or reformation of the 1944 settlement, but about replacing it' (Hall, 1988, p. 4).

Notes

1 It has been pointed out by Baron and Howell in *The Government and Management of Schools* (1974) that governors and managers have traditionally had remarkably little say in curriculum matters. 'In very many cases, governors take only a perfunctory interest in the curriculum, merely noting what the head chooses to tell them. This is exactly what is wanted by many heads, as they feel their governors are not competent to express an opinion.' (p. 125)
2 It is true that in 1945 the Council for Curriculum Reform produced a carefully-argued document *The Content of Education*, which made the case for a common curriculum for secondary schools. Unfortunately for the cause of rational curriculum planning, the Council lacked any political power base, and its recommendations were virtually ignored.
3 The reference to 'Suggestions' here is to *Handbook of Suggestions for the Consideration of Teachers in Public Elementary Schools* (London, 1937). This Handbook was, in fact, very vague on the subject of school curricula: 'it is not possible to lay down any rule as to the exact number of subjects which should be taken in an individual school . . . the curriculum must vary to some extent with the qualifications of the teaching staff'.
4 Interestingly, the reason cited here for the enforcement of uniformity in the Soviet Union is the same as that given in England in the sixteenth century for insisting upon the use of *one* Latin grammar in all grammar schools. The problems caused by a pupil moving from one area to another were referred to in Educational Canons of Convocation of Canterbury (1529): 'Of Schoolmasters and a Uniform Method of Teaching': 'Whereas . . . it often happens that a boy who has begun to learn grammar for a year or two under one teacher, is obliged to leave him and go to a new teacher . . .' (quoted in Leach, 1911, p. 447). The same issue was also used as a justification for the imposition of a National Curriculum in the 1987

consultation document: 'a national curriculum will . . . secure that the curriculum offered in all maintained schools has sufficient in common to enable children to move from one area of the country to another with minimum disruption to their education' (DES, 1987c, p. 4).

5 This description of the Schools Council's composition and purposes is based on the paragraph which appeared on the contents page of the later numbers of its newsletter *Dialogue* which was published regularly between 1968 and 1977.

6 To be fair, Professor Lawton has since argued (1984) that the evidence suggests that it was not really until the mid-1970s that the DES was moving away from its non-intervention stance on curriculum to a much more positive, *dirigiste*, centralist role (p. 8).

7 Sir Edward Boyle was Education Minister in 1962–64; Anthony Crosland was Education Secretary in 1965–67.

8 For a full discussion of this subject, see chapter 4.

9 Reference has already been made in the Introduction to the curious but revealing fact that it was political intervention which secured this important change at the top of the DES (see Donoughue, 1987, p. 111).

10 These are discussed in detail in chapter 6.

11 The Secretaries of State referred to in this and the following DES documents were the Secretary of State for Education and Science and the Secretary of State for Wales.

12 This refers to *Primary Education in England: A Survey by HM Inspectors of Schools*, published in September 1978 and *Aspects of Secondary Education in England: A Survey of HM Inspectors of Schools*, published in December 1979.

13 The implications of the Initiative for the differentiating and vocationalizing strategies of the government are discussed in the following chapter.

14 Interviewed about TVEI in a *Panorama* programme 'Good enough for your child?' broadcast on 28 February 1983, Sir Keith claimed that the DES and the MSC had complementary objectives.

15 This speech is printed in full in a Supplement to *The Director*, May 1982, pp. 3–5.

16 More recently Welsh Secretary Peter Walker has echoed Sir Keith's views by advocating that 'lessons in capitalism should be held in every school as part of a concerted political programme to increase participation in the free enterprise system'. (Quoted in *The Independent*, 4 March 1987)

Chapter 6

Differentiation and Vocationalization

Differentiation

In the period following the Ruskin speech and the Great Debate, the
Labour government was anxious to placate right-wing critics of the state
education system without actually *abandoning* the comprehensive school.
Education Secretary Shirley Williams believed firmly in the principle of
parental choice, and this meant that within the state system, there should
be a variety of provision with no concession to the concept of
'neighbourhood' or 'community' schools. Choice and diversity would be the
new watchwords for the comprehensive school. Within any given area, the
number of schools to choose from would ensure the availability of courses to
suit all tastes and requirements.

In a letter to her colleague Denis Healey, dated 2 March 1977, in
response to one that he had passed on to her from a headteacher in his
constituency, Mrs. Williams made clear her commitment to greater
differentiation *within* the system:

> I know that at present many authorities with comprehensive
> systems in operation are able to allow parents to select the schools
> they wish their children to attend — whether county schools or
> voluntary schools, denominational, single sex or mixed, and I
> hope in the future, as some schools begin to specialize in
> particular subjects such as sciences or languages, that parents will
> be allowed to choose schools for their children to attend on this
> basis.[1]

In the meantime, falling rolls brought about by a marked decline in the
birthrate made it essential to rationalize provision at the sixth-form level:

> Authorities will find it necessary to concentrate sixth-form
> resources so as to avoid unduly small groups of pupils if they are to
> make a reasonably economic use of highly-qualified teachers and

expensive equipment and buildings and, at the same time, provide an adequate choice of courses and subjects.[2]

In 1976, the Labour government had introduced a minor Education Act requiring that 'education is to be provided only in schools where the arrangements for the admission of pupils are not based (wholly or partly) on selection by reference to ability or aptitude'[3]. But in 1977 Mrs. Williams was anxious to draft an important new Education Bill whose chief provision would be to guarantee to parents a place for each of their children at the secondary school of their choice. The consultative document on the subject issued by the DES was widely circulated among leading members of the Labour Party and caused considerable alarm. Tony Benn, who was at that time Secretary of State for Energy, raised the matter at a meeting of the Cabinet and then wrote to the Prime Minister on 26 October 1977 to express his anxieties and doubts. In the first place, he felt that the proposed Bill would simply raise expectations that could not possibly be met:

> The legislation proposes to secure for every parent a right to choose his or her child's school — which involves suggesting that something might be done which no government can possibly do. The subsequent qualifying clauses in the consultative document do make this clear, but the question is whether it is wise to appear to hold out a promise which cannot really be kept. To raise expectations in this way might lead to greater dissatisfaction and parental anxiety, and would certainly lead to a terrific pressure on the local education authorities, on the ministers and, of course, MPs as well.[4]

It was also reasonable to point out that the vast majority of local authorities already took parental choice into account and operated successful admissions procedures. Furthermore, in Benn's view, the continued existence of grammar schools in many areas made it impossible to legislate for parental choice of secondary school without, at the same time, giving harmful legislative recognition to selection at 11 +:

> While grammar schools still remain in being, as they do, any parental choice set out as an objective in legislation must also provide that that choice cannot be exercised into a grammar school by children who do not have the requisite ability . . . Since the consultative document suggests that parental choice shall be limited by 'the age, ability and aptitude of the pupils', the Bill could actually appear to be, and the Courts might make it become, a route back to the legalization of selective secondary

education at a time when our real task is to complete the comprehensive development in the secondary sector.[5]

Shirley Williams was forced to take note of the criticism that her proposals had aroused and in a letter to the Prime Minister dated 28 October 1977, she appeared to accept that it would be impracticable to undertake a large-scale reorientation of all admissions procedures. She did, however, outline her long-term aims of seeing that (i) admissions procedures 'take account of parental wishes'; (ii) authorities set out their admissions criteria clearly; and (iii) appeals machinery be made uniform.[6] This more cautious approach would avoid causing unnecessary controversy in the Party and elsewhere. With its uneasy and, at times, equivocal support for the comprehensive principle, the Labour government found it very difficult to cope with the problem of parental choice, and, despite the fact that the majority of admissions procedures were working perfectly satisfactorily, the issue remained one which could be exploited by right-wing critics of the comprehensive system.

The policies of widening parental choice and of creating as much differentiation as possible within the education system were continued by Mark Carlisle (Secretary of State in 1979–81) and, more particularly, by Sir Keith Joseph (1981-86), though always against a background of concerted right-wing pressure to abandon the system altogether in favour of wholesale privatization. Sir Keith became particularly interested in strategies for curricular differentiation *within* schools when it proved singularly difficult to resurrect the grammar schools. Yet this did little to satisfy his former right-wing supporters who were already demanding more radical measures. In the eyes of the Right, Sir Keith's emphasis on vocational courses and the needs of the less able represented a fruitless dissipation of his energies (see, for example, Seldon, 1986).

The term 'differentiation' actually became an important feature of the political vocabulary after Sir Keith Joseph's speech to the North of England Education Conference meeting in Sheffield in January 1984[7]. Here, Sir Keith argued that in both the primary and secondary phases, the curriculum should accord more than was already the case with four key principles: breadth, relevance, differentiation and balance. As with the other principles, differentiation should be applied deliberately and in the interests of all pupils:

> There should be differentiation within the curriculum for variations in the abilities and aptitudes of pupils. This is a task that has to be tackled within each school, as well as between schools, where this is relevant. (Joseph, 1984, p. 141)

Interviewed a month later by Brian Walden for the ITV programme *Weekend World*, Sir Keith again emphasized the importance of differentiation *within* schools and particularly in the light of the recent failure to reintroduce selection in Solihull and elsewhere. If high standards were to be maintained, there must, he argued, be different educational routes within the comprehensive school:

> If it be so, as it is, that selection *between* schools is largely out, then I emphasize that there *must* be differentiation *within* schools. (Reported in *The Times Educational Supplement*, 17 February 1984) (my emphasis).

In fact, of course, even at the time of this revealing *Weekend World* interview, there was still a considerable amount of differentiation *between* schools, even if it fell short of the Secretary of State's own wishes. Even in Solihull itself, where the grammar school lobby was defeated, the comprehensive system was based on clearly-defined catchment areas which served to ensure that local or 'community' schools meant schools serving a relatively homogeneous social class intake. As Walford and Jones have pointed out (1986, p. 251), children from the affluent middle-class areas in the south of the borough were well catered for, attending prestigious schools well supported by active parent-teacher associations. There was certainly no social mixing with the Birmingham overspill children living in the north of the borough. This probably helps to explain why large numbers of middle-class parents felt there was really no need to reintroduce eleven-plus selection.

In a BBC TV *Panorama* programme, 'Schools — Selling the children short', shown in March 1986, Margaret Jay visited Cheshire, a large education authority with seventy-seven comprehensive county high schools, whose social structure was said to be typical of the country as a whole. Her survey revealed a three-tier structure of secondary schools that could doubtless be mirrored in many other parts of Britain: a top tier consisting of well-endowed, well-resourced private schools; a middle tier embracing comprehensive schools with prosperous middle-class catchment areas and parents able to find the money for expensive books and equipment; and a bottom tier where school buildings were crumbling and books were scarce.[8]

Yet none of this went far enough to satisfy the Secretary of State, and Sir Keith's period in office was notable for a number of curriculum initiatives designed to foster the differentiating process. The DES-funded LAPP (Lower Attaining Pupils' Programme) for the so-called 'bottom 40 per cent' of the ability range (see Hutchinson, 1986; Weston, 1986) and the

TVEI (Technical and Vocational Education Initiative), funded from outside education by the Manpower Services Commission, can be seen as calculated attempts to introduce further differentiation into the system. The second of these provides a fascinating insight into the government's thinking.

While the TVEI was clearly seen by ministers as a differentiating strategy, there was, in fact, considerable confusion as to the exact *nature* of the target-group (see Chitty, 1986; Chitty and Worgan, 1987). David Young, for example, who, as Chairman of the Manpower Services Commission, had played a leading role in devising the Initiative, clearly did not see it as being intended for either the *most* or the *least* able pupils. Shortly after the launching of the scheme, he said courses would be aimed at 'the 15 to 85 percentiles of the ability range in schools' (quoted in *Education*, 19 November 1982, p. 386). Later he again conceded that the TVEI was not designed for pupils who were taking 'good' 'O' and 'A' levels: 'They are not going to join the scheme. My concern is for those who are bright and able and haven't been attracted by academic subjects . . .' (reported in *Education*, 24 December 1982, p. 490). Upon his appointment as Secretary of State for Employment in the Cabinet reshuffle of September 1985, he outlined his vision of the future:

> My idea is that, at the end of the decade, there is a world in which 15 per cent of our young go into higher education . . . roughly the same proportion as now. Another 30 to 35 per cent will stay on doing the TVEI, along with other courses, ending up with a mixture of vocational and academic qualifications and skills. The remainder, about half, will go on to two-year YTS. (Reported in *The Times*, 4 September 1985)

This would seem to be a clear statement of the role of TVEI in Young's concept of secondary and tertiary tripartism.

Sir Keith Joseph, on the other hand, saw the Initiative as having special significance for the lower half of the ability range. In discussing the target-group for the scheme in a BBC TV *Panorama* programme 'Good enough for your child?', broadcast on 28 February 1983, he talked about:

> . . . the very large proportion of children who are not getting a benefit from school. They're certainly not getting a parity of esteem. They're either dropping out, or they're emerging from school without what they themselves, their parents or their future potential employers would expect them to have got at school . . . These are the children who will benefit from the government's new plans.

The Education Secretary claimed to be deeply concerned about the education being offered to the lower end of the ability range in secondary schools, particularly in years four and five; and this was certainly reflected in the speech he delivered at Sheffield in January 1984. Yet he could also talk in terms of TVEI being appropriate for a wider clientele:

> Sir Keith, stressing that the [TVEI] courses would cater for a wide ability range, said that the options they would offer would prepare pupils for qualifications such as City and Guilds and TEC and BEC awards. But there would be nothing to prevent them picking up 'O' levels on the way. (Interview with *The Times Educational Supplement*, 19 November 1982)

The government's general vagueness about the TVEI 'target-group' meant that in the early stages of the Project, there were significant variations both *between* and *within* different schemes. A review of three local authority schemes that had just got underway (*The Times Educational Supplement*, 14 October 1983) revealed that most of the programmes were for pupils not on 'O' level courses, and that even when 'flyers' were added, they were there in small numbers as 'token additions' and their work was not integrated. Wigan's TVEI coordinator, Stan Cooper, admitted in an interview with *The Guardian* (4 October 1983) that:

> ... the inability of the tutors to explain exactly where two years of technical and vocational education might lead in terms of qualifications largely explains the schools' inability to persuade many potential 'O' level candidates to take part.

In Leicestershire, on the other hand, it was intended from the very beginning that the TVEI should embrace pupils, both girls and boys, across the whole ability range.

If LAPP and TVEI represent examples of the government's differentiating strategy for comprehensive schools, the decision to introduce a common system of examining at 16+ might at first sight seem to be evidence of a countervailing tendency. Yet as the details for the new GCSE (General Certificate of Secondary Education) unfolded in 1985/86, it became clear that it was not going to be the common examination that so many educationists and teachers had campaigned for since 1966. As Gipps observed in 1986:

> Teachers wanted and originally thought they were going to get *a common examination* which would do away with the divisiveness of the old system. What they are actually getting is *a common*

examining system (with the GCE boards responsible for the higher grades and the old CSE boards for the lower grades) with differentiated examination papers and/or questions in many subjects . . . Differentiation means that the system will still be divisive: that there will be separate routes to the examination; that some candidates will not be eligible for higher grades (if they take the less difficult route); that teachers will still have to decide which students are suited for which route/course/range of grades; that in some cases these decisions will still have to be made as early as 14. (pp. 14–15)

Yet it is important to point out that the emphasis on differentiation was not a Conservative innovation. The concept of differentiated papers first appeared as DES policy in a government White Paper in 1978, during Shirley Williams's period as Education Secretary, where one of the recommendations was 'to ensure that alternative papers are used wherever this is necessary to maintain standards' (DES, 1978b, p. 11). In implementing their plans for an 'uncommon' examination, Sir Keith Joseph and Kenneth Baker were simply building on the policy pursued by their Labour predecessor. It was not a policy designed to remove existing anomalies and injustices.

Moreover, the DES White Paper *Better Schools*, published in March 1985, acknowledged that the new GCSE, with its first candidates in 1988, would be only one of a number of different examinations competing for the custom of aspiring 16-year-olds:

Some schools prepare pupils for pre-vocational examinations other than 'O' level and CSE (e.g. those of the City and Guilds of London Institute, the Royal Society of Arts, and the Business and Technician Education Council) during the years of compulsory schooling. Such courses will continue to be available to complement GCSE examinations as well, in the service of a curriculum which is broad, balanced, relevant, and differentiated in accordance with pupils' abilities. (DES, 1985c p. 32)[9]

The White Paper went on to announce the setting up of a working party 'to draft national criteria for pre-vocational and vocationally oriented examination courses taken by pupils of statutory school age' (*ibid.*). The working party would also be asked to consider progression from such courses to post-16 courses leading to vocational qualifications. It spent a year on its various tasks and produced its report, the Johnson Report, in June 1986 (DES, 1986c), but its terms of reference were severely criticized by, among others, the Further Education Unit which argued that the Report's preoccupation with single-subject courses had led to an emphasis on the examinable parts of the curriculum, to the neglect of other crucial aspects (reported in *The Times Educational Supplement*, 12 December 1986).

At the same time, the Joint Board for Pre-Vocational Education, set up in May 1983 to administer the new Certificate of Pre-Vocational Education (CPVE), was preparing its own plans for the 14–18 age range. A press release was issued in January 1984 to announce that:

> BTEC (the Business and Technician Education Council) and CGLI (City and Guilds of London Institute) see their decision to adopt a joint approach to pre-vocational education as a major contribution to helping schools and colleges provide young people with a more effective transition from school to work. The two bodies want to create a new curriculum pathway for that majority of those between the ages of 14 and 18 for whom the traditional academic curriculum is unsuitable.

This was followed by a further statement in September 1985 announcing that:

> The Councils of BTEC and City and Guilds have agreed jointly to develop and operate a new pre-vocational provision for students aged 14 to 16 which will offer a national alternative to traditional subject-based school courses.

These resulted in the publication in May 1986 of *The Framework Description of BTEC-City and Guilds Pre-Vocational Programmes for Pupils Age 14–16* incorporating the different existing programmes, City and Guilds 365 and Foundation Courses and BTEC Preparatory Programmes, into one common framework.[10]

With the development of these initiatives, there seemed little cause for optimism that the term 'comprehensive education' would actually come to mean anything significant beyond the age of 14. It will be interesting to see how the increased prevalence of pre-vocational courses for the 14–16 range will be affected by the introduction of the National Curriculum.

Towards a New Vocationalism

An account of differentiating strategies leads inevitably to the debate about the vocationalization of education. This has assumed a special significance in the past ten or so years with repeated demands for the curriculum of schools and colleges to be more closely related to the requirements of industry. Indeed, it has been common practice to view the Ruskin speech as the actual starting-point of the whole debate (see, for example, Holt, 1983b; Lawton, 1985; Chitty, 1986; Wellington, 1987; Shilling, 1988). As we have already seen, Callaghan's initiative was certainly an important event in the post-war history both of secondary schools and of other institutions providing education and training beyond the age of 16. Yet it is also important to take account of Reeder's argument (1979) that recent complaints emanating from employers and politicians about the contribution being made by schools and colleges to industrial development and the quality and attitudes of the labour force represent only 'the most recent phase of a long-standing controversy about the role of schooling in a modern industrial society' (p. 115). Differences of outlook were clearly apparent in early nineteenth-century arguments about education and industry associated with the rise of the factory system, but the debate acquired a special significance with the passing of the Forster Education Act of 1870 which laid the first foundations of a universal system of elementary schools for the newly-enfranchised working class. It has continued unabated ever since.

At the end of the First World War, for example, H. A. L. Fisher, the author of the 1918 Education Act, told a group of 'paternalistic' employers whose interest in 'works schools' had led them to form the Association for Education in Industry in 1911:

> I have always felt the great problem for the next years is to bring the world of business and the world of education into clear connection. We have the same interests, and I believe that the solution of all the difficulties between capital and labour will ultimately lie, not in the sphere of wages at all, not in any material sphere, but in the kind of improvement in the general condition which is due to the spread of knowledge and intelligence amongst the people and amongst the employers. (Inaugural Address to the Association, *Proceedings*, 1 May 1919, in the archives of the British Association for Commercial and Industrial Education quoted in Reeder, 1979, p. 122)

A few years later, in a speech at an Advertising Convention at Olympia, Lord Eustace Percy, President of the Board of Education in 1924–29, urged businessmen to put pressure on schools to teach subjects relevant to commercial and industrial needs. The Board, he said, was currently working out standards for the new forms of post-primary education, but 'our success...must depend...upon the advice and assistance...from organized commerce and industry and upon the standards which organized commerce and industry can set for these schools' (Percy's speech at the Advertising Convention at Olympia, 20 July 1927 quoted in White, 1975, p. 32).

Not that all views of schooling saw it simply as a means of adapting future generations to the conditions of living and working involved in modern industry. Such utilitarian thinking conflicted with ideas about schooling embodied in another important tradition of educational thought which rejected many of the more divisive features of urban-industrial society. Within that second and more humane tradition, education was viewed as a means of combating the disruptive and dehumanizing effects of technology and 'technicism' in modern industry and of thereby creating a more civilized society. It was also — and this was a cause of some concern to industrialists and employers — a powerful means of showing the working class how society could be changed according to developing aspirations.

As Reeder has shown (1979, p. 117), the ideological conflict, at the heart of the vocational argument, between those concerned with transforming the social order and those concerned with simply improving its effectiveness, was not peculiar to Britain. It emerged also in another form in the United States, in the early years of this century, in the debate between the educationist John Dewey and those who articulated the fears and grievances of the American business community by pressing for educational reform in the interest of social order. Both Dewey and the industrialists shared the view that modern schooling should prepare pupils for living in a complex industrial society, but they disagreed as to the precise nature of that preparation. As Dewey expressed it in 1915:

> The kind of education in which I am interested is not one which will adapt workers to the existing industrial regime; I am not sufficiently in love with the regime for that. It seems to me that the business of all those who would not be educational time servers is to resist every move in this direction, and to strive for a kind of vocational education which will first alter the existing industrial system, and ultimately transform it.[11]

A slightly different model to clarify the terms of the debate of the last hundred or so years was put forward in 1961 by Raymond Williams in his book *The Long Revolution* where he argued that the nineteenth-century reorganization of elementary and secondary education was a clear reflection of a radically changing society in which the growth of industry and of democracy were the leading elements. Two major factors could be distinguished as the century progressed: the rise of an organized working class, which demanded education, and the needs of an expanding and changing economy. In Williams's view, the justification for the 1870 Education Act rested clearly on two main arguments: one democratic and the other industrial. The democratic argument saw the legislation as either a protective (in the view of the right-wing Liberal Robert Lowe, it would be 'absolutely necessary to compel our future masters to learn their letters') or a genuine response to the enlargement of the franchise; while it was the practical impulse which led the Act's principal architect, W. E. Forster, to use as his main argument in the House of Commons: 'upon the speedy provision of elementary education depends our industrial prosperity'. According to Williams, this economic argument was even more central in the growth of secondary education, with the curriculum which the nineteenth century evolved being, in effect, a compromise between the views of the public educators, the industrial trainers and the old humanists, with those of the industrial trainers predominant:

> The democratic and the industrial arguments are both sound, but the great persuasiveness of the latter led to the definition of education in terms of future adult work, with the parallel clause of teaching the required social character-habits of regularity, 'self-discipline', obedience, and trained effort. Such a definition was challenged from two sides, by those with wider sympathies with the general growth of democracy, and by those with an older conception of liberal education, in relation to man's health as a spiritual being . . . On the one hand, it was argued, by men with widely differing attitudes to the rise of democracy and of working-class organization, that men had a natural human right to be educated, and that any good society depended on governments accepting this principle as their duty. On the other hand, often by men deeply opposed to democracy, it was argued that man's spiritual health depended on a kind of education which was more than a training for some specialized work, a kind variously described as 'liberal', 'humane', or 'cultural'. The great complexity of the general argument, which is still unfinished, can be seen from the fact that the public educators, as we may call the first group, were frequently in alliance with the powerful group which promoted education in terms of training and disciplining the poor, as workers and citizens, while the defenders of 'liberal education' were commonly against both: against the former because liberal education would be vulgarized by extension to the 'masses'; against the latter because liberal education would be

destroyed by being turned into a system of specialized and technical training. Yet the public educators inevitably drew on the arguments of the defenders of the old 'liberal' education, as a way of preventing universal education being narrowed to a system of pre-industrial instruction. These three groups — the public educators, the industrial trainers, and the old humanists — are still to be distinguished in our own time . . . . (Williams 1961, pp. 162–3)

According to Beck (1983, pp. 221–2), the 'recurring debate' entered a new phase in the second half of the 1970s when industry's contribution took a dual form. On the one hand, larger employers and the Department of Industry were putting forward the criticism that the education system's longstanding academic bias had, in Beck's words, 'played a major part in creating and maintaining the situation . . . in which wealth creation, the profit motive and engineering were accorded less status in Britain than in most other manufacturing countries'. One important consequence of this was said to be that teachers, consciously and unconsciously, discouraged their most gifted pupils from aspiring to careers in industry. On the other hand, in Beck's view, a campaign against comprehensive schools, generated mainly in the press, argued that 'the growth in progressive teaching methods, the increased autonomy of the teaching profession, and certain unintended consequences of comprehensive reorganization' had resulted in 'falling standards of attainment in basic subjects, a growth in negative attitudes to work and to authority especially among school-leavers, and a curriculum which was teacher-dominated and increasingly irrelevant to the nation's economic needs'. In short, 'too many of the nation's schools were making pupils unemployable at the very time when youth unemployment was rising at an alarming rate'. With its refusal to acknowledge the 'benefits' of vocational education, at least for the lower half of the ability range, and its encouragement of anti-capitalist attitudes, it was Britain's education system which was held to be chiefly responsible for the country's relative economic decline. This, in Beck's view, explained the content and timing of the Ruskin speech.

Throughout the period of the Great Debate, and in the years after 1977, the term 'vocational education' was, in fact, used to cover three different and separate — though not necessarily mutually incompatible — areas where traditional approaches to schooling could be said to have failed. As Dale has argued (1985), it was often defined in opposition, or contrast, to the ills it was meant to remedy:

(a) the teacher-based progressive ideology which allegedly leads to a neglect of, or even contempt for, rigour and standards, and produces pupils with attitudes inimical to the disciplinary and moral requirements of many employers, who prefer, therefore, to offer jobs to older, more mature and more 'stable', if less qualified, people; (b) the fact that the things that pupils are taught at school are inappropriate, and often do not equip them to do the jobs they are offered; (c) the fact that they do not know enough about the world of work, and especially about the economic importance of industry. (p. 47)

As an answer to all these perceived short-comings, a vocationally-oriented education has, however, proved difficult to define and even more difficult to prescribe in detail.

As we have seen in chapter 2, the views of industrialists and employers exerted a powerful influence on James Callaghan when he was preparing the final draft of the Ruskin speech. In the interview he gave to BBC Radio 4 in December 1987, he mentioned particularly the influence of Sir John Greenborough, shortly to become President of the CBI.[12] As Jamieson has observed (1985) 'the Ruskin speech did not conjure up the schools-industry debate out of thin air; rather it gave a focus and added legitimacy to many existing complaints about the education system' (p. 26).

Education Secretary Fred Mulley had, in fact, already made a speech in March 1976 in which he identified education as 'a key to our industrial regeneration':

I am concerned that young people appear to attach little esteem to careers in the wealth-generating industries and in commerce, upon which the country's economic future depends. The problem goes far beyond my ministerial sphere of responsibility, but I believe it provides a key to our industrial regeneration. A start could be made by an attempt to change the attitudes of our ablest students . . . If the country does not concentrate more of its talents on the basic necessity of earning its own living, our present problems are almost certain to multiply. (CBI, 1976, p. 27 quoted in Beck, 1983, p. 224)

The timing of this speech was highly significant in that it was made within four months of the unveiling of the government's revised Industrial Strategy proposals in November 1975, which accorded education a key role in the economic regeneration of Britain.

In preparing his own speech, the Prime Minister had the benefit of the considered opinions of the DES as revealed in the Yellow Book which also drew attention to employers' reservations about the typical school leaver:

> Many employers — some probably recruiting from lower levels of ability than was formerly the case — complain that school leavers cannot express themselves clearly and lack the basic mathematical skills of manipulation and calculation and hence the basic knowledge to benefit from technical training. (DES, 1976a, p. 7)

The DES document proceeded to argue the need 'to explore and promote further experiment with courses of a higher level of vocational relevance likely to appeal to a significant number of 14- and 15-year-olds (*ibid.*, p. 22); though it seems likely that, at this stage, leading members of the Department did not fully share the politicians' sense of urgency about the need to vocationalize the curriculum for what was perceived to be the 'non-academic' section of the school population. Drawing on his experience as Specialist Adviser to the 1976/77 Education, Arts and Home Office Select Committee enquiry into the attainments of the school leaver, Professor Ted Wragg concluded that the DES was 'singularly unenthusiastic' about most aspects of the school-to-work debate (Wragg, 1976, p. 11). Since this attitude clearly changed over the next ten years, culminating with the warm endorsement of vocational courses so evident in *Better Schools*, this was obviously one respect in which the civil servants were happy to follow the politicians' lead.

The need for schooling to be more related to the needs of industry was clearly uppermost in the Prime Minister's mind when he took the unusual step of including two paragraphs devoted to education in his speech to the Labour Party Annual Conference at the end of September 1976. This section of his speech, written by Bernard Donoughue, foreshadowed his address at Ruskin College three weeks later:

> We *are*, we *always have been*, we *remain* a party of social reform, and far more needs to be done to prepare young people for the time when they leave school. There should be much closer cooperation between employers and schools; and employers could do more to make their requirements known to teachers. Heads of schools could extend their sphere of interest to obtaining and acting upon the advice of local firms about their requirements. Firms could provide practical help of various kinds to local schools, and so discover how they could make better use of school leavers. Personnel officers in industry could ask teachers to appraise their training techniques in industry. Cooperation in these ways would help industrial and commercial training to flow naturally from the last years at school. Some schools, perhaps

many, need to give their careers departments more serious attention than they have done.

> I am concerned at the gap that exists at many levels between education and industry today, not only at this level but at other levels too. Let us begin by helping our young people to fit themselves for life in their work, as well as in their leisure . . . There are new ways of learning that were unknown to us, vouched for by the teachers. This is good. But let me emphasize that the greatest gifts a teacher can give to a child are the basic tools of learning and a desire for knowledge. A literate and numerate child has the key to open the door of learning and the key to the freedom of the mind. (Labour Party, 1976, p. 191)

In the Ruskin speech itself, James Callaghan argued that schools were failing, in that young people were not being trained in the skills necessary to find employment in industry and commerce:

> I am concerned on my journeys to find complaints from industry that new recruits from the schools sometimes do not have the basic tools to do the job that is required.
>
> I have been concerned to find that many of our best trained students who have completed the higher levels of education at university or polytechnic have no desire to join industry. Their preferences are to stay in academic life or to find their way into the Civil Service. There seems to be a need for a more technological bias in science teaching that will lead towards practical applications in industry, rather than towards academic studies. Or, to take other examples, why is it that such a high proportion of girls abandon science before leaving school? Then there is concern about the standards of numeracy of school leavers. Is there not a case for a professional review of the mathematics needed by industry at different levels? To what extent are these deficiencies the result of insufficient coordination between schools and industry? Indeed, how much of the criticism about basic skills and attitudes is due to industry's own shortcomings, rather than to the educational system? Why is it that 30,000 vacancies for students in science and engineering in our universities and polytechnics were not taken up last year, while the humanities courses were full? . . .
>
> The goals of our education, from nursery school through to adult education, are clear enough. They are to equip children to the best of their ability for a lively, constructive place in society

and also to fit them to do a job of work. Not one or the other; but both. For many years, the accent was simply on fitting a so-called inferior group of children with just enough learning to earn their living in the factory. Labour has attacked that attitude consistently, during sixty or seventy years and throughout my childhood. There is now widespread recognition of the need to cater for a child's personality, to let it flower in the fullest possible way.

The balance was wrong in the past. We have a responsibility now to see that we do not get it wrong in the other direction. There is no virtue in producing socially well-adjusted members of society who are unemployed because they do not have the skills.

This can be seen as a classic statement of the 'skills-deficit model' of unemployment which argued that one of the key factors in the rise of unemployment was the shortage of relevant skills. Schools and teachers could then be blamed for failing to teach those skills (whatever they might be) which would make their pupils more employable.

The same emphasis on the reluctance of schools to train pupils to meet the needs of wealth-producing industry was evident in the subsequent Green Paper, *Education in Schools: A Consultative Document*, published by the DES in July 1977. Here reference was made to the criticisms voiced at the regional conferences which followed the Ruskin speech:

> It was said that the school system is geared to promote the importance of academic learning and careers with the result that pupils, especially the more able, are prejudiced against work in productive industry and trade; that teachers lack experience, knowledge and understanding of trade and industry; that curricula are not related to the realities of most pupils' work after leaving school; and that pupils leave school with little or no understanding of the workings, or importance, of the wealth-producing sector of our economy. (DES, 1977b, p. 34)

In the view of the Green Paper, the education service was answerable to the society which it served and should therefore take account of such criticisms:

> It is vital to Britain's economic recovery and standard of living that the performance of manufacturing industry is improved, and that the whole range of government policies, including education, contribute as much as possible to improving industrial performance and thereby increasing the national wealth. (*ibid.*, p. 6)

The Department of Employment White Paper, *A New Training Initiative: A Programme for Action,* published in December 1981, reaffirmed a strictly utilitarian view of education and training:

> To get a better trained and more flexible workforce, we need to start with better preparation for working life in schools and better opportunities for continuing education and personal development in the early years at work... The last two years of compulsory education are particularly important in forming an approach to the world of work. Every pupil needs to be helped to reach his or her full potential, not only for personal development, but to prepare for the whole range of demands which employment will make. The Government is seeking to ensure that the school curriculum develops the personal skills and qualities as well as the knowledge needed for working life, and that links between schools and employers help pupils and teachers to gain a closer understanding of the industrial, commercial and economic base of our society. (DoE, 1981, p. 5)

This was one of the key documents leading to the launching of the Youth Training Scheme (YTS) in September 1983.

The 1981 White Paper contained three paragraphs outlining two implicit models of the nature and causes of unemployment and of the role of vocational training in a modern competitive economy:

> The skill shortages which have held back our economic progress in the past could reappear when the economy recovers. They cannot be met solely by training the new intake of young people, but will require considerable readaptation of the existing labour force. Skill needs will continue to change and require updating. Wider opportunities for training and retraining of people in their twenties, thirties and later in life are bound to be required in the future. (paragraph 48)

> For the immediate future, the government sees an increase of public expenditure... as the only way of plugging the gap in the training provision required if we are to be ready to meet the skill needs of the economy as trading conditions improve and to offer adequate opportunities to the current generation of young people. It is applying these extra resources to help secure longer-term reforms in the quality of training and bring about a change in the attitudes of young people to the value of training and acceptance of relatively lower wages for trainees. (paragraph 58)

For many years now, our system of training has failed to produce the numbers of skilled people required by a modern competitive economy. This paper sets out a framework within which employers, employees, unions, educationists and government can more clearly see what they need to do for the system to work. (paragraph 61)

As Wellington has pointed out (1987, p. 23), these paragraphs are interesting because they tacitly rely on two distinct models of unemployment. All three paragraphs make use of the 'skills-deficit model' (previously adopted by Callaghan) which argues that a shortage of relevant skills is one of the key factors in unemployment. The second model of unemployment, which Wellington calls the 'cyclical model', suggests that an upturn in the economy is to be expected in the very near future and that unemployment will decrease as 'trading conditions improve' and the economy recovers. The role of the teacher is, then, to train pupils to be ready to respond to the skill needs of a revived economy. But it can also be argued (see, for example, Jenkins and Sherman, 1979; Stonier, 1983) that unemployment patterns are caused by structural changes within society in undergoing a revolution from an industrial to a post-industrial era. According to this view, these patterns are not fundamentally altered by skills shortages or by cyclical changes in trading conditions. Of far greater significance is the fact that primary and secondary industry have both declined sharply while only the service industries have grown.

The Technical and Vocational Education Initiative

The Technical and Vocational Education Initiative (TVEI), launched, as we have noted, by Margaret Thatcher in a Commons written statement in November 1982[13], was designed, in the words of the accompanying Department of Employment press release, 'to stimulate technical and vocational education for 14–18-year-olds as part of a drive to improve our performance in the development of new skills and technology' (DoE, 1982, p. 1). It was also seen as a follow-up to the 1981 White Paper in acknowledging 'the importance of the last two years of compulsory education and the need for more vocationally-orientated courses for those continuing full-time education past 16' (*ibid.*). In a letter to all LEA Directors of Education in England and Wales in January 1983, David Young outlined the main objectives of the TVEI in the eyes of the MSC:

First, our general objective is to widen and enrich the curriculum in a way that will help young people to prepare for the world of work, and to develop skills and interests, including creative abilities, that will help them to lead a fuller life and to be able to contribute more to the life of the community. Secondly, we are in the business of helping students to 'learn to learn'. In a time of rapid technological change, the extent to which particular occupational skills are required will change. What is important about this Initiative is that youngsters should receive an education which will enable them to adapt to the changing occupational environment. (Young, 1983, p. 2)

Yet the TVEI fits uneasily into any account of moves to vocationalize the secondary school curriculum for 'non-academic' pupils largely because the term 'vocational' in the title was never clearly defined and, as we saw in the first half of this chapter, there was also considerable vagueness about the Initiative's intended 'target group'. Over the years, many teachers and local authorities have tried to make the Initiative attractive to *all* sections of the ability range, which was not the original intention of either David Young or Sir Keith Joseph (see Chitty and Worgan, 1987, pp. 32–4). This helps to explain why the Initiative has incurred the hostility of leading members of the New Right who are prepared to tolerate courses of a vocational nature only if they are reserved for pupils who can be labelled as 'non-academic' or 'non-examinable' (see Quicke, 1988, p. 15).

While Sir Keith Joseph remained Secretary of State, the TVEI was regarded as one of the great achievements of the Conservative government. As late as March 1985, it was awarded many column inches in the DES White Paper *Better Schools*:

The TVEI embodies the government's policy that education should better equip young people for working life. The courses are designed to cater equally for boys and girls across the whole ability range and with technical or vocational aspirations, and to offer in the compulsory years a broad general education with a strong technical element followed, post-16, by increasing vocational specialization. The course content and teaching methods adopted are intended to develop personal qualities and positive attitudes towards work as well as a wide range of competence, and more generally to develop a practical approach throughout the curriculum. The projects are innovative and break new ground in many ways, being designed to explore curriculum organization and development, teaching approaches and learning styles, cooperation between the participating institutions, and enhanced careers guidance supported by work experience, in order to test the feasibility of sustaining a broad vocational commitment in full-time education for 14–18-year-olds. (DES, 1985c, pp. 16–17)

How different is the treatment accorded TVEI in the 1987 National Curriculum Consultation Document (DES, 1987e). Here the Initiative warrants only two brief mentions, in the first of which it is put forward simply as *an example* of a curriculum development programme that might be built on the framework offered by the new National Curriculum:

> ... The government intends that legislation should leave full scope for professional judgment and for schools to organize how the curriculum is delivered in the way best suited to the ages, circumstances, needs and abilities of the children in each classroom. This will, for example, allow curriculum development programmes such as the Technical and Vocational Education Initiative (TVEI) to build on the framework offered by the National Curriculum and to take forward its objectives. (paragraph 27)

And:

> ... For the final two years of compulsory schooling, the national extension of TVEI will also help LEAs in the development and establishment of the National Curriculum, particularly in the areas of science and technology, and in enhancing the curriculum's relevance to adult and working life. (paragraph 85)

Nowhere in the Consultation Document, as Low has pointed out (Low, 1987), is there any mention of the many new subjects, such as hotel and food services, robotics, microelectronics or manufacturing technology, which teachers have been able to introduce — for at least some of their pupils — as part of the TVEI project.

The current treatment of TVEI as a major vocationalizing strategy is, on the face of it, very curious. In a period of less than ten years from 1983 onwards, well over £1 billion will have been spent by the Conservative government on TVEI and its extension. It is the most expensive intervention in curriculum development ever undertaken in Britain. In a sense, it is still at the developmental stage, with many evaluation reports in the process of being compiled. Yet the experience gained by those working on the project is in no way reflected in the thinking behind the National Curriculum — either in its content or in its organization. As TVEI has steadily gained credibility with both teachers and parents, the government appears to have lost interest in it. Why should this be so?

I have argued elsewhere that:

> It could well be that so much energy is now being devoted to undermining comprehensive education by the dismantling of the state system that there is less need to concentrate on initiatives designed to promote differentiation within existing schools. (Chitty and Worgan, 1987, p. 33)

At the same time, the New Right clearly finds it difficult to approve of the new subjects and the new styles of learning which TVEI courses have helped to pioneer. In this matter, as in so many others, their thinking has influenced the civil servants of the DES.[14] The Consultation Document is a monument to the view that traditional subjects are 'safe' and help to prevent the spread of subversive doctrines.

Whatever the chief reason, the decline in government support for TVEI has proved a cause for some concern among leading TVEI practitioners. They argue that the Initiative will survive only if the mandatory subjects in the government's National Curriculum are taught within the TVEI's modules and if the syllabuses simply lay down what must be covered and not how it should be taught. Keith Evans, Director of Education for Clwyd, the first authority to extend the Initiative to all its secondary schools (at its own expense), has argued that the only practicable way to provide *both* the National Curriculum *and* the TVEI is to 'receive' the Curriculum into the Initiative's framework. The basic TVEI approach, which relies heavily on experiential learning and practical work, covering the curriculum in modules rather than dividing it up into self-contained subjects, could not, in his view, be delivered through a conventional subject timetable (reported in *The Times Educational Supplement*, 12 August 1988). As the debate on the National Curriculum continues, it will be interesting to see if the attempt to reintroduce the traditional curriculum into TVEI schools will mean disrupting and destroying the culture on which the courses are based.

Notes

1 From the Private Political Papers of Tony Benn, 2 March 1977, in the Benn Archives.
2 *Ibid.*
3 This statement is taken from the preamble to the 1976 Act. The Act was repealed when the Conservative government took office in 1979.
4 From the Private Political Papers of Tony Benn, 26 October 1977, in the Benn Archives.

5 *Ibid.*
6 From the Private Political Papers of Tony Benn, 28 October 1977, in the Benn Archives.
7 This speech is printed in full in *Oxford Review of Education*, 10, 2, 1984, pp. 137–46.
8 Margaret Jay's findings were written up in an article in *The Listener*, 20 March 1986.
9 The White Paper's enthusiastic support for TVEI is discussed later in the chapter.
10 It was certainly fashionable at this time to envisage a divided curriculum from the age of 14. At a conference held in Devon in September 1984 on 'The management of change in the 14–19 sector', Joslyn Owen, the County's Chief Education Officer, stated firmly that 'we must decide to vocationalize the education of those who will not pass examinations and tackle the main problem which has arisen, namely that we have to identify two halves of a school population which are now educated together'. Taking note of what has actually happened (or not happened) to 'half our future' in the twenty or so years following the publication of the *Newsom Report* in 1963, Devon must, in his view, consider 'putting vocational education and examination-aimed education into separate categories of education from the age of 14' (Devon County Council/Institute of Local Government Studies, 1984). I am grateful to Maurice Holt for supplying me with this reference.
11 These observations were made by Dewey in *The New Republic* dated 5 May 1915, and are quoted in Reeder (1979, pp. 117–18). *The New Republic* was one of the liberal papers in the United States at this time and one to which Dewey was a frequent contributor after his arrival in New York in 1904 (see Skilbeck, 1970, pp. 10–11).
12 Professor Ted Wragg interviewed Lord Callaghan for a programme in the series *Education Matters*, broadcast on BBC Radio 4 on 6 December 1987.
13 See chapter 5 for a discussion of this statement.
14 This point is developed further in the final chapter.

Chapter 7

Early Attempts at Privatization: Choice, Competition and the Voucher

Two Aspects of Privatization

Pring has argued on a number of occasions (1983, 1986, 1987a and 1987b) that the privatization of education in the 1980s has assumed at least two major forms: the purchasing at *private* expense of educational services which should be free within the *public system*; and the purchasing at *public* expense of educational services in *private institutions*. A third category would be privatization in the sense of impoverishing the maintained sector in order to encourage parents to select private education for their children. Whatever form it takes, the privatization of education can be usefully defined as the systematic erosion, and possibly even abandonment, of the commitment to a common educational service based on pupil needs rather than upon private means. It has taken place in this country against a background of sustained criticism of the achievements of the public sector and as part of the process of subjecting the education service to the same kind of market pressures that any commercial commodity would be subjected to.[1]

Pring's first category would include the various ways in which parents and private firms have been asked to pay for both essential and inessential services within the public sector: special lessons or curriculum areas, resources and books, repairs and maintenance, basic facilities and buildings, even teaching posts[2]. It may be argued that there are a number of extra-curricular activities — for example, visits to the theatre or school trips abroad — for which parents might well be asked to make a contribution. Yet in many cases, parents have been expected not simply to enrich the curriculum for a few but actually help ensure basic curriculum provision for all. Successive HMI reports have pointed to the need for parents to contribute large sums of money in order to compensate for a desperate shortage of books and other essential equipment. The report of the 1985 survey, for example, published at a time when Sir Keith Joseph was being much criticized for his refusal to demand more money for education, showed that the gap between rich and poor schools was widening because of differing parental contributions. Schools in affluent middle-class areas were in a better position to compensate for LEA economies:

> Contributions overall ranged from £50 to £15,000 per year, the latter sum being on top of a capitation allowance of £38,000. In one exceptional case, one secondary school received £45,000, which was 25 per cent more than its capitation, though a considerable proportion of this sum came from convenants made by parents . . . Schools in the shire counties received proportionately the greatest level of contribution: over one-third of the schools visited received contributions in excess of £6 per pupil, while this was so in only one-fifth of the schools in the metropolitan districts and London authorities. Compared with previous years, schools in all three types of authority are receiving more contributions from parents than ever before. (DES, 1986c, p. 46)

These contributions were being used to provide or enhance a wide variety of teaching resources and activities:

> Most commonly, the money was used to help towards the cost of educational visits (764 schools), followed by the purchase of computers, audio-visual equipment, library and reference books, PE and games equipment, school mini-buses, musical instruments, textbooks and reprographic equipment. The most notable change since last year was the increased number of references to parental contributions being used to improve school premises (417 such references). For example, in one school, the whole of the first floor was rewired using the funds provided by parents, while in many others, the funds were used to provide the materials to redecorate parts of the school. (*ibid.*, p. 47)

A notable example of Pring's second category would be the Assisted Places Scheme introduced in September 1981. It was argued by its proponents that this would enable children of proven intellectual ability from poor homes to enjoy the benefits of a private education. Yet the interim evaluation report on the scheme (see Whitty, Fitz and Edwards, 1986) showed that it had not attracted significant numbers of pupils from poor or deprived areas of the country or from the working class as a whole. The offspring of the clergy had benefited most from the scheme, along with the children of single-parent middle-class families. Moreover, a significant proportion of the recipients of Assisted Places would have attended private schools anyway and indeed had done so at the preparatory stage. In the light of this evidence, it could well be argued that privatization schemes tend to favour those who are already fully paid-up members of the enterprise society.

Yet none of this goes far enough to satisfy the Prime Minister's more radical and enthusiastic supporters on the Far Right. For them, the way ahead requires choice, and choice requires private enterprise. In their view, the quality of education will be improved only by the speedy introduction of the voucher.

The Campaign for the Voucher

Mrs. Thatcher's policy advisers in the Centre for Policy Studies and the Downing Street Policy Unit advocated two main educational strategies in the early 1980s: to make the education system both more responsive to the needs of industry and at the same time more susceptible to market forces.[3] The chosen instrument for the former was the Manpower Services Commission; the preferred means of achieving the latter was parental choice and, if possible, the voucher. The first objective harked back to the educational consensus established in 1976; the second looked forward to a new era epitomized by the 1988 Education Reform Act.

The voucher has been described by Arthur Seldon, formerly Editorial Director of the right-wing Institute of Economic Affairs, as:

> . . . . a highly flexible instrument, with many variations, that would replace the financing of schools through taxes under political control and bureaucratic supervision by payments direct from parents thus equipped with a new ability (for the 95 per cent with middle and lower incomes) to compare schools and move between them. (Seldon, 1986, p. 1)

It would, or so it has been claimed, create choice and competition, while, at the same time, establishing consumer sovereignty in education. People with higher incomes could already send their children to the very best schools, either by paying the fees to private schools or by meeting the higher housing costs of districts with the superior state schools; now the voucher would make these privileges available to all. The scheme has assumed many forms over the years, but the first voucher systems put forward in this country were based on the simple principle that all parents should be issued with a free basic coupon, fixed at the average cost of schools in the local authority area. This would entitle them to a minimum standard place at the school of their choice, but those who could afford to do so would be free to supplement the basic voucher out of their own pocket and shop around for a more expensive place. Right from the outset, this implied a system of two-tier provision: the 'minimum price' school place and the 'more expensive' school place where the education on offer would somehow be 'better' or more exclusive. It was not always clear whether any right of selection rested with the school itself or whether, in fact, the top grammar and independent schools would be forced to accept all the children whose parents could afford to send them there.

The idea of enabling, and indeed encouraging, all parents to break free of the state system by distributing earmarked purchasing power as a substitute for nil-priced schooling was advocated by Milton Friedman, a relatively little-known economist at the University of Chicago, as long ago as 1955[4]. According to Seldon, if education ministers in this country had paid proper attention to Friedman's views, many of the damaging developments of the 1960s and 1970s would have been avoided:

> Britain's grammar schools would have been saved, parents would have learned to choose schools and insist on rising standards, numeracy and literacy among the school population would now be higher than ever, taxation would be much lower, the official-dom smaller, the state would not have encroached on civil life to the point at which it is now difficult to roll back. (Seldon, 1986, p. 12)

Nine years after the Friedman paper, Professors Alan Peacock and Jack Wiseman were the first economists in Britain to argue that parents should be enabled by vouchers, grants or loans to shop around in a free market (Peacock and Wiseman, 1964).

The campaign to promote 'parent-power' through the voucher began effectively with a motion in favour of experimental vouchers at the September 1974 Conference of the National Council of Women. The support it received encouraged the sponsors to establish the Friends of the Education Voucher Experiment in Representative Regions (FEVER) in December 1974.

The cause was taken up by Dr. Rhodes Boyson, a former headteacher and now Conservative MP, in 'The developing case for the educational voucher', one of the contributions to *Black Paper 1975: The Fight for Education*. The article included a glowing account of the voucher experiment in Alum Rock, California, which had been inaugurated in 1972. As part of the experiment, each school offered a variety of courses, so that parents could choose not only *between* schools, but between specific courses *within* schools. According to Boyson, the whole scheme was proving an unqualified success:

> It is interesting that the variety of courses offered within the schools has brought about a form of optional 'tracking' or streaming whereby pupils themselves, with the help of their families and their teachers, have chosen their courses to suit their intellectual abilities and technical aptitudes. Such 'tracking', being chosen by pupils themselves to maximize their achievements, has brought none of the resentment occasionally arising from streaming in British schools . . . Under this Alum Rock programme, the involvement of parents has broken all records, the attendance of the pupils has improved, and the teaching staff, at first hostile and suspicious, has been won round by the keener interest of parents and pupils despite the greater demands made upon them. (Boyson, 1975a, p. 27)

From this, it was argued that the time was ripe for the establishment of at least two full voucher experiments in Britain in areas where local education authorities were anxious to cooperate:

> A non-transferable voucher could be issued for each pupil and the parents would be able to pay it into the school of his choice, either state or private . . . Popular schools in the areas would continue and expand, and unpopular schools would decline and close. (*ibid.*)

The introduction of voucher schemes, on a local or national basis, would have positive benefits for all concerned:

> It is likely that under the voucher, the quality of all schooling would rise so much that even the worst school would then be better in absolute quality than the general run of today's schools. Parents would also probably insist on different courses within the monolithic, egalitarian comprehensive schools before they sent their children there . . . The later 1970s could be an ideal time to introduce the voucher because the falling birthrate would mean that there would be redundant school buildings in which new independent schools could be opened by teachers, trusts, churches and other voluntary bodies subject to enforcing a minimum requirement on the record and qualifications of the teaching staff. (*ibid.*)[5]

Yet a very different view of the Alum Rock experiment, and of the practical benefits of voucher schemes, was provided by David Mandel in an article published a year after Boyson's eulogy (*The Times Educational Supplement*, 21 May 1976). According to Mandel, one school lost 17 per cent of its previous enrolment in the first year of the scheme and another had to rent portable classrooms to accommodate the excess demand. Changes of similar proportions were still taking place in the third year, shifts of 10 per cent being common. In this experiment, since vouchers represented personally disposable property, transfers from one school to another could take place at any time and as often as parents wished. This placed the public sector in the unenviable position of having to utilize tax-payers' money to balance a continuously moving see-saw.[6]

Despite misgivings right across the political spectrum, the prospect of political action on the voucher quickened with the election of the first Thatcher administration in May 1979. Little progress was made under Mark Carlisle, but at the 1981 Conservative Party Conference, the newly-appointed Education Secretary, Sir Keith Joseph, received spontaneous applause when he said:

> I personally have been intellectually attracted to the idea of seeing whether eventually, *eventually*, a voucher might be a way of increasing parental choice even further . . . I know that there are very great difficulties in making a voucher deliver — in a way that would commend itself to us — more choice than the 1980 Act will, in fact, deliver. It is now up to the advocates of such a possibility to study the difficulties — and there are real difficulties — and see whether they can develop proposals which will really cope with them.[7]

On 18 November 1981 two pressure groups, the National Council for Educational Standards and the Friends of the Education Voucher Experiment in Representative Regions, wrote to Sir Keith asking for an account of the problems that would need to be resolved before an education voucher scheme could be defined, and its implications assessed, for the purposes of educational policy. The Education Secretary asked his civil servants to prepare a paper on the voucher scheme which was sent to FEVER on 16 December with a covering letter from Sir Keith himself. In this letter, he reiterated that he was 'intellectually attracted to the idea of education vouchers as a means of eventually extending parental choice and influence yet further and improving educational standards' (reprinted in Seldon, 1986, p. 36). Yet the memorandum itself, which was hardly sympathetic to the concept of vouchers, stated categorically in its first paragraph, that 'the Secretary of State for Education and Science has made it clear that he has no plans for the general introduction of a voucher scheme' (DES, 1981c, p. 1). The memorandum made it clear that the DES civil servants were anxious to see the whole idea quietly dropped.

Despite this opposition, Sir Keith himself continued to give public backing to the voucher concept. Questioned after a speech to the Institute of Directors in March 1982 as to how far the government was prepared to go in backing parental choice by the introduction of a voucher system across the entire country, the Education Secretary replied:

> I have declared that I, myself, am intellectually attracted by the voucher scheme [but] I am not committing the government in any way. I have published the obstacles that stand in the way of introducing vouchers. I have now received answers to those problems from the partisans of vouchers, and my officials, at my request, are studying how practical it would be to go in the direction of the vouchers. Intellectual interest — certainly. Commitment — not yet, if at all. (Joseph, 1982, p. 5)

After further questioning from members of his audience, Sir Keith went on to say:

> The voucher, in effect, is a cash facility for all parents, only usable in schools instead of money. It would come from the taxpayer, and it would give parents, however poor, a choice of schools regardless of how much those schools cost, be they in the private sector or the maintained, that is, the public sector. The idea of the voucher is a noble idea. It is the idea of freeing parents from all money considerations in choosing a school for their children ... A voucher would provide an equal moral treatment for all parents. It would not provide an equal background for all children, because the home is very important in the education of a child, and homes differ from each other in the combination of love, discipline and encouragement that is given to the child. (*ibid.*)

Sir Keith appeared to go even further at the 1982 Conservative Party Conference, though by this time, the civil servants in his Department were quite determined that there should be no voucher experiment, either on a local or a national basis:

> [We] are concerned not only with the rich and the clever. We want to extend choice to every person ... The voucher would create a pressure for standards to rise. I believe that there would be an increase in the number of good popular independent schools. I believe that if vouchers were combined with open

enrolment, some of the least good state schools would disappear, and increased competition might galvanize the less good state schools to achieve better results. These are the prospects that attract me to a combination of the voucher idea and open enrolment.

Yet whatever he might say at a Conservative Party Conference, Sir Keith was unable to proceed without the support of his civil servants; and it has been suggested (Wilby, 1987) that he may himself have been at least partially convinced by their arguments. His cerebral approach demanded coherent solutions that would stand up; he seemed over the years to arrive at the painful conclusion that a 'market' in compulsory education was a logical impossibility. Others were quite happy to blame his failure on the combined opposition of bureaucrats and teachers. Lord Harris of High Cross, for example, saw 'the rejection of the voucher' as the triumph of 'the concentrated, articulate producer interests of organized teachers and entrenched bureaucracy' over 'the dispersed, muted interests of consumer-parents' (Seldon, 1986, p. viii). Apart from any other considerations, the voucher scheme certainly challenged the structure and processes of the civil service itself. But there were also very real practical difficulties. Would the schools that did not find favour with parents be allowed simply to wither away and die? How could schools cope with the logistical problems of fluctuating demand? How could independent and grammar schools continue to ensure a selective entry? In addition, there was the ideological argument voiced, for example, by Morris (1976, p. 19) that the voucher scheme was, in reality, a thinly-disguised plot to ensure that 'the wealthier can obtain a superior education at the expense of the disadvantaged and the taxpayer'.

By the end of 1983, the idea had been dropped. Speaking at the 1983 Conservative Party Conference, Sir Keith said: 'the voucher, at least in the foreseeable future, is dead'. He repeated this in a written statement to the House of Commons in June 1984:

I was intellectually attracted to the idea of education vouchers because it seemed to offer the possibility of some kind of market mechanism which would increase the choice and diversity of schools in response to the wishes of parents acting as customers. In the course of my examination of this possibility, it became clear that there would be great practical difficulties in making any voucher system compatible with the requirements that schooling should be available to all without charge, compulsory· and of an acceptable standard. These requirements — difficult though the latter two are to achieve effectively under any dispensation — were seen to limit substantially the operation, and the benefits, of free market choices; and to entail an involvement on the part of the state — centrally and locally — which would be both financial and regulatory and on a scale likely to necessitate an administrative effort as great as under the present system. These factors would have applied, whether vouchers were available only within the maintained system or could be used in the independent sector as well.

A change of this magnitude would desirably be preceded by pilot schemes undertaken by volunteer LEAs. These would require legislation, and there was serious doubt whether they could adequately establish the feasibility of a voucher scheme within a manageable time scale.

I concluded that the difficulties which would arise from the many and complex changes required to the legal and institutional framework of the education system, and the additional cost of mitigating them, were too great to justify further consideration of a voucher system as a means of increasing parental choice and influence.

For these reasons, the idea of vouchers is no longer on the agenda. (*Hansard*, H. of C., Sixth Series — Vol. 62, Col. 290, written answers to questions, 22 June 1984)

The Thatcher government was clearly not ready in 1984 to risk alienating a large number of its traditional supporters. The abandonment of the voucher (temporary or otherwise) could be seen as a victory for the conservative forces at the heart of the political establishment. At the beginning of 1986, *The Daily Telegraph* argued that:

... measures dear to [the Prime Minister] which fell by the wayside include education vouchers, student loans, repeal of rent control ... Though her aspirations reflect popular feeling, they run counter to those of the political classes ... the establishment, by now accustomed to rule whomever *demos* elects. (*The Daily Telegraph*, 13 January 1986)

According to FEVER Chairperson Marjorie Seldon, speaking on a BBC2 programme 'Decision-making in Britain', first shown in March 1983:

The bureaucrats, if told to do so, would produce a perfectly workable scheme. There is no difficulty that cannot be overcome with ingenuity. But it requires political will.

This view was echoed by Arthur Seldon in 1986 who argued that the reason for Sir Keith's decision was 'not administrative impracticability but official feet-dragging and political underestimation of potential popular acclaim' (p. 97).

It could, of course, be argued that under Sir Keith's successor, and as part of the new dynamic thrust of the third Thatcher administration, the voucher scheme has now re-emerged in a slightly different guise. The decision to abandon the voucher was never popular with the Government's right-wing supporters. The Prime Minister herself said, in an interview broadcast on Channel 4 in July 1985: 'I am very disappointed that we were not able to do the voucher scheme; I think I must have another go' (quoted in Seldon, *ibid.*, p. xii). An editorial in *The Times Educational Supplement* (22 May 1987) saw the 1987 Conservative election manifesto as embracing 'the ideology of vouchers in all but name'. In the circumstances, it is hardly surprising that the Baker Education Bill, with its proposals for grant-main-tained schools and open enrolment, should be seen as something of a victory for the right-wing campaigners of the Institute of Economic Affairs. What we are being offered is a series of halfway measures designed to educate the public to accept the feasibility of alternatives to the traditional state system. As Glennerster has observed (1987) 'the Government's strategy is, in fact, more sweeping than Mr. Baker and the DES will say or perhaps want' (p. 18).

According to the authors of *The Reform of British Education*, the Hillgate Group pamphlet published in September 1987, the proposals in the 1987 Baker Education Bill were perfectly compatible with the principles enshrined in the concept of the voucher. In their view, government plans should be seen as 'the first steps towards the goal of providing an inde-pendent education for all' (Hillgate Group, 1987, p. 41). Yet certain add-itional measures were needed in the cause of the total liberation of schools. As well as allowing maintained schools to 'opt out' of local authority control, the government should, for example, allow independent schools to 'opt in' to the state system, thereby becoming new direct grant schools. These would enjoy the same privilege as other independent schools in not being subject to the constraints of the National Curriculum. All this would then take us nearer to the ultimate goal of the establishment of nationally-recognized 'pupil entitlements', available not to schools, but directly to parents:

> All the initiatives included in the new Education Bill are compat-
> ible with the establishment, within the lifetime of this Parlia-
> ment, of a nationally-recognized *pupil entitlement*, which would
> cover the full cost of providing education for each pupil in the
> primary, secondary (11–16), or 16–19 age groups. Once this pupil

entitlement had been established, it would be both easy and desirable to make it available not to schools, but directly to parents, to be used in any school — LEA, grant-maintained, direct grant or independent. Then, at last, parents would have the maximum freedom to choose an education for their children and the maximum control over those who provide it . . . It is . . . important to harmonize all the new initiatives, so that no unnecessary bureaucratic obstructions are created which will prevent these desirable outcomes. (*ibid.*)

In its analysis of the reasons for the government's failure to introduce a voucher scheme in the early 1980s, the IEA booklet *The Riddle of the Voucher*, published in 1986, argued that the privatization of education at one go was, perhaps, too much for politicians and the public to accept. What was needed was a more subtle way of incorporating the principle of the voucher, 'possibly under a different name', into education policy (Seldon, 1986, pp. 15 and 96). The Baker Education Bill would appear to fit this strategy perfectly.

Notes

1   It is interesting to point out that Pring's own attitude towards privatization has changed over time. In his 1987 paper, he finds it necessary to explain why he has modified the uncompromising stance he adopted in 1983: 'I feel that, in adopting too dogmatic a stance against all forms of privatization, I may be reinforcing a divide between public and private that can, under present circumstances, only re-inforce the advantages of the private, thereby exacerbating the impoverishment and thus the disillusionment within the public sector. I don't feel (reluctantly and sadly) that I can be so exhaustively condemning of privatization in all its forms as I was when I wrote the paper for RICE in 1983'. (Pring, 1987, p. 295)
2   The inclusion of 'teaching posts' in this list is justified by a case of sponsorship cited by Pring in his 1987 paper: 'One town in the South West is dominated by one firm and its factories; local houses have been built by the firm, the town's bypass has been partly financed by it, and some teachers' salaries in the public sector are paid by it. The conditions for their so doing have been agreed with the LEA and the firm's contribution to staffing must be over and above what would be provided by the LEA — that is, in no way is the publicly-funded provision affected'. (*ibid*, p. 292)
3   For further discussion of this point, see Low (1988) p. 219.
4   Some advocates of the voucher trace the idea back to Tom Paine, author of *The Rights of Man*, who in 1790 worked out in Virginia a scheme whereby poor families could receive an annual grant of £4 for each child under the age of 14, which they had to spend on the education of their children.
5   In 1978, a Kent county public survey, based on Ashford, actually revealed strong parental desire for more choice in education, and seemed to suggest that the number who would switch schools would not be unmanageable.

6   The Alum Rock experiment was discontinued in 1976, with supporters blaming the failure on the lack of cooperation from the main teachers' unions.
7   These extracts from Sir Keith Joseph's speech to the 1981 Conservative Party Conference (and later on in the chapter from his speech to the 1982 Party Conference) are taken from the Open University television programme 'Decision-making in Britain', first shown on BBC2 in March 1983.

Chapter 8

1987 and Beyond:
The New Right Education Offensive

The Early Stages of Thatcherism

According to Marquand (1988b), the main objective of moderate socialists in the 1960s and 1970s, following in a tradition going back as far as the Chartists, was to bring the market economy under social and political control:

> ... the central project of the Democratic Left has been to de-mystify the market: to show that the allegedly iron laws of market economics can and should be broken if the outcomes they produce are unjust or anti-social; to make the market the servant, instead of the master, of democratic politics.

If Marquand is correct, this project should have been abruptly halted by the election in May 1979 of a Conservative government headed by Margaret Thatcher and pledged to diminish the role of the State and enhance the role of the individual (Conservative Party, 1979, p. 6).

Yet it can be argued that the novelty of Thatcherism as a major break in social and economic policy has often been overstressed. For one thing, the monetarist policies pursued by the new government as part of its social market strategy for reversing British decline were not as innovative as the Prime Minister herself often liked to claim. As Gamble has pointed out (1985):

> One of the great advantages enjoyed by the new government was that it could pursue its monetarist experiment in a political climate in which opinion had already shifted decisively towards monetarism as the necessary framework for controlling the impact of the recession. The Thatcher government did not have to

abandon the old Keynesian demand-management policies. That had already been done by Labour. It was a Labour government that had presided over a doubling of unemployment between 1975 and 1977 without resorting to traditional Keynesian remedies. It was a Labour government that had introduced cash limits in 1975 to exert much stricter control over public expenditure. It was a Labour government during the sterling crsis of 1976 that had accepted a formal commitment to monetary targets and pledged itself to contain and reduce the burden of public expenditure in order to reassure the international financial markets about the direction of government policy and ministers' intentions... The main contribution of the Thatcher government to this evolution of British economic management away from Keynesianism was a much more doctrinal and ideological politics. (p. 193)

Gamble's view has been endorsed by Skidelsky who has similarly argued (1987) that the so-called Thatcher Revolution had been gestating in previous governments and in previous events:

Monetarism started under Callaghan, as did the first resolute attempt to rein in public spending... Trade union reform was on the agenda long before Mrs. Thatcher implemented it. The collapse of Callaghan's pay policy in the 'winter of discontent' made it unlikely that any successor government would return in a hurry to incomes policy. In social policy, the sale of council houses to tenants was seriously considered by both Wilson and Callaghan; it was Callaghan who started the debate on the 'quality' of education.

For Tony Benn, who had responsibility for first industry then energy in the 1974–79 Labour administrations, there is no doubt that the period of 'welfare capitalist consensus' which had begun in 1945 had already ended by 1976: 'the "monetarist consensus" was... born three years before Mrs. Thatcher came to power' (Benn, 1987, pp. 301 and 304).

At the same time, despite repeated assertion of the values of self-help and self-reliance and a readiness to embrace unreservedly the monetarist ethic, the first two Thatcher administrations were marked by a certain degree of caution in the actual implementation of radical social policies. The clear priorities of the period 1979–87 were two-fold: to bring down the rate of inflation (even at the risk of sustaining very high levels of unemployment) and to curb the power and influence of such extra-Parliamentary institutions as the big trade unions. Much of the welfare state was left intact, and there was little evidence of truly innovative thinking in the areas of housing, health and education. Indeed, this was a source of some dissatisfaction among those Conservatives who were anxious to press on with what they saw as the logical third stage in the transformation of Britain. A private and confidential memorandum drawn up after the 1987 election and proposing the setting up of a 'Free Market Secretariat', designed to service a small group of right-wing Conservative MPs anxious to promote free-market policies in Parliament, argued that Conservative ministers had not done enough to achieve a liberalization of society. In the words of the memorandum:

> Despite the Prime Minister's success in changing the climate of opinion in Britain, the first two Thatcher governments have failed to bring about many urgently needed reforms in the economy, particularly deregulation. In the field of welfare, things are much as they were eight years ago. (Reported in *The Independent*, 28 March 1988)

In an interview published in *The Independent* on 4 April 1988, the former Chairman of the Conservative Party, Norman Tebbit, argued that on the whole the Thatcher governments had been 'fairly successful'. The major task ahead was clearly to transform the dependency culture. The climate of opinion was improving, but 'ministers still had a way to go in changing public attitudes'. This view that much remained to be done was reiterated by Sir Geoffrey Howe, the Foreign Secretary, in a speech to a meeting of Conservatives in the City of London at the beginning of June 1988:

> The new frontier of Conservatism — or, rather, the later stage in that rolling frontier — is about reforming those parts of the state sector which privatization has so far left largely untouched: those activities in society such as health and education which together consume a third of our national income but where market opportunities are still hardly known. (Quoted in *The Independent*, 7 June 1988)

Looking back over the whole period 1976–86, particularly in matters relating to educational policy-making, one is certainly aware of a remarkable unity of purpose, a kind of linear progression. This view of the period has been endorsed by both those who were at the heart of the decision-making process and those who were avid observers of the educational scene. According to Bernard Donoughue, for example (Donoughue, 1987, p. 113), the principal lesson that Conservative administrations after 1979 learned from the Callaghan years was the need to make efficient use of limited resources. This was the unifying factor of the ten-year period following the Ruskin speech which cut across party divisions, notwithstanding differences in style:

> Ironically, the Ruskin speech became the Whitehall blueprint for what Sir Keith Joseph later attempted, and partly achieved, under Mrs. Thatcher's subsequent administrations, although from quite different motives. Our intention had been to make the educational system meet the needs of education and serve the children of this country, rather than to effect cutbacks in public expenditure. Had Labour enjoyed the time and demonstrated the will necessary to implement the Ruskin proposals, I believe they would have made teaching and schooling (the most important of human endeavours) a more satisfactory experience, without the battles and demoralization which resulted from the later tactics of confrontation in the field of education. (*ibid.*)

Sheila Browne has also argued[1] that, as far as HMI was concerned, the Conservative victory of 1979 had comparatively little influence on policy-making, and her analysis takes full account of the curriculum initiatives of the period:

> There was no marked change of policy in 1979, although in a number of key areas — the broadening of the 16–19 curriculum, the movement towards a core or common curriculum for the 11–16 age range, the discussion about a new system of examining at 16+ — the change of government slowed things up temporarily because the plans had to be checked out again in detail.

Two prominent journalists of the period have seen the Ruskin speech as marking a genuine watershed in educational thinking, with consequences spanning the first two Thatcher administrations. In the words of Maureen O'Connor, education correspondent of *The Guardian*, writing in 1987:

> In 1976 Prime Minister James Callaghan shattered the complacency of parts of the educational establishment by launching a major political attack on Britain's schools... In the succeeding ten years, following the Great Debate of 1976/77, a consensus has emerged which has survived changes of government and Secretaries of State. (p. 2)

That consenssus was to be broken by the more radical elements in the Baker Education Bill of 1987/88 but, even here, there was one proposal which could be said to be in line with the trends and developments of the previous ten years. According to Stuart Maclure, editor of *The Times Educational Supplement*, the 1987 National Curriculum could be seen as the culmination of a process which began in 1976:

> The Callaghan speech and the Great Debate which followed (something of a damp squib) changed the relationship between the DES and the education system. The long-term trend towards central control was strengthened. The taboo on government intervention in the curriculum was broken. It would be another ten years before ministers would talk quite openly of their desire for a national curriculum, but the process of achieving one began at Ruskin. (Maclure, 1987a, p. 11)

If these analyses are correct, it can be argued that for at least the first seven years of its existence, the new Conservative government was prepared to operate largely within the terms of the educational consensus constructed by the Labour leadership of 1976. Education was accorded comparatively little space in the 1979 and 1983 Conservative election manifestos and on each occasion the programme outlined was unexceptional. The changes proposed were hardly far-reaching and there was no suggestion that the system itself should be overhauled.

In the 1979 manifesto, plans to maintain and improve standards in education were included as part of a broader section with the title 'Helping the family'. Very little was actually proposed beyond the repeal of those sections of the 1976 Education Act which required local authorities to carry out comprehensive reorganization, more effective use of the Assessment of Performance Unit and of HMI, the introduction of a new Parents' Charter and the setting up of an Assisted Places Scheme to ensure the restoration of the Direct Grant principle:

> ... We must restore to every child, regardless of background, the chance to progress as far as his or her abilities allow.
>
> We will halt the Labour government's policies which have led to the destruction of good schools; keep those of proven worth; and repeal those sections of the 1976 Education Act which compel local authorities to reorganize along comprehensive lines and restrict their freedom to take up places at independent schools.
>
> We shall promote higher standards of achievement in basic skills. The government's Assessment of Performance Unit will set national standards in reading, writing and arithmetic, monitored by tests worked out with teachers and others and applied locally by education authorities. The Inspectorate will be strengthened.

In teacher training, there must be more emphasis on practical skills and on maintaining discipline ...

Extending parents' rights and responsibilities, including their right of choice, will also help raise standards by giving them greater influence over education. Our Parents' Charter will place a clear duty on government and local authorities to take account of parents' wishes when allocating children to schools, with a local appeals system for those dissatisfied. Schools will be required to publish prospectuses giving details of their examination and other results.

The direct grant schools, abolished by Labour, gave wider opportunities for bright children from modest backgrounds. The direct grant principle will therefore be restored with an Assisted Places Scheme. Less well-off parents will be able to claim part or all of the fees at certain schools from a special government fund. (Conservative Party, 1979, pp. 24–6)

The 1983 manifesto reflected on the achievements of the previous four years and went on to outline a six-point programme for the new administration, some of which was already being implemented:

Until now, HM Inspectors' reports have remained secret. Now we are publishing them and making sure they are followed up, too.

We are not satisfied with the selection or the training of our teachers. Our White Paper sets out an important programme for improving teacher training colleges.

We shall switch the emphasis in the Education Welfare Service back to school attendance, so as to reduce truancy.

We have given special help for refresher courses for teachers, research into special schools, and play groups and nursery schools where they are most needed.

We shall also encourage schools to keep proper records of their pupils' achievements, buy more computers, and carry out external graded tests. The public examination system will be improved, and 'O' level standards will be maintained.

We are setting up fourteen pilot projects to bring better technical education to teenagers. The success of these will play a vital part in raising technical training in Britain to the level of our best overseas competitors. (Conservative Party, 1983, pp. 29–30)

Of these proposals, perhaps the most significant concerned the introduction of the Technical and Vocational Education Initiative in fourteen selected areas, although this had, in fact, already been announced by the government in the previous November[2]. Apart from a general reference to the public examination system being improved, no mention was made of progress towards a single system of examining at 16+, plans for which were announced by the Secreatry of State in the House of Commons in June 1984.

Under Mark Carlisle (Secretary of State in 1979–81) and, more particularly, under Sir Keith Joseph (1981–86), attempts were made to create differentiation and selection within the education system[3] but, as we have already seen, these fell far short of the demands being pressed upon the Prime Minister by her doctrinaire supporters on the Far Right. After leaving office, Sir Keith (now Lord) Joseph himself admitted that the creation of differentiation had not been a big enough contribution to the Thatcherite revolution:

> What we haven't done, but still need to do, are in the obvious areas of education and health . . . In my view, there's a lot still to be done to give people more choice in education . . . and to change the dependency-creating aspects of the social security arrangements. (Quoted in *The Independent*, 13 November 1987)

This was indeed a curious admission, coming as it did from a politician who was originally one of the principal advocates of monetarist philosophy (and who might himself have stood for the leadership of the Conservative Party in 1975 had he not been widely criticized for a controversial speech he delivered to the Birmingham Conservative Association in October 1974 in which he argued for a 'remoralization' of the national life[4]). Yet Sir Keith's view of the limited nature of Conservative achievement in education, and of the consequent need for a more positive and dynamic approach, had already been foreshadowed by the Prime Minister in clear and revealing statements made on the eve of the 1987 election. In an interview with the editor of *The Daily Mail*, published on 13 May 1987, she said:

> We are going much further with education than we ever thought of doing before. When we've spent all that money per pupil, and with more teachers, there is still so much wrong, so we are going to do something determined about it . . . There is going to be a revolution in the running of the schools.

This revolution would apparently embrace: a reduction in the powers of the local education authorities, a reversal of 'this universal comprehensive thing,' and 'the breaking-up of the giant comprehensives' (*ibid.*). A month later, the same determination was clearly evident. Asked by a caller to a pre-election radio and television programme in the BBC series *Election*

Call, broadcast on 10 June 1987, what she regretted she had not actually achieved during eight years of Conservative government, the Prime Minister replied:

> In some ways, I wish we had begun to tackle education earlier. We have been content to continue the policies of our predecessors. But now we have much worse left-wing Labour authorities than we have ever had before — so something simply has to be done. (Reported in *The Guardian*, 11 June 1987)

After eight years of Conservative education policy, the *real* break with past traditions and accepted procedures came in 1987/88. The third Thatcher administration possessed the confidence and determination to adopt truly radical strategies for dismantling both the comprehensive secondary system so painstakingly built up since the 1950s and 1960s and the constitutional settlement devised in 1944. According to Simon (1988), the educational objectives of the victorious politicians of 1987 were twofold: 'first, to break the power of the local authorities which traditionally had been directly responsible for running their own "systems" of education . . . and second, to erect (or reinforce) an hierarchical system of schooling both subject to market forces and more directly under central state control' (p. 15). In Warnock's view (1988, p. 173), competition had emerged, by the third term of the Conservative government, as 'the central Thatcherite concept'. This involved the search for new types of school to make parental choice a reality. While it could be argued that a competitive education service was not 'necessarily incompatible' with an education policy that was for *everyone*, it was Warnock's contention that 'competition can best and most fruitfully take place in a condition of justice, where everyone may enter the race and do his best' (*ibid.*). Not that the issues at stake here were purely educational. Jackson Hall, formerly Director of Education for Sunderland, has argued that the change of direction in policy-making was also of the utmost *constitutional* significance:

> We should remind ourselves that until a few years ago, the changes in the school system foreshadowed in the 1987 Education Reforn Bill would have caused a first-class political row. The issues are as clear as they are contentious — the enhanced powers which promote the Secretary of State from senior partner to supremo of the service, the relegation of the local education authorities from partnership to monitorial status, the revision of the 1944 settlement with the churches, something approaching dominion status for the individual school, and the fabrication of a

market economy for the schools. The Bill is not about the
development or reformation of the 1944 settlement but about
replacing it. (Hall, 1988, p. 4)

To fully understand how this situation came about, we need to go back to
the appointment of Kenneth Baker as Education Secretary in May 1986.

The Development of New Policies

By the spring of 1986, it was clear that Conservative education policy was
in a state of disarray and, furthermore, that Sir Keith Joseph himself had
incurred widespread hostility and resentment as Education Secretary. Talk
of 'crisis' was now being used in the service of a comprehensive indictment
of Conservative management or mismanagement of the system. Central to
the whole debate was the question of funding. The BBC TV *Panorama* programme 'Schools — Selling the children short', broadcast on 17 March
1986, investigated the alleged under-resourcing of the state education
system by visiting Cheshire to see how the national statistics and political
debate translated into practical experience for one community. The Chairman of the Education Committee was quite realistic about the impact of
reduced funding on many Cheshire schools:

> They're becoming gloomy and dilapidated, and this does affect
> pupils' performance. We're £40 million behind in our decoration
> programme. The government is saying, 'raise standards', but at
> the same time it is cutting our resources. It's cutting the prospects
> of achieving success, because we haven't got enough books, we
> haven't got enough equipment.

In an accompanying article in *The Listener*, the programme's presenter
Margaret Jay talked of the lack of resources in terms of a new 'crisis in
education' in which children were 'likely to be the main casualties (Jay,
1986, pp. 2–3)[5]. Figures gathered by the National Confederation of Parent-
Teacher Associations (NCPTA) in 1984 and 1985 showed that parents were
being asked to buy textbooks in more than half of the country's secondary
schools, and that, in 84 per cent of schools, parents' funds were being spent
on items listed as 'essential educational equipment' for science, home
economics, art and music (*ibid.*). Much of the blame for all this was laid at
Sir Keith's door. He had constantly reiterated, throughout his period of
office, that the education service could not expect increased resources, and
he clearly alienated a large section of the teaching profession: indeed, his
speech to the NAS/UWT National Association of Schoolmasters and Union
of Women Teachers conference on 3 April 1986 was received in total silence

— an extraordinary snub for a serving minister. The announcement on 2 February 1986 of his impending retirement waas followed by demands right across the political spectrum — including leading articles in *The Times* (27 March) and *The Daily Telegraph* (8 April) — that if he really intended to go, he should go quickly[6]. Moreover, the state of the nation's schools was considered by many commentators to be one of the main reasons for the government's electoral reverses in the municipal elections in early May (see Simon, 1986, pp. 20–6 and 1988, pp. 28–9).

The appointment of Kenneth Baker as Sir Keith's successor in May 1986 meant that the government could now abandon its defensive posture by constructing a package of radical proposals to be put before the electorate in the next election manifesto. There is evidence (see below) that many of the ideas supported by Mr. Baker were circulating in the DES and in the Downing Street Policy Unit in the time of his predecessor, but Sir Keith's attitude towards them was often ambivalent, and it was only in the period 1986/87 that they acquired the status of viable measures. Reference has already been made to the supreme irony that it was not Sir Keith Joseph, one of the founding intellects of Thatcherism, who was able to bring all the new ideas together on to the statute book. In a number of ways, Sir Keith proved a great disappointment to Mrs. Thatcher's more right-wing supporters in the Hillgate Group and the Institute of Economic Affairs. He failed to promote the cause of the education voucher[7]; and he seemed more concerned with the needs of the less able than with devising new ways of privatizing the system. It may be that he was defeated by his own civil servants; or it may be, as Wilby has suggested (Wilby, 1987), that he was unable to find ways of achieving his objectives that would satisfy his own need for coherent solutions to problems. Kenneth Baker, on the other hand, is seen by Wilby as 'the supreme pragmatist':

> There is something curiously fragmented about Baker's approach. Read his speeches and articles and you will rarely find a connected argument, a sense of an intellect grappling with problems and journeying towards coherent solutions. His speeches have been aptly compared to those of a man drawing on a mixture of old Chinese proverbs and Christmas cracker mottoes . . . Joseph's cerebral approach demanded coherent solutions that would stand up . . . Pragmatists, because they are not interested in placing ideas within a coherent political framework, are more easily seduced by the superficially attractive. (*ibid.*)

Wilby's view has been endorsed by Morris and Griggs (1988, pp. 21–2) who, comparing Baker with Joseph, have described the new Secretary as 'a minister more direct, less subtle, with an air of absolute certainty, a man not beset by any intellectual doubts as was his more thoughtful and philosophically-minded predecessor'. Certainly many commentators have made reference to Kenneth Baker's obvious ambition, suggesting that he sees himself as a future occupant of 10 Downing Street[8].

One of the earliest initiatives to be announced by the new Education Secretary concerned the setting up of a number of city technology colleges (CTC) financed by private capital to provide a new choice of school in inner-city areas. It has been suggested (*The Sunday Times*, 26 July 1987) that these new colleges were the brainchild of Professor Brian Griffiths, who took over as Head of the Downing Street Policy Unit in 1985[9]. He may well have taken a keen interest in the venture; but it could also be argued that it was the scheme which eventually became the Technical and Vocational Education Initiative at the end of 1982 that was the CTC concept in embryonic form[10]. As we have already seen, the original TVEI proposal envisaged, in the words of the Prime Minister's House of Commons statement of 12 November 1982, 'new institutional arrangements for technical and vocational education for 14–18-year-olds, within existing financial resources, and, where possible, in association with local education authorities'. Moreover, David Young, the then Chairman of the Manpower Services Commission, made it quite clear in November 1982 that, in the absence of wholehearted LEA support, the MSC would be quite happy to open its own technical establishments. He even suggested that it would be a nice idea to get financial backing from industry and call them 'Young schools' (interview with *Education*, 19 November 1982, pp. 385–6). In the event, and for reasons already discussed, the more 'radical' aspects of the original TVEI scheme were shelved; but the basic idea of a new system of technical schools or colleges for children just below the top ability band refused to lie down even after it was discreetly dropped by the progenitors of TVEI. There was, for example, reference to a revival of the original TVEI idea and, therefore, to an early version of the CTC concept in *The Sunday Times* in December 1985. In a short article headed 'Technology school plan for the young elite', plans were revealed for the establishment of '16–20 technology schools in main urban areas'. The article confidently asserted that:

> Each would take 1,000 pupils, who would be specially selected and would not pay fees . . . The LEAs would not be responsible for the new schools . . . They would be funded directly by the taxpayer via a National Education Trust. (*The Sunday Times*, 22 December 1985)

Baker's official announcement of the CTC plan was made in a speech to the 1986 Conservative Party Conference held at the beginning of October. It was emphasized that the new colleges — some twenty in number — would be completely independent of local education authority control, a fact which drew sustained and rapturous applause from Mr. Baker's audience and which apparently 'chilled the blood' of Philip Merridale, the Conservative leader on the Council of Local Education Authorities and later to be a founding member of the moderate Conservative Education Association[11]. Mr. Baker also made it clear that he had Treasury approval for extra public money to finance the new colleges but that an important part of the plan was that private sector sponsors would be encouraged to contribute to capital and running costs. The colleges would develop enterprise, self-reliance and responsibility, and would broaden parental choice. There would be no 11 + style entry examination for the colleges, but there would be selection procedures and these would lay particular emphasis on the 'attitudes' of pupils and their parents and on their commitment to making the most of a technology-oriented education. Among the Conservative faithful, there was clearly much enthusiasm for the new scheme; and at least one national newspaper was moved to comment that Mr. Baker's announcement helped to present the final period of Mrs. Thatcher's second administration as 'the vigorous prelude to a third term, rather then the dogged performance of a team that has run out of steam' (*The Guardian*, 8 October 1986).

The original concept of the city technology college was clearly outlined in *A New Choice of School: City Technology Colleges*, the glossy brochure published by the DES in October 1986 (DES, 1986e):

> Their purpose will be to provide a broadly-based secondary education with a strong technological element, thereby offering a wider choice of secondary school to parents in certain cities and a surer preparation for adult and working life to their children. (*ibid.*, p. 2)

The CTCs would be *new* schools for 11–18-year-olds established in urban areas *alongside* existing secondary schools. The new schools would be registered independent schools and therefore independent of local authority control, but would charge no fees. Each CTC would serve a substantial catchment area, the composition of the intake being broadly representative of the local community. The main principle of funding would be that individual promoters would meet all or a substantial part of the initial capital costs, with the Secretary of State paying the running costs at a level of assistance per pupil comparable with that provided by LEAs for maintained schools serving similar catchment areas. As far as the curriculum was concerned, there would be a large technical and practical element within a broad and balanced diet.

The brochure announced that the government was prepared to fund up to twenty CTCs in the first period of development. It actually listed twenty-seven possible locations, including Hackney and Notting Hill in London, the St. Paul's area of Bristol, Handsworth in Birmingham, Chapeltown in Leeds, Knowsley on Merseyside and Highfields in Leicester (*ibid.*, p. 15). A number of the areas listed were suffering acute social deprivation and receiving attention in other ways through the Inner City Initiative.

The CTC proposal may have earned Mr. Baker a standing ovation at the Conservative Party conference, but it received a notably hostile response from large numbers of teachers, educationists, union leaders and journalists (see Chitty, 1987a, 1987b and 1989). Writing in *The Listener* in October 1986, John Clare, at that time BBC Radio Education Correspondent, argued that CTCs were irrelevant to the needs of the majority of schoolchildren and potentially damaging to the British school system (Clare, 1986a, p. 5). They would have the effect of robbing comprehensive schools of both 'their most able and highly motivated pupils' and 'scarce teachers' in such areas as maths, physics, design and technology (*ibid.*). Taking part in a BBC Radio 4 *Analysis* programme, broadcast on 3 December 1986, Professor Ted Wragg argued that the CTC plan would undermine the existing comprehensive system in at least two ways: it would encourage early and narrow specialization by forcing parents and pupils to make a specific commitment to a certain type of schooling at the age of 10 or 11 and, more invidiously, it must involve a return to selection. In the view of Fred Jarvis, General Secretary of the National Union of Teachers, the CTC scheme should be seen as 'just another device to ensure that a minority of children get privileged treatment'; and David Hart, General Secretary of the National Association of Head Teachers, observed: 'there is an urgent need for *all* secondary schools to have more technology-based teaching, not just for what will become the privileged few in the inner-city areas' (reported in *The Guardian*, 8 October 1986). At their annual conference in May 1987, the National Association of Schoolmasters/Union of Women Teachers went as far as to vote for a boycott of the goods and services of any company offering financial support for a CTC.

Despite the opposition that would inevitably be aroused, it was clear by the end of 1986 that the government was preparing to introduce further radical changes affecting the whole of the education system in England and Wales. Kenneth Baker voiced his dissatisfaction with the existing arrangements in an interview with Terry Coleman published in *The Guardian* on 6 December. He said that, plainly, there would have to be a major reform bill in the next Parliament to cure the malaise that had crept into the system. He felt that he had 'an inchoate mandate' to sort out the mess that he had inherited. In his view:

> Rab Butler, if he were alive today, would barely recognize the system he tried to set up in 1944. Standards were low. There was far too much experiment. Central government, at the hub, had to take greater control of the curriculum. At the same time, at the rim of the wheel, the schools and the parents (not the local authorties) had to have a greater say in administration. (*ibid.*)

It was on a television programme, albeit a prestigious one, that the Education Secretary chose to unveil details of his forthcoming legislative reforms. Interviewed by Matthew Parris on the London Weekend Television programme *Weekend World*, broadcast on 7 December 1986, Mr. Baker made it clear that he had plans to introduce the biggest changes in schools for more than forty years. He said that if the government won the next election, it would introduce a major education bill, the most far-reaching since 1944, legislating principally for a 'national core curriculum' with set objectives. Detailed benchmarks would be established 'in a wide range of subjects' at the ages of 9, 11 and 14[12]. Although there was no intention to 'chill and destroy the inventiveness and creativity of teachers', Mr. Baker warned that 'there would have to be more direction from the centre as far as the curriculum was concerned'. The proposed 'national curriculum' should be seen as part of the move towards central control in the interest primarily of the pupils, far too many of whom were at present allowed to be 'aimless and drifting'. In Mr. Baker's view, the comprehensive system was 'seriously flawed'; the great hopes of those early believers that 'comprehensive schools were going to solve everything' had been cruelly dashed — which was 'a great pity'. Only a national core curriculum, centrally imposed, could ensure an all-round improvement in standards, particularly at the secondary level.

Other changes in the pipeline announced by Mr. Baker in the same programme included giving schools responsibility for their own budgets and allowing them to recruit as many pupils as they wished. Despite the introduction of a national curriculum, there should in future be more choice and differentiation at the secondary level and this would include an emphasis on courses of a more vocational nature for academically less able children — the so-called bottom 40 per cent — from the age of 11 or 12. The new CTCs would provide a greater variety of schools but as 'prototypes' for the entire secondary school system. They would be independent of local authority control following curriculum guidelines laid down by the government, and, 'a very important principle', there would be no fixed limit to the number of pupils they could take if they gained the support of parents. Moreover, future colleges, beyond the first twenty to be established within the next two years, would not have to be technology-oriented: they could, for example, be 'language schools' and could perhaps be 'created from existing schools'[13].

The Education Secretary went on to develop his case for a national core curriculum in a speech delivered to the North of England Education Conference in Rotherham in January 1987. He described the English education system as 'a bit of a muddle, one of those institutionalized muddles that the English have made peculiarly their own'. It could, moreover, be compared unfavourably with that operating elsewhere in Europe:

> In England we are eccentric in education as in many other things. For at least a century, our education system has been quite different from that adopted by most of our European neighbours. They have tended to centralize and to standardize. We have gone for diffusion and variety. In particular, the functions of the State have largely been devolved to elected local bodies; and the school curriculum has largely been left to individual schools and teachers. (DES, 1987a, p. 1)

Mr. Baker went on to complain about the lack of agreement concerning the curriculum for the 14–16 age group, stressing the confusion in schools over the question of balance and the failure to work out satisfactory objectives. Here again, these problems did not arise elsewhere in Europe:

> These weaknesses do not arise in those West European countries where schools follow more or less standard national syllabuses. In those countries, the school system produces results which overall are at least as satisfactory as those produced here; and the teachers are no less professional than ours. Nor do these countries show any sign of wanting to give up the advantages of national syllabuses. So it would be foolish to reject out of hand the idea of moving much nearer to the kind of curricular structure which obtains elsewhere in Western Europe. For my part, I am sure that we must so move . . . (*ibid.*, p. 20)

In Mr. Baker's view, we must both 'preserve the good features of our present arrangements *and* do away with the bad ones' by 'establishing a national curriculum which works through national criteria for each subject area of the curriculum' (*ibid.*).

A sense of urgency was conveyed to the Education Secretary in a second important speech in January 1987, this time to the Society of Education Officers' conference. Here Mr. Baker made it clear that he would not be diverted from his chosen path by the views of 'professional educators':

> ... I believe that, at least as far as England is concerned, we should now move quickly to a national curriculum. By that I mean a school curriculum governed by national criteria which are promulgated by the Secretary of State but in consultation with all concerned — inside and outside the education service — and which are sufficiently flexible to allow schools and teachers to use professional enterprise and judgment in applying them to individual pupils in their particular schools. I want to finish up with criteria which are broadly accepted by those who have to apply them because they have had a say in their determination...
>
> ... I realize that the changes I envisage are radical and far-reaching and may, therefore, be unwelcome to those who value what is traditional and familiar and has often served well in the past. But I believe profoundly that professional educators will do a disservice to the cause of education, and to the nation, if they entrench themselves in a defence of the status quo. More and more people are coming to feel that our school curriculum is not as good as it could be and needs to be, and that we need to move nearer to the kind of arrangements which other European countries operate with success, but without sacrificing those features of our own traditional approach which continue to prove their worth. (DES, 1987b, pp. 4–5)

In a further statement at the beginning of April 1987, Mr. Baker announced that two working groups, on mathematics and science, would be set up to advise on attainment targets for children of different ages and abilities and on programmes of study to enable children to reach those targets. They would be the first of a number of working groups with similar tasks. The government wanted to ensure that pupils received 'a well-balanced foundation curriculum' including not only mathematics and English, but also science, foreign languages, history, geography and technology. At the same time, 'clear and challenging attainment targets were needed for the key ages of 7, 11 and 14'. Once these were established, it would also be possible to 'define the essential content, skills and processes to be taught in each subject' (DES, 1987c).

While working towards a system of greater uniformity in curriculum provision, Mr. Baker was anxious to stress that the main emphasis of the remaining aspects of his forthcoming Education Reform Bill would be on differentiation and choice. In an interview with Stuart Maclure for the TVS series *Promises and Piecrust* (an edited version of which appeared in *The Times Educational Supplement* at the beginning of April 1987), the Education Secretary argued that within any education system, there had to be a large element of selection. In response to the question: 'Do you think that we should end up with a series of quasi-independent schools and no system at all?' he replied:

> No, I think that's a rather extreme manifestation of what I'm saying. I want a much greater degree of variety and independence in the running of schools. I do want to see a greater amount of variety and choice...I think that when it comes to the independent sector, what we have is 7 per cent or so in the independent sector, probably going to rise to 10 per cent, and on the other side a huge continent, 93 per cent in the state maintained sector. I'm responsible for that state sector. What I think is striking in the British education system is that there is nothing in between...Now the city technology colleges are a half-way house. I would like to see many more half-way houses, a greater choice, a greater variety. I think many parents would as well. (Maclure, 1987a and 1987b)

The 1987 Conservative Party election manifesto devoted over four pages to 'raising standards in education'. It acknowledged that not enough had been done in eight years of Conservative rule to create the sort of system of which Conservatives could be truly proud. Extra resources had been provided; but money alone was not enough:

> Increased resources have not produced uniformly higher standards. Parents and employers are rightly concerned that not enough children master the basic skills, that some of what is taught seems irrelevant to a good education and that standards of personal discipline and aspirations are too low. In certain cases, education is used for political indoctrination and sexual propaganda. The time has now come for school reform. (Conservative Party, 1987, p. 18)

The manifesto moved on to outline four major reforms designed to establish choice and competition as dominant features of a new education system. First, a 'national core curriculum' would be established, with prescribed syllabuses, attainment levels and forms of assessment at the ages of 7, 11, 14 and 16. All pupils between the ages of 5 and 16 would study a basic range of subjects, including maths, English and science. In the words of the manifesto, the government would 'consult widely among those concerned in establishing the curriculum'. Second, within five years, governing bodies and headteachers of all secondary schools, and of many primary schools, would be given control over their own budgets. This would draw on the experience of heads already involved in pilot schemes for financial devolution such as those operating in Cambridgeshire and Solihull. Third, a number of reforms would be introduced designed to increase parental choice. These would include: requiring heads to enrol children up to a school's agreed physical capacity instead of 'artificially restricting pupil numbers'; establishing a pilot network of city technology colleges; and expanding the Assisted Places Scheme to 35,000. And fourth, state schools would be allowed to opt out of local authority control and become independent charitable trusts financed centrally. (*ibid.*, pp. 18–20)

Compared with the education proposals outlined in the Conservative Party manifesto, those put forward in tbe SDP/Liberal Alliance and Labour Party documents seemed bland and unexceptional. Both talked in terms of widening access to education, raising standards of performance in schools and providing more effective training and skills (SDP/Liberal Alliance, 1987, pp. 14–16; Labour Party, 1987, p. 9), but neither could match the Conservative manifesto for detailed radical proposals. This prompted *The Times Educational Supplement* to argue that the Labour and Alliance manifestos appeared to be trapped in a time-warp while the government had embarked on a truly innovative course of its own:

> There is a lot in the opposition party policies which reads like an intelligent commentary on *Better Schools*. They have done Sir Keith Joseph the honour of taking him seriously, only to find the Tories have got bored with the nuts and bolts of *Better Schools* and gone for the ideology of vouchers in all but name. (*The Times Educational Supplement*, 22 May 1987)

It was soon obvious that right-wing ministers and their supporters were confident that they had hit upon an idea whose time had come. Education Junior Minister Bob Dunn told right-wing campaigners within the Conservative Party at a meeting in May 1987 that government proposals to allow schools to take as many pupils as they could physically cope with, in tandem with plans to give heads control of school budgets and the right to 'opt out' of council control, were all parts of a strategy that would eventually lead to the 'denationalization of education' (reported in *The Times Educational Supplement*, 15 May 1987). And at a pre-election press conference, Margaret Thatcher argued that heads and governing bodies who 'opted out' of local education authority control should be free to establish their own admissions policies and would not necessarily be prevented from raising extra funds through parents — thereby giving rise to much media speculation that the new plans might include a fee-paying element (reported in *The Guardian*, 23 May 1987). Indeed, Kenneth Baker conceded during a BBC Radio 4 *World At One* discussion broadcast on 10 June 1987 that there would be nothing to stop 'better-off parents' raising additional resources for a particular school so that the headteacher would be able to purchase expensive books and items of equipment and pay the teachers higher salaries.

Yet at the same time, it was widely reported, in the press and elsewhere, that the Education Secretary was not himself a wholehearted supporter of all the features of the new Conservative education programme. Professor Ted Wragg suggested in a BBC TV *Panorama* programme 'A class revolution', broadcast on 2 November 1987, that it was 'an open secret' that Kenneth Baker had had a number of policies foisted upon him as a condition of taking the education portfolio in May 1986. In the weeks before the 1987 election, the Minister was certainly anxious to deny that he had been stampeded by right-wing elements in his own party, while, at the same time, claiming full responsibility for the curriculum proposals in the education package. Interviewed at the beginning of June, he said:

> The national core curriculum — that was my idea. At the time it was seen as very heretical. But in just a few months, all the political parties have come round to accepting it. (*The Times Educational Supplement*, 5 June 1987)

The June 1987 election was followed by the publication in quick succession of six consultation papers to prepare the way for the introduction in parliament of a major education bill. These papers provoked a great deal of public debate, despite being published at the beginning of the holiday season. They dealt with the following matters: (i) the introduction of a national curriculum in maintained schools in England and Wales; (ii) the devolution of financial responsibility for running schools very largely to governing bodies; (iii) the greater freedom of parents to send their children to the school of their choice; (iv) the creation of opportunities for schools to opt out of the locally maintained system; (v) the reconsideration of what educational services would be charged for; and (vi) the reappraisal of the governance, financing and legal basis of further education[14].

The National Curriculum consultation document, published in July 1987 (DES, 1987e), listed ten foundation subjects to be taken by all pupils during their compulsory education: English, maths, science, a modern foreign language (except in primary schools), technology, history, geography, art, music and physical education. Of these, English, maths and science would form the 'core' of the curriculum, and the majority of curriculum time at primary level would be devoted to these three subjects. Secondary schools would be expected to devote 30 to 40 per cent of their time to the three core subjects and, in years four and five, 80 to 90 per cent of their time to the foundation subjects. Themes such as health education and information technology would have to be taught through foundation subjects.

Attainment targets would be set for the three core subjects for 7-, 11-, 14- and 16-year-olds. They might also be set for other foundation subjects, but for art, music and physical education, there would be 'guidelines' rather than specific attainment targets. The attainment targets would provide standards against which pupils' progress and performance could be assessed. It was envisaged that much of the assessment would be done by teachers as an integral part of normal classroom work. But in the words of the document (page 11):

> At the heart of the assessment process, there will be nationally prescribed tests done by all pupils to supplement the individual teachers' assessments.

The consultation document was greeted with a chorus of disapproval and disbelief from large numbers of teachers and educationists (see, for example, Lawton, 1987b; Golby, 1987; Lawton and Chitty, 1988). It was pointed out that the curriculum was conceived of entirely in terms of traditional subjects, with little or no acknowledgment of the curriculum debate which had been going on both inside and outside the DES since at least 1976. At the same time, important areas of human experience were almost wholly neglected: there was no mention of integrated subjects like humanities or environmental studies, or of the 'pastoral curriculum' or personal and social education, or of 'newer' subjects like psychology, sociology, politics or economics. Moreover, as Aldrich pointed out (1988, p. 29), the curriculum could hardly be called 'national' in that it did not apply to the independent sector:

> What concept of a national curriculum and of a national education, indeed what concept of a nation, underlies this document? Is it that teachers in independent schools can be trusted to

provide a balanced curriculum and appropriate standards of education whilst teachers in state schools can not? Is it that pupils in independent schools can be trusted to make the right choice of subjects and to work hard, whilst those in state schools can not?[15]

The government took no notice of these criticisms in steering its Education Bill through Parliament. Only in two curriculum areas was there evidence of a change of heart. The Education Secretary was forced to abandon his idea that the core curriculum should take up at least 80–90 per cent of the secondary school timetable. Launching the Bill on 20 November 1987, Mr. Baker said:

> We don't intend to lay down either in this Bill or in secondary legislation a precise percentage of subjects. It was never the original intention. It will be up to schools, heads and local authorities to deliver the national curriculum and bring children up to the level of attainment targets. (Reported in *The Guardian*, 21 November 1987)

A few months later, following concessions made by the Education Secretary in the House of Commons, religious education became the one and only *basic* subject, supervised locally and with no national assessment.

Cordingley and Wilby argued (1987, p. 6) that, of the remaining consultation papers, those on devolution of budgets, open enrolment and opting-out were of special significance for the future of the state education system. Taken together, they would introduce market principles to education:

> Each of these subjects might, on its own, be unobjectionable. Together, they represent a proposal for a fundamental shift in how the education service works, a shift, essentially, from the principles that underly a universal, public, non-market service to those that underly a selective, privatized (and hence differentiated and inequitable) market service. (*ibid.*)

Many commentators pointed out that these proposals would inevitably have the effect of destabilizing, and even disrupting, local systems of comprehensive education. As indicated by Mr. Baker in his TVS interview, they seemed to be designed to expand and strengthen the independent sector in education at the expense of the maintained sector. Alliance spokesperson Anne Sofer wrote that opting-out would not be a liberating but 'a profoundly conservative force'; future planning would be 'paralyzed' (*The Times Educational Supplement*, 17 July 1987). Tessa Blackstone, Master of Birkbeck College, London, argued that children's futures were now 'threatened by a scheme casually destructive of the best in the maintained system, dangerously divisive, and administratively unworkable' (*The Guardian*, 9 June 1987). In the view of *The Times Educational Supplement* (17 July 1987), the main effects of the government's proposals would be to 'raise costs and lower efficiency'. Open enrolment signified 'the negation of planning'. If market forces were allowed to prevail, planning would, in future, be retrospective: 'a matter of picking up the bits and presiding over the bankruptcies after the consumers have made their educational purchases'. Once the measures were implemented, it was extremely doubtful whether it would any longer make any sense 'to talk about a "system" at the local level'. A 'blight' would be put on 'all plans for restructuring, closures and mergers'. Some regarded this as unnecessarily alarmist, but one thing agreed upon by all commentators was that the new proposals represented something of a victory for New Right pressure groups and for those in charge of the Downing Street Policy Unit.

The Influence of New Right Thinking

The philosophy of the so-called New Right can be seen as one expression of the new politics which emerged in the 1970s in response to the world economic recession, the exhaustion of Fordism as a regime of accumulation and the break-down of American hegemony. The New Right encompasses a wide range of groups and ideas, and there are many internal divisions and conflicts. What the term could not be said to signify is either a unified movement or a coherent doctrine. Yet according to Gamble (1988), there are certain important beliefs which are common to all adherents of New Right philosophy:

> What all strands within the New Right share . . . is the rejection of many of the ideas, practices and institutions which have been characteristic of social democratic regimes in Europe and of the New Deal and the Great Society programmes in the United States. The New Right is radical because it seeks to undo much that has been constructed in the last sixty years. New Right thinkers question many of the assumptions which have become accepted for the conduct of public policy while New Right politicians have sought to build electoral and policy coalitions which challenge key institutions and key policies . . . As a political programme, the New Right is identified with opposition to state involvement in the economy. They are fierce critics of Keynesian policies of economic management and high public expenditure on

welfare. But New Right politicians are also renowned as advocates of national discipline and strong defence ... To preserve a
free society and a free economy, the authority of the state has to be
restored. (pp. 27–8)

There is, then, a paradox at the very heart of New Right philosophy; and
this is why, for Gamble, the phrase which best summarizes the doctrine of
the New Right and the hegemonic project which it has inspired is 'free
economy/strong state'. Different meanings are attached to these two terms
and they are given different weight by different factions within the New
Right, but if the New Right has a unity and can be distinguished from previous right-wing groupings, what makes it special is the unique combination of a traditional liberal defence of the free economy with a traditonal
conservative defence of state authority.

This combination of potentially opposing doctrines means that New
Right philosophy has contradictory policy implications and the ambiguity
owes much to a basic division between those, on the one hand, who emphasize the free economy, often referred to as the neo-liberals, and those on the
other who attach more importance to a strong state, the so-called neo-conservatives. Using Belsey's useful summary of the main points of difference:
neo-liberalism prioritizes freedom of choice, the individual, the market,
minimal government and *laissez-faire*, in contrast to neo-conservatism
which prioritizes notions of social authoritarianism, the disciplined society,
hierarchy and subordination, the nation and strong government (Belsey,
1986). As Gamble has pointed out, it is hardly surprising that New Right
philosophy often represents a confused set of messages to those outside its
ranks:

> The idea of a free economy and a strong state involves a paradox.
> The state is to be simultaneously rolled back and rolled forward.
> Non-interventionist and decentralized in some areas, the state is
> to be highly interventionist and centralized in others. The New
> Right can appear by turns libertarian and authoritarian, populist
> and elitist. This ambiguity is not an accident. It derives, in part,
> from the fact that the New Right has two major strands: a liberal
> tendency, which argues the case for a freer, more open, and more
> competitive economy; and a conservative tendency, which is
> more interested in restoring social and political authority
> throughout society. What makes matters more confusing is that
> not only do those within the New Right regard the importance of
> these tendencies differently, but those who have written on the

New Right often concentrate upon one of them to the exclusion of the other. (*ibid.*, pp. 28–9)[16]

As far as the formulation of education policy is concerned, three New Right groups are of special significance: the Institute of Economic Affairs which was established as a research and educational trust in 1955 and began issuing regular publications in 1957; the Centre for Policy Studies which was set up by Margaret Thatcher and Sir Keith Joseph in 1974; and the Hillgate Group, comprising Caroline Cox, Jessica Douglas-Home, John Marks, Lawrence Norcross and Roger Scruton, whose first major pamphlet *Whose Schools? A Radical Manifesto*, was published at the end of 1986. Other groups exist, but these three have played the major role in influencing government policy. Quicke (1988) has argued that 'in education, it seems to be the neo-conservative rather then the neo-liberal wing who have taken the lead in controlling the debate and constructing the framework for a "new consensus"' (p. 9). Yet it could be argued that, in reaching this conclusion, he tends to rely rather heavily on the writings of the Hillgate Group in general and of Roger Scruton in particular.

Roger Scruton believes that for Conservatives, the state is always an end, not a means to some other end, like the achievement of maximum freedom in civil society. Individuals always belong to the state, whose authority comes not from the mandate of citizens, but from the exercise of established power. Scruton remains implacably hostile to liberalism in all its forms and sometimes finds it very difficult to co-exist with the more 'libertarian' strand of New Right opinion. In his book *The Meaning of Conservatism*, published in 1980, he describes the philosophy of liberalism as 'the principle enemy of conservatism', and denounces all 'liberal' notions of 'individual autonomy' and the 'natural' rights of man. His description of a genuine conservative attitude is one which:

> . . . seeks above all for government, and regards no citizen as possessed of a natural right that transcends his obligation to be ruled. Even democracy . . . . can be discarded without detriment to the civil well-being as the conservative conceives it. (Scruton, 1980, p. 16)

For Scruton and his colleagues, the institutions that sustain capitalist economic activity are more important than the concept of a free market. Markets and free competition are not ends in themselves for New Right Conservatives but only means to those ends. The emphasis is always on authority, hierarchy and the maintenance of social order. Socialism and social democracy are to be equated with permissiveness and the erosion of established values. It is generally believed that enemies of the ordered society have penetrated the schools and the universities and must therefore be exposed and challenged. The main purpose of schooling is to instil respect for the family, private property and all the bodies which uphold the authority of the bourgeois state. The traditional curriculum must be defended as the only one based on genuinely educational principles. Anti-racist and anti-sexist education, peace studies, world studies and various other dubious subjects are seen as the main components of a politicized curriculum which has to be rejected if traditional moral values are to survive. (Hillgate Group, 1986 and 1987)

Yet it should not be assumed that the views of Roger Scruton or of the Hillgate Group are necessarily representative of New Right education and social philosophy as a whole. The Institute of Economic Affairs, for example, could be said to be very much influenced by the writings of Milton Friedman and to lay particular emphasis on the privatization of the system. At the same time, it is fair to point out that even the Hillgate Group, while placing special emphasis on the need to specify the type of curriculum to be taught in schools, still believes that a return to established moral values will be achieved only if schools are wrenched free of local authority control, thereby depriving the authorities of 'their standing ability to corrupt the minds and souls of the young' (Hillgate Group, 1986, p. 18). In this respect, neo-conservatives are able to make common cause with neo-liberals.

For the liberal New Right, the central issue is always the conditions under which markets function most effectively. It is taken as axiomatic that markets are inherently superior to any other way of organizing human societies. This point was made by Sir Keith Joseph in a pamphlet published in 1976:

> The blind, unplanned, uncoordinated wisdom of the market is over-whelmingly superior to the well-researched, rational, systematic, well-meaning, cooperative, science-based, forward-looking, statistically respectable plans of governments, bureaucracies and international organizations... The market system is the greatest generator of national wealth known to mankind: co-ordinating and fulfilling the diverse needs of countless individuals in a way which no human mind or minds could even comprehend, without coercion, without direction, without bureaucratic interference. (pp. 57 and 62)

Along with this profound belief in the inherent superiority of the free-market economy goes the associated conviction that the key to economic success and individual happiness lies in rapid and widespread privatization. Only the wholesale abandonment of public ownership can bring democratic capitalism to fruition and signal the absolute demise of socialism. According to Oliver Letwin, formerly special adviser to Sir Keith Joseph at the DES and then an influential member of the Downing Street Policy Unit, the Conservative governments of Margaret Thatcher will merit a whole chapter in history on account of their outstanding contribution to 'the global revolution wrought by privatization'. In his view:

> Privatization . . . is the point at which the economic and political Thatcher revolutions converge. The idea of selling state assets was born out of a gut feeling in the seventies that businesses would run better if they were free of government's dead hand. There have been other benefits: popular capitalism; cutting the national debt with the proceeds; expanding the City's financial capacity. But few imagined that it would lead to the multi-billion asset sales of British Telecom, British Gas, British Petroleum . . . Yet the most important benefit is still only dimly-perceived: a transformation in the way government thinks and behaves . . . Nationalized industries drag officials and ministers into opposing the customers' interest. Once privatization is complete, the role of ministers in running everything will never be restored . . . Britain is moving back into a position where people in government do not think it is their business to run anything. Four hundred years from now, people will still be talking about Mrs. Thatcher. And it will be because of that profound shift in the way government thinks. (Quoted by Hughes, 1988)

This represents a very important strand of liberal New Right thinking. Sir Alfred Sherman, a former adviser to the Conservative Party, wrote an article in *The Daily Telegraph* on 6 August 1987 advocating the privatization of all schools.

A key point of disagreement among those members of the New Right specializing in educational matters and one which reflects essential differences between the conservative and liberal wings of the movement concerns the desirability or otherwise of a centrally imposed national curriculum. As long ago as 1975, Dr. Rhodes Boyson was arguing, from a neo-conservative standpoint, for a nationally enforced curriculum which would have the support of parents:

> The malaise in schools in Britain has followed from a breakdown in accepted curriculum and traditional values. There was little concern about either political control or parental choice so long as there was an 'understood' curriculum which was followed by

every school. Schools may have differed in efficiency but their common values or curriculum were broadly acceptable. The present disillusionment of parents arises from their resentment that their children's education now depends upon the lottery of the school to which they are directed. Standards decline because both measurement and comparisons are impossible when aims and curriculum become widely divergent . . . These problems can be solved only by making schools again accountable to some authority outside them. The necessary sanction is either a nationally enforced curriculum or parental choice or a combination of both. (Boyson, 1975, p. 141)

The Hillgate Group also believes in the desirability of a national curriculum, provided it upholds the values of a traditional education:

We believe that a national curriculum is essential . . . The curriculum should have a core: reading, writing and arithmetic. It should also have a settled range of proven subjects from which secondary education may be constructed. The tradition which we have inherited is, we believe, a good one. Foreign languages, mathematics, science, history and literature are of lasting value to the person who learns them. Such subjects involve a testable and coveted body of knowledge which it is the duty of any educational system to pass on from generation to generation, and which can broaden the mind and the experience of anyone who has the good fortune to be initiated into it. (Hillgate Group, 1986, p. 7)

For others who belong to the liberal New Right, the imposition of any sort of national core curriculum is simply not compatible with the idea of providing greater variety and choice in education. They have always favoured as much diversity as possible both *between* schools and *within* schools. In an article in *The Times Educational Supplement* on 18 September 1987, Dennis O'Keeffe argued that the national curriculum was clearly an anomaly, a logical inconsistency:

All the economic successes since 1979 have come from shifting power to the consumer and trusting markets to do the rest . . . The government should have considered financial changes such as tax relief which would allow more parents effective rights of exit from the system: this would create competition and generate efficiency. The government believes in capitalism. Why then does it favour coercive education? The surest advantage of markets is that they cannot be controlled politically.

Similar reservations were expressed by Stuart Sexton, Director of the Education Unit of the Institute of Economic Affairs and a former adviser to Mark Carlisle and Sir Keith Joseph, in a letter to *The Independent* in November 1987:

> One of the government's mistakes is over the national curriculum, which is not a natural development from earlier Conservative policies and enactments. National curriculum proposals are really old hat, going back at least to the late 1960s, dusted down off the shelf for each successive Secretary of State to consider. The nearest we need to a national curriculum is the reassertion of the three Rs on behalf of parents, which was inherent in Sir Keith Joseph's paper *Better Schools*... The best 'national curriculum' is that resulting from the exercise of true parental choice by parents and children acting collectively, and being provided collectively by governors and teacher in response to that choice. The substitution for that freely adopted curriculum, geared to the needs of the particular children in question, of a government-imposed curriculum is poor second best. (Letter to *The Independent*, 19 November 1987)

Sexton reiterated his views in an article published in *The Times* in the following May:

> The government's proposals will put the schools' curriculum into a straitjacket, removing all flexibility and retarding the continual process of improvement and updating. Once these proposals are put into tablets of legislative stone, it will be years before the bureaucracy wakes up to its own mistakes and to necessary changes... The opportunity remains for the Government to respond to its critics by returning to a national curriculum dictated by the 'market' instead of a *nationalized* one dictated by government. (Sexton, 1988)

Former Secretary of State for Education and Science Sir Keith (now Lord) Joseph also argued that the government's plans would put the secondary school curriculum into 'too tight a straitjacket' in a debate in the House of Lords in April 1988. He told peers as the House began its second reading debate on the Education Reform Bill that he strongly supported most of its proposals but joined critics in declaring that the proposed core curriculum was far too rigid (reported in *The Guardian*, 19 April 1988). And this view was also shared by the Centre for Policy Studies which was Joseph's own creation. In the CPS pamphlet *Correct Core: Simple Curricula for English,*

Maths and Science, published in March 1988, Sheila Lawlor argued that a national curriculum should be confined to the three subjects of the title; beyond this, individual schools should have freedom what and how to teach.

Despite the marked reservations of the neo-liberals, there is a very real sense in which the National Curriculum is not necessarily incompatible with devolution of power or with market principles. As I have argued elsewhere (Chitty, 1988, p. 46), the Curriculum does, after all, act as justification for a massive programme of national testing at 7, 11, 14 and 16 which will, in turn, provide evidence to parents for the desirability or otherwise of individual schools. As Cordingley and Wilby have observed (1987)

> In some senses, a market system demands attainment targets, with, in addition, the publication of results. A market can work effectively only if there is maximum consumer information. Without national tests and test results, parents would have little hard information on which to base choices. (p. 8)

The Centre for Policy Studies might well retort that the same result could be achieved with a national curriculum restricted to English, maths and science.

As we saw in chapter 6, the New Right is also confused and divided over its attitude towards vocational studies. New Right academics dislike, for example, the main methodological and cross curricular concerns of TVEI, but they are prepared to welcome any initiative which circumvents the power of the LEAs and are happy to support vocational studies provided they are restricted to those pupils who, in their view, cannot and indeed do not wish to be educated (see Hillgate Group, 1986, p. 15; Quicke, 1988, pp. 15–16).

Not only are there differences among those who would see themselves as members of the New Right, but it is also clear that the Prime Minister and her right-wing advisers have not been *totally* successful in colonizing the DES bureaucracy. Kenneth Baker has made a determined effort to preserve a certain degree of independence for the DES machine. In an interview with *The Independent*, published on 14 September 1987, Mrs. Thatcher looked forward to a situation where 'most schools' would choose to opt out of the state system; whereas Mr. Baker argued on television (2 November 1987) that only a *minority* of schools would choose to do so. Mrs. Thatcher hoped that popular comprehensive schools which opted out of the system would soon elect to change their character and become selective; whereas Mr. Baker expected most comprehensives to remain comprehensive (*The Observer*, 20 September 1987). Finally, a leaked letter from the Prime Minister's Private Secretary to the Secretary of State's Office, dated 21 January 1988 (reproduced in full in *The Independent*, 10 March 1988), showed that Mr. Baker did not have the Prime Minister's full support in welcoming the major recommendations of the Task Group on Assessment and Testing (see Lawton, 1989, chapter 7).

What of the Future?

The Education Reform Act (with 238 clauses and thirteen schedules) received the royal assent on 29 July 1988 and was much longer than the Education Reform Bill (with 147 clauses and eleven schedules) which had been introduced into the House of Commons in November 1987. The Act was described by Peter Wilby and Ngaio Crequer in *The Independent* (28 July 1988) as 'a Gothic monstrosity of legislation', its scope having grown remarkably during its passage through Parliament, with most of the ninety-one additional clauses being tabled by the government itself. Yet the legislation in its final form showed little sign of being influenced by the many trenchant criticisms of the original Bill. It emerged virtually unscathed from 370 hours of often heated debate in the House of Commons and the House of Lords. Only in a limited number of areas was the government forced to take note of the views of its critics, notably in having to make religious education the one and only *basic* subject in the National Curriculum (already discussed in this chapter) and in having to modify the arrangements for allowing a school to opt out of the state system and acquire grant-maintained status. On this latter point, the Lords voted by a majority of nineteen votes to insist that the opting-out process must be backed by a majority of parents *eligible to vote* — rather than simply by a majority of those taking part in the voting. This was later modified by the government so that as the Act now stands, the result of a ballot on opting-out is determined by a simple majority of those voting, so long as 50 per cent of the registered parents have taken part. But if less than 50 per cent vote, a second ballot must be held within fourteen days of the result of the first ballot. The outcome of the second ballot is conclusive, irrespective of turn-out[18].

The central purpose of the Education Reform Act is that power should be gathered to the centre and, at the same time, devolved on to school and parent, both processes being at the expense of mediating bureaucracies, whether elected or not. On the one hand, the Act opens up education to the forces of competition; alongside this process, the arrangements for the school curriculum are designed to ensure that pupils will not be exposed to controversial material which challenges accepted values and ways of thinking.

Stuart Maclure attaches particular importance to the provisions in the 1988 Act for financial delegation, the object of which is to make local authorities distribute funds to their primary and secondary schools by means of a weighted, *per capita* formula. Governing bodies are then made responsible for controlling the budgets delegated to them. Maclure sees this development, viewed in conjunction with the provisions for open enrolment and opting out, as a subtle means of adapting the education system in such a way as to make a future transition to vouchers possible without undue disruption:

> The financial delegation provisions have a direct connection with those on open enrolment . . . because they effectively ensure that funding follows the pupil; and with grant-maintained schools . . . because they provide a mechanism for determining how much money the government can recoup from a local authority if one of its schools opts out . . . The result is to create a situation in which the resources — *per capita* payments — which a school receives depend directly on the choices which parents exercise. The school has ceased to be 'maintained' as an institution independently of those choices. Under schemes of delegation, the *per capita* payments are still paid to the school; but the circumstances have been engineered in which it would be a relatively simple matter to give the money directly to the parents instead — in the form of vouchers or warrants — thereby completing the transfer of power from the institutions and the local authority to the parents. (Maclure, 1988, pp. 42–3)

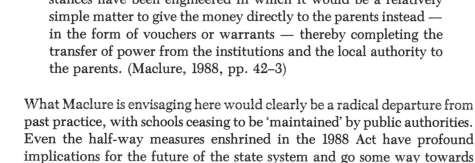

What Maclure is envisaging here would clearly be a radical departure from past practice, with schools ceasing to be 'maintained' by public authorities. Even the half-way measures enshrined in the 1988 Act have profound implications for the future of the state system and go some way towards satisfying the demands of the voucher lobby[19]. It is, of course, fair to concede that there have been few periods since the passing of the 1944 Act when there has not been conflict between central government and individual local authorities. What was rarely questioned, however, was the essential validity of a national education system, locally administered. Now the system itself is under threat; and it would appear that the 1988 Act is part of a clearly designed strategy to undermine existing structures. 'The return of a Conservative government today', forecast Peter Wilby writing in *The Independent* on 11 June 1987, 'will mean the break-up of the state education system that has existed since 1944'.

Yet, despite the confidence, some might say arrogance, of government ministers and right-wing politicians, it can be argued that, for a number of reasons, the government will find it comparatively difficult to implement all its plans. For one thing, the 1988 Act does not share the advantage of its 1944 predecessor in being the outcome of a lengthy period of genuine consultation. No attempt has been made to create a consensus among teachers, educationists, union leaders, local authority administrators and the churches. At the same time, there is a wide-spread belief that the Act has been introduced for *political* rather than *educational* reasons. In her interview with the editor of *The Daily Mail* in May 1987, Mrs. Thatcher made it clear that her education programme had a central part to play in the realization of her ultimate objectives which were to see 'the elimination of socialism from Britain' and the creation of 'a new political alignment': a two-party system with a Conservative Party 'fundamentally committed to liberty, effort and responsibility' and a Labour Party 'committed to the high ideals of freedom and democracy' but 'totally non-socialist' (*The Daily Mail*, 13 May 1987). Speaking to about 200 members of the Conservative backbench 1922 Committee a few weeks after the Conservative victory in the 1987 election, the Prime Minister described her new Education Bill as 'the key to the future'. She said she regarded it as the biggest and most important legislation of the forthcoming parliamentary session. Above all, it would help to secure a fourth electoral victory:

> Just as we gained great political support in the last election from people who had acquired their own homes and shares, so we shall secure still further our political base in 1991/92 by giving people a real say in education and housing. (Quoted in *The Independent*, 17 July 1987)

The 1988 Act might well be 'the key to the future', but it is not clear that the government is sufficiently aware of the possible consequences of weakening the structure of elected representative local government. As Tomlinson (1988) has pointed out:

> It must ... be open to question whether the new-style governing bodies and the responsibilities to be devolved upon them will be attended with the success necessary to achieve the Bill's objectives. The delegation to governors of powers of staff appointment and dismissal is problematic (especially while retaining the local education authority as employer). The consequent loss of opportunity for strategic deployment of teachers by the local education

authority is unproven as a better way to optimize the use of scarce human resources. And the prospect of school appointments being decided at the scale of the parish pump is not encouraging. The retreat from such procedures has been part of the development of the local education authority this century. The schemes of devolved financial management remain to be constructed, still less implemented and proved. The procedures and systems needed to support grant-maintained schools do not yet exist and those for city technology colleges are yet elementary. (pp. 11–12)

Alongside these reservations, there remains the very real doubt as to whether the larger number of school governors, each bearing greater financial and managerial responsibility, can be recruited from the economic and social communities around the schools. The Act's ambitions in this respect could be said to imply the existence of a 'political nation' whose actuality remains to be proved.

The opting-out proposals in the Act pose particular problems as far as local planning is concerned. Interestingly, of the thirty or so secondary schools which have held opt-out ballots in the first six months following the passing of the 1988 Act, a majority have been those threatened by closure or amalgamation under local plans for reorganization[20]. The Shadow Education Secretary, Jack Straw, has commented that 'opting-out is effectively paralyzing the sensible reorganization of schools which Mr. Baker himself has demanded' (*The Guardian*, 23 February 1989). Moreover, the organization of post-16 education will be particularly difficult in the future, since any attempt to rationalize sixth-form provision in a given area by, for example, the creation of a system of tertiary colleges, will be negated by the arrival of an 11–18 CTC or the decision of a comprehensive school, threatened with the loss of its sixth form, to opt out of the system altogether and acquire grant-maintained status.

Nor can it be easily shown that the opting-out provision will necessarily widen parental choice. It can be argued that the present government is interested in creating competition not choice. The provision for open enrolment and for opting out will cause some schools to expand at the expense of others. A number of very good schools may well be allowed to wither away and die if they find it impossible to compete with neighbouring establishments. Nor will parental choice be enhanced if large numbers of successful grant-maintained schools are allowed to change their selection procedures in a bid to further upgrade their image.

Furthermore, the possibility that the emphasis on so-called parental choice and the modification of the criteria which determine pupil admission limits could lead to a system of racially-segregated schools was highlighted in the recent controversy in Dewsbury and should give the government serious cause for concern. Here was a case where a group of parents in Dewsbury, West Yorkshire campaigned for eleven months in 1987/88 to send their 7-and 8-year-old children to local junior schools where the majority of the children were white instead of to the school which they had been allocated where 85 per cent of the pupils were of Asian origin. The ensuing court case ended in July 1988 when the Kirklees Education Authority acceded to the parents' demands. 'Triumph for parent power' proclaimed the headline on the front page of *The Daily Mail* (13 July 1988): 'Education chiefs surrender in school choice battle'. It was successfully argued on the parents' behalf that the Council had failed to publish clear guidance on school catchment areas or to identify the criteria which determined pupil admission limits. Yet the grave implications of this case went far beyond the observance of such bureaucratic niceties. As Howard Roberts, Secretary of the local National Union of Teachers Association, commented at the time: 'The real issue, about multi-cultural education, has gone by default' (reported in *The Independent*, 13 July 1988).

As far as city technology colleges are concerned, it can be argued that the original concept has been changed dramatically in the light of severe recent setbacks (see Chitty, 1989). This is particularly true in the case of funding and the provision of suitable sites. Of 1800 firms approached for help with financial contributions, fewer than twenty have so far responded positively. The result is that the Exchequer is now having to bear most of the capital costs. In the case of the CTC in Nottingham, for example, due to open in the autumn of 1989, the government has agreed to donate £9.05 million from the Treasury to augment the £1.4 million which has been subscribed by public companies. As *The Times Educational Supplement* commented on 27 May 1988:

> Just what sort of a public education initiative is it which puts up £9 million from public funds for a private school? And just what sort of priorities are being pursued when one, as yet unbuilt, private school gets £9.05 million, while the county of Nottinghamshire's entire capital allocation is less than £2.5 million?

Since only £28 million has been forthcoming from industry, the state has been forced to set aside £86 million of taxpayer's money. The government will have spent £33 million on two or three CTCs in 1989 — some £3 million more than the money set aside to facilitate the introduction of the National Curriculum into all 30,000 schools in the country. More officers within the DES have been set aside to deal with the CTCs than have been delegated to cope with the consequences of abolishing the Inner London Education Authority with its 1000 schools and 250,000 pupils. And in answer to a parliamentary question from Jack Straw in June 1988, the Education Secretary said that 16.7 DES personnel were employed in the CTC Unit at a monthly salary cost of £25,000 (*The Times Educational Supplement*, 17 June 1988). Yet, despite this feverish activity, only five CTCs will actually be in operation by the end of 1991. And in an interview with *The Times Educational Supplement* in June 1988, Cyril Taylor, special CTC adviser to Kenneth Baker and Chairman of the CTC Trust, admitted that all the original plans were doomed to fail. It had been diffi-cult to meet the government's target for industrial sponsorship; and the costs of refurbishing and equipping redundant schools and green-field sites were, he said, 'woefully underestimated by the Department of Education and Science'. The aim now was to buy up schools already in use and 'phase in' the CTCs over a period of up to six years. Mr. Taylor thought that this would help the government to rescue its project while at the same time 'broadening' the CTC concept:

> We are approaching councils like Croydon, Bexley and Kent and asking them to sell us the most deprived or failing school . . . Instead of creating a new school which then threatens others, we try to make the existing school better . . . The CTCs are no longer a pilot scheme. I predict that eventually one in four secondary schools will become CTCs. (*The Times Educational Supplement*, 17 June 1988)

This would explain why the Haberdashers' Aske's Schools in Lewisham were offered £4 million for refurbishment and resources provided parents agreed to turn them into CTCs (*The Times Educational Supplement*, 5 August 1988). It also explains why great efforts have been made to re-organize Riverside Comprehensive School which serves Thamesmead in Bexley, despite the fact that it can in no way be described as a 'failing school' and regardless of a massive vote by parents (89 per cent to 11 per cent) in favour of keeping it as a thriving state school (*The Times Educational Supplement*, 24 June 1988).[21]

A delegate to the Young Conservative Conference meeting in Southport in February 1989 received rapturous applause when he told his right-wing audience that it was time both to 'proclaim education a com-modity to be bought and sold' and to 'disclaim the Marxian view that education is a right' (*The Guardian*, 13 February 1989). Yet there are many who would argue that a market in education is a contradiction in terms.

Far from being a commodity to be purchased and consumed, education should be seen as 'one of the processes by which more and more individuals and groups in society might be enfranchised and drawn into full membership of that society' (Tomlinson, 1988, p. 9). Nor is disillusionment with the government's market values necessarily restricted to long-established critics of government policy. Speaking in the House of Commons in February 1989, George Walden, a former Conservative Education Minister with responsibility for higher education, warned against the 'indiscriminate application' of the government's free market philosophy:

> There is a great danger in this country that when we get an idea, we go on and on with it. We did that with egalitarianism and caused the damage that we now all know about. Now we have a new idea called market forces, and like children with a pot of paint, we daub it all over the damned place. If we do that in education, or in broadcasting, we shall cause infinite damage to the people least well placed to cope with it. (Reported in *The Times Educational Supplement*, 17 February 1989)

This is perhaps the major criticism levelled against the establishment of grant-maintained schools and city technology colleges: that quality education for a few will be secured at the price of a decent education for the majority.

As far as the requirements of the National Curriculum are concerned, there are a number of possible teacher reactions: ranging from opposition or resistance at one extreme to compliant acquiescence at the other. Somewhere in between come a large number of proposals for modifying or manipulating the National Curriculum framework to make it compatible with recent significant initiatives in curriculum planning. According to O'Connor (1989), the chief purpose of these proposals is to ensure that 'the professionals can, in the short term at least, live with the National Curriculum, and, in the long term, come to feel that they own it, which is the prerequisite of any effective teaching and learning'. Even the Education Secretary has shown some awareness of the need to encourage the enterprise and initiative of teachers. In his Notes of Guidance to the Cox Committee on the Teaching of English which was set up in April 1988, he argued that:

> Within the overall programme of study, there must be space to accommodate the enterprise of teachers, offering them sufficient flexibility in the choice of content to adapt what they teach to the needs of the individual pupil, and scope for different teaching approaches. (DES, 1988, p. 67)

It is at the higher levels of secondary school that teachers will face very real problems in trying to implement the 1988 Act. With one eye on the National Curriculum, many schools are also having to come to terms with the Technical and Vocational Education Initiative extension. Some may look for new modular or integrated examination courses to help them fit all the various demands into the school week. Others may try to fit the subject-based National Curriculum into the broader framework of TVEI with its powerful emphasis on new subject areas and cross-curricular themes.

Despite initial reservations, many teachers have worked hard to transform recent pre-vocational and vocational initiatives into genuinely worthwhile and educational experiences for their pupils. Now they face the prospect of seeing this work either marginalized or ignored. According to Pring, White and Brockington:

> What has been remarkable about rcent pre-vocational and vocational developments, despite the critics of TVEI, YTS and CPVE, is the response that they have evoked in schools throughout the country — a kind of catalyst that has enabled educationally valuable courses to be developed. It has meant a major shift in attitudes, in teaching styles, in curriculum content, and in the organization of schools. But the process is already well established in many local education authorities, with schools committed to an educational programme that stresses the value of a broad range of experiences, achievements and skills ... This process needs to be carefully nurtured, especially in the light of the 1988 Education Act ... There is a real danger that much of what is currently exciting and creative in schools will be destroyed as the educational clock is put back many decades by the 1988 Act. (Pring, White and Brockington, 1988, pp. 60–1)

The Government would appear to have changed its mind quite dramatically over the past five years, from lending its support to a programme of narrow vocationalism for the majority of young people to laying down the content of a curriculum that is decidedly subject-based and academic. What seems to have got lost along the way is the concept of an 'entitlement curriculum' as outlined by Her Majesty's Inspectorate between 1977 and 1983 which saw curriculum development in terms of a synthesis between the academic, the vocational, the technical and the practical. It remains to be seen whether teachers can preserve the balance between individual and social needs that many would hold to be an essential characteristic of any worthwhile educational experience.

As long ago as 1961, Raymond Williams argued in *The Long*

Revolution that, once the privileges and barriers of an inherited kind had been abolished, we would have to choose between two competing philosophies of the organization of education and society:

> It is a question of whether we can grasp the real nature of our society, or whether we persist in social and educational patterns based on a limited ruling class, a middle professional class, a large operative class, cemented by forces that cannot be challenged and will not be changed. The privileges and barriers, of an inherited kind, will in any case go down. It is only a question of whether we replace them by the free play of the market, or by a public education designed to express and create the values of an educated democracy and a common culture. (p. 176)

The education debate may, therefore, not be new, but it needs now to be addressed with a greater sense of urgency than ever before. As far as secondary schooling is concerned, the 1988 Act can be seen as a frontal attack on locally organized systems of comprehensive education. Those who are still committed to the principles of comprehensive schooling have to seize upon and exploit the contradictions and tensions within New Right and therefore government thinking. The question mark in the title of this book remains firmly in place and will not easily be dislodged.

Notes

1 Interview with Sheila Browne, 24 July 1986.
2 Various aspects of the TVEI proposal are discussed in chapters 5 and 6.
3 In 1985/86, for example, in accordance with the provisions of the Assisted Places Scheme introduced in 1981, around 24,500 pupils were sent to various public schools at an estimated cost to the taxpayer of £39.45m, two-fifths of them having their fees paid in full (figures quoted by Labour Research Department, 1987, p. 20).
4 The speech was considered controversial because it appeared to argue that the nation was moving towards degeneration on account of the high and rising proportion of children being born to mothers 'least fitted to bring children into the world':

> These are mothers who were first pregnant in adolescence in social classes four and five (the unskilled and lower skilled). Many of these girls are unmarried; many are deserted or divorced or soon will be . . . Some are of low intelligence; most of low educational attainment. They are unlikely to be able to give children the stable emotional background, the consistent combination of love and firmness which are more important than riches. They are producing problem children, the future unmarried mothers, delinquents, denizens of our borstals, subnormal educational establishments, prisons, hostels for drifters. Yet these mothers, the under-twenties in many cases, single parents from classes four and

five, are now producing a third of all births. A high proportion of these births are a tragedy for the mother, the child and for us . . . If we do nothing, the nation moves towards degeneration, however many resources we pour into preventive work and the over-burdened educational system. (Reported in *The Sunday Times*, 20 October 1974)

Sir Keith proposed that birth control facilities should be extended — presumably free of charge — to the destitute, poor and inadequate.

5   Further evidence of the serious consequences of the under-funding of the state system was provided by HMI in their 1986 report on the effects of local authority expenditure policies on education provision in England:

> The condition of much of the accommodation used by pupils, students, teachers and lecturers continues to deteriorate. Last year's report warned that without urgent attention, the cost of putting things right would become prohibitive. There has been no such improvement. In fact, there has been no improvement overall in the state of school buildings since 1981, and the current programmes of maintenance in many LEAs suggest that the situation is likely to continue to worsen . . .
>
> In some schools and colleges, the conditions in which teaching and learning take place adversely affect the quality of pupils' and students' work and do nothing to encourage their sense of enjoyment and pride in their school or college. In many more, the environment is shabby and uninviting and does little to stimulate learning or to impress parents or other visitors. The cost of attending to these problems . . . . is mounting and has now reached proportions where it is difficult to see how on present funding the education service can prevent further decline, let alone reverse the situation . . . .
>
> There are sharp polarizations between schools in different parts of the country and within the same local authority. Where hard decisions about priorities have to be made at LEA level, it tends to be building maintenance, redecoration and furniture replacement programmes that suffer. At school level, it is the least able in all types of school and top junior and early year secondary pupils who appear to bear the brunt of reduced or inappropriate provision. In addition, many schools are finding it increasingly difficult to replace old books, equipment and furniture; to implement curricular change; and to respond to planned changes in assessment and examination procedures. (DES, 1986c, pp. 9, 10 and 11)

6   As Simon has pointed out (1986, p. 24), the wording of the leader in *The Daily Telegraph* was somewhat reminiscent of Macbeth's famous soliloquy in Act 1, Scene 7 of Shakespeare's play: 'Sir Keith has announced he is going soon anyway, and what will have to be done in the end would be better done quickly'. 'Is the leader writer here calling for assassination?' Simon asks.

7   This is discussed in some detail in chapter 7.

8   To take a fairly recent example: having interviewed the Education Secretary for a profile in *The Independent* in August 1988, Colin Brown reflected that 'in his replies . . . there was little attempt to conceal the fact that he sees the Education Reform Act as a test of his qualities for the leadership when the time comes' (*The Independent*, 23 August 1988).

9   As we have already seen in the Introduction, Professor Brian Griffiths has certainly been one of Mrs. Thatcher's most influential policy advisers. The same article in *The Sunday Times* goes on to suggest that after the 1987 general election, there was a scheme to make Griffiths a life peer in the Dissolution Honours List and then a

Junior Minister at the Department of Education. But, or so we are told, 'Kenneth Baker . . . strongly disliked the thought of having within his Department a spy from No. 10'. (*The Sunday Times*, 26 July 1987)

10 For a full discussion of the origins of this Initiative, see chapter 5.

11 Mr. Merridale made this confession at a press conference to launch the Conservative Education Association (CEA) at the end of March 1987 (reported in *The Times Educational Supplement*, 3 April 1987).

12 This was later modified to the ages of 7, 11, 14 and 16.

13 A detailed account of this interview was given by John Clare in *The Times* (8 December 1986) with the headline: 'Baker unfolds far-reaching school reform'.

14 Kenneth Baker's request for comments and advice from interested parties drew more than 20,000 responses. Mr. Baker refused to make this material available to the public, but an interesting selection was collected together by Julian Haviland in *Take Care, Mr. Baker!*, published in the spring of 1988. The government was clearly embarrassed by the generally hostile response to most of its proposals and tried to create the impression that there was, in fact, popular support for its major reforms. For example: Mrs. Angela Rumbold, the Minister of State, told a supporter on 19 January 1988 that of 11,790 representations on the National Curriculum examined in the DES, only 1536 were opposed in principle. Her answer was accurate but it was also incomplete. Not one of the responses actually endorsed without reservation the structure for the curriculum which the Government was proposing. (Haviland, 1988)

15 It is also true that city technology colleges do not have to adhere to the national curriculum framework in a strict sense (see DES, 1987d, p. 15).

16 An example of this would be *After the New Right*, Nick Bosanquet's excellent study of the so-called liberal New Right, published in 1983.

17 In its evidence to the DES prior to the publication of the Education Reform Bill in November 1987, the Centre for Policy Studies argued that if there had to be a national curriculum in this country, it should not apply to those schools which opted out of the local authority control:

> Grant-maintained schools should not be subject to the legal framework of a National Curriculum, but should be in exactly the same position in relation to a National Curriculum as an independent school . . . We believe . . . that the best way of deciding the school curriculum (mix of subjects, teaching styles, aims and characters of schools) is by the market. This serves the independent sector well. Schools are subject to HM Inspection, but within this limit, are free to experiment and provide the variety of choice that a pluralistic society requires. The government may wish to issue guidelines, but independent and grant-maintained schools should not be subject to statutory requirements to follow them. (Haviland, 1988, pp. 106–7)

18 New guidelines on opting-out were issued by the Education Secretary in February 1989 after a speech to the Young Conservatives' Conference at Stockport in which he claimed that Labour councils were using 'bully-boy tactics', including threats to headteachers' careers and school funding, in an attempt to prevent schools from opting for grant-maintained status. According to Mr. Baker:

> . . . there is an unscrupulous war of misrepresentation and intimidation which it appears is being waged by some Labour local education authorities, with the connivance and even assistance of some Labour MPs . . . This is the sort of blatant intimidation which the Labour Party has countenanced upon picket-lines and in town halls. It is the bully-boy tactics which have made the Labour Party unelectable for the past ten years. (Reported in *The Independent*, 13 February 1989)

19 The IEA paperback *The Riddle of the Voucher*, already referred to in chapter 7, put forward a number of suggestions for half-way houses and stepping-stones — changes in the way education was organized which fell short of the introduction of a proper voucher scheme, but which would pave the way for such a move later on. One of the IEA proposals was for the central government grant-in-aid for education to local authorities to be paid as a *per capita* payment for each pupil. This was a variation of the scheme which eventually found its way into chapter 3 of the 1988 Act. What both schemes have in common is the establishment of something approaching a fee-structure. Once this is established, the advocates of the voucher believe it will be comparatively simple to proceed to the next stage and make the *per capita* payment to the parent instead of to the school.

20 Skegness Grammar School in Lincolnshire and Audenshaw High School in Tameside, Greater Manchester were the first two schools to be given grant-maintained status by the Secretary of State, the decision being announced in February 1989. Tameside Council, which wanted to close Audenshaw High, has been forced to abandon its reorganization plans, saying it can no longer afford to put any school up for closure. (Reported in *The Guardian*, 23 February 1989)

21 By the beginning of 1989, the parents of Thamesmead were able to celebrate a remarkable victory. The CTC sponsoring body had withdrawn its offer of funding; and it was decided that Riverside should remain a thriving community comprehensive school.

Bibliography

ABBS, P. *et al* (1987) 'Criticism of the proposed national curriculum', *The Independent*, 14 October.

ALDRICH, R. (1988) 'The National Curriculum: An historical perspective', in LAWTON, D. and CHITTY, C. (Eds) *The National Curriculum*, Bedford Way Paper 33, Institute of Education, University of London, pp. 21–33.

ALDRICH, R. and LEIGHTON, P. (1985) *Education: Time for a New Act?*, Bedford Way Paper 23, Institute of Education, University of London.

ALTHUSSER, L. (1971) 'Ideology and ideological state apparatuses', in *Lenin and Philosophy and Other Essays*, London, New Left Books, pp. 123–73.

AULD, R. (1976) *William Tyndale Junior and Infants Schools Public Inquiry: A Report to the Inner London Education Authority by Robin Auld, QC*, London, Inner London Education Authority, July.

BALL, S. J. (1981) *Beachside Comprehensive: A Case Study of Secondary Schooling*, Cambridge, Cambridge University Press.

BALL, S. J. (1984) 'Introduction: Comprehensives in crisis?', in BALL, S. J. (Ed) *Comprehensive Schooling: A Reader*, Lewes, Falmer Press, pp. 1–26.

BANTOCK, G. H. (1975) 'Progressivism and the content of education', in COX, C. B. and BOYSON, R. (Eds) *Black Paper 1975: The Fight for Education*, London, Dent, pp. 14–20.

BARNES, A. (1977) 'Decision making on the curriculum in Britain', in GLATTER, R. (Ed) *Control of the Curriculum: Issues and Trends in Britain and Europe*, Proceedings of the fifth annual conference of the British Educational Administration Society, London, September 1976, Studies in Education (new series) 4, Institute of Education, University of London.

BARON, G. and HOWELL, D. A. (1974) *The Government and Management of Schools*, London, Athlone Press.

BATES, I. (1984) 'From vocational guidance to life skills: Historical perspectives on careers education', in BATES, I. *et al.* (Eds) *Schooling for the Dole? The New Vocationalism*, London, Macmillan, pp. 170–219.

BECK, J. (1983) 'Accountability, industry and education — Reflections on some aspects of the educational and industrial policies of the Labour administration of 1974–79', in AHIER, J. and FLUDE, M. (Eds) *Contemporary Education Policy*, London, Croom Helm, pp. 211–32.

BELL, R., FOWLER, G. and LITTLE, K. (1973) *Education in Great Britian and Ireland: A Source Book*, London, Routledge & Kegan Paul in association with the Open University Press.

BELSEY, A. (1 986) 'The new right, social order and civil liberties', in LEVITAS, R. (Ed) *The Ideology of the New Right*, Cambridge, Polity Press.

BENN, C. and SIMON, B. (1972) *Half Way There: Report on the British Comprehensive School Reform* (2nd edn), Harmondsworth, Penguin.

BENN, T. (1987) 'British politics 1945–87: One of four perspectives', in HENNESSY, P. and SELDON, A. (Eds) *Ruling Performance: British Governments from Attlee to Thatcher*, Oxford, Basil Blackwell, pp. 301–8.

BENNETT, N. (1976) *Teaching Styles and Pupil Progress*, London, Open Books.

BERNBAUM, G. (1979) 'Editorial introduction', in BERNBAUM, G. (Ed) *Schooling in Decline*, London, Macmillan, pp. 1–16.

BLACKBURN, F. (1954) *George Tomlinson*, London, Heinemann.

BLAKE, R. (1966) *Disraeli*, London, Eyre & Spottiswoode.

BLISHEN, E. (1957) 'The potentialities of secondary modern school pupils', in SIMON, B. (Ed) *New Trends in English Education*, London, Macgibbon & Kee, pp. 74–82.

BOLTON, E. (1987a) *The Control of the Curriculum*, Occasional Paper 3, School of Education, University of Durham.

BOLTON, E. (1987b) 'The debate on a national agreement on the curriculum and its implications for standards', *NUT Education Review*, 1, 1, spring, pp. 8–13.

BOSANQUET, N. (1983) *After the New Right*, London, Heinemann.

BOURDIEU, P. and PASSERON, J. C. (1977) *Reproduction in Education, Society and Culture*, London, Sage.

BOWLES, S. and GINTIS, H. (1976) *Schooling in Capitalist America: Educational Reform and the Contradictions of Economic Life*, London, Routledge & Kegan Paul.

BOYLE, E. (1972) 'The politics of secondary school reorganization: Some reflections', *Journal of Educational Administration and History*, 4, 2, June, pp. 28–38.

BOYLE, E. and CROSLAND, A. (1971) *The Politics of Education*, Harmondsworth, Penguin.

BOYSON, R. (1969) 'The essential conditions for the success of a comprehensive school', in COX, C. B. and DYSON, A. E. (Eds) *Black Paper Two: The Crisis in Education*, London, Critical Quarterly Society, pp. 57–62.

BOYSON, R. (1975a) 'The developing case for the educational voucher', in COX, C. B. and BOYSON, R. (Eds) *Black Paper 1975: The Fight for Education*, London, Dent, pp. 27–8.

BOYSON, R. (1975b) *The Crisis in Education*, London, Woburn Press.

BRIAULT, E. (1976) 'A distributed system of educational administration: An international viewpoint', *International Review of Education*, 22, 4, pp. 429–39.

BRIAULT, E. and SMITH, F. (1980) *Falling Rolls in Secondary Schools*, Windsor, NFER.

BROADFOOT, P. (1979) *Assessment, Schools and Society*, London, Methuen.

BROUDY, H. S., SMITH, B. O. and BURNETT, J. R. (1964) *Democracy and Excellence in American Secondary Education*, Chicago, IL, Rand McNally.

BROWNE, S. (1977) 'Curriculum: An HMI view', *Trends in Education*, 2, autumn, pp. 37–43.

BTEC (1986) *The Framework Description of BTEC — City and Guilds Pre-vocational Programmes for Pupils Aged 14–16*, London, Joint Unit for 14–16 Pre-vocational Education, May.

BURGESS, R. G. (1983) *Experiencing Comprehensive Education: A Study of Bishop McGregor School*, London, Methuen.

CALLAGHAN, J. (1987) *Time and Chance*, London, Collins.

CANNON, C. (1964) 'Social studies in secondary schools', *Educational Review*, 17, pp. 18–30.

CARNOY, M. (1974) *Education as Cultural Imperialism*, New York, David McKay Co.

CBI (1976) *CBI Education and Training Bulletin*, 6, 2, May.

CCCS (1981) *Unpopular Education: Schooling and Social Democracy in England Since 1944*, London, Hutchinson.

CHITTY, C. (1969) 'Non-streaming in comprehensives: A review', *Comprehensive Education*, 12, summer, pp. 2–8.

CHITTY, C. (1979) 'Inside the secondary school: Problems and prospects', in RUBINSTEIN, D. (Ed) *Education and Equality*, Harmondsworth, Penguin, pp. 150–63.

CHITTY, C. (1981) 'Why comprehensive schools?', *Forum*, 24, 1, autumn, pp. 4–6.

CHITTY, C. (1986) 'TVEI: The MSC's trojan horse', in BENN, C. and FAIRLEY, J. (Eds) *Challenging the MSC: On Jobs, Education and Training*, London, Pluto Press, pp. 76–98.

CHITTY, C. (1987a) 'The commodification of education', *Forum*, 29, 3, summer, pp. 66–9.

CHITTY, C. (1987b) 'City technology colleges: A bad idea in a bad cause', in CHITTY, C. (Ed) *Aspects of Vocationalism*, London, Post-16 Education Centre, Institute of Education, University of London, pp. 55–70.

CHITTY, C. (1988) 'Two models of a national curriculum: Origins and interpretation', in LAWTON, D. and CHITTY, C. (Eds) *The National Curriculum*, Bedford Way Paper 33, Institute of Education, University of London, pp. 34–48.

CHITTY, C. (1989) 'City technology colleges: A strategy for elitism', *Forum*, 31, 2, spring, pp. 37–40.

CHITTY, C. and REIN, N. (1969) 'Blackwards', *Tribune*, 14 November.

CHITTY, C. and WORGAN, J. (1987) 'TVEI: Origins and transformation', in CHITTY, C. (Ed) *Aspects of Vocationalism*, London, Post-16 Education Centre, Institute of Education, University of London, pp. 19–36.

CLARE, J. (1986a) 'Tomorrow's schools created at the expense of today's?', *The Listener*, 23 October.

CLARE, J. (1986b) 'Baker unfolds far-reaching school reform', *The Times*, 8 December.

CLARK, R. H. (1971) 'From secondary modern to comprehensive', *Comprehensive Education*, 19, autumn, pp. 14–17.

COE, J. (1988) 'Primary schools' in MORRIS, M. and GRIGGS, C. (Eds) *Education: The Wasted Years? 1973–86*, Lewes, Falmer Press, pp. 55–71.

CONSERVATIVE PARTY (1979) *The Conservative Manifesto*, London, Conservative Central Office, April.

CONSERVATIVE PARTY (1983) *The Conservative Manifesto*, London, Conservative Central Office, May.

CONSERVATIVE PARTY (1987) *The Next Moves Forward* (Conservative Party Election Manifesto), London, Conservative Central Office, May.

CORDINGLEY, P. and WILBY, P. (1987) *Opting Out of Mr Baker's Proposals*, London, Education Reform Group, Ginger Paper 1.

COUNCIL FOR CURRICULUM REFORM (1945) *The Content of Education*, London, University of London Press.

COX, C. B. and BOYSON, R. (Eds) (1975) *Black Paper 1975: The Fight for Education*, London, Dent.

COX, C. B. and BOYSON, R. (Eds) (1977) *Black Paper 1977*, London, Maurice Temple Smith.

COX, C. B. and DYSON, A. E. (Eds) (1969a) *Fight for Education: A Black Paper*, London, Critical Quarterly Society.

COX, C. B. and DYSON, A. E. (Eds) (1969b) *Black Paper Two: The Crisis in Education*, London, Critical Quarterly Society.

COX, C. B. and DYSON, A. E. (Eds) (1970) *Black Paper Three: Goodbye Mr Short*, London, Critical Quarterly Society.

CURRIE, D. (1983) 'World capitalism in recession', in HALL, S. and JACQUES, M. (Eds) *The Politics of Thatcherism*, London, Lawrence and Wishart, pp. 79–105.

DALE, R. (1979) 'The politicization of school deviance: Reactions to William Tyndale', in BARTON, L. and MEIGHAN, R. (Eds) *Schools, Pupils and Deviance*, Driffield, Nafferton Books, pp. 95–112.

DALE, R. (1981) 'Control, accountability and William Tyndale', in DALE, R. *et al* (Eds) *Education and the State Volume 1: Schooling and the National Interest*, Lewes, Falmer Press.

DALE, R. (1983) 'Thatcherism and education', in AHIER, J. and FLUDE, M. (Eds) *Contemporary Education Policy*, London, Croom Helm, pp. 223–55.

DALE, R. (1985) 'The background and inception of the technical and vocational education initiative', in DALE, R. (Ed) *Education, Training and Employment: Towards a New Vocationalism?*, Oxford, Pergamon Press in association with the Open University, pp. 41–56.

DAVID, T. (1988) 'The funding of education', in MORRIS, M. and GRIGGS, C. (Eds) *Education: The Wasted Years? 1973–86*, Lewes, Falmer Press, pp. 28–54.

DENNISON, W. F. (1981) *Education in Jeopardy: Problems and Possibilities of Contraction*, Oxford, Basil Blackwell.

DENT, H. C. (1958) *Secondary Modern Schools: An Interim Report*, London, Routledge & Kegan Paul.

DEPARTMENT OF EDUCATION AND SCIENCE (1965) *The Organization of Secondary Education* (Circular 10/65), London, HMSO.

DEPARTMENT OF EDUCATION AND SCIENCE (1967) *Children and Their Primary Schools* (2 vols) (The Plowden Report), London, HMSO.

DEPARTMENT OF EDUCATION AND SCIENCE (1970a) *The Organization of Secondary Education* (Circular 10/70), London, HMSO.

DEPARTMENT OF EDUCATION AND SCIENCE (1970b) *HMI Today and Tomorrow*, London, HMSO.

DEPARTMENT OF EDUCATION AND SCIENCE (1972) *Education: A Framework for Expansion* (Cmnd 5174), London, HMSO.

DEPARTMENT OF EDUCATION AND SCIENCE (1974) *Educational Disadvantage and the Educational Needs of Immigrants* (Cmnd 5720), London, HMSO, August.

DEPARTMENT OF EDUCATION AND SCIENCE (1975) *A Language for Life* (The Bullock Report), London, HMSO.

DEPARTMENT OF EDUCATION AND SCIENCE (1976a) *School Education in England: Problems and Initiatives*, London, HMSO, July.

DEPARTMENT OF EDUCATION AND SCIENCE (1976b) *Schools in England and Wales: Current Issues — An Annotated Agenda for Discussion*, London, HMSO, November.

DEPARTMENT OF EDUCATION AND SCIENCE (1977a) *Educating Our Children: Four Subjects for Debate. A Background Paper for the Regional Conferences, February and March 1977*, London, HMSO, January.

DEPARTMENT OF EDUCATION AND SCIENCE (1977b) *Education in Schools; A Consultative Document* (Cmnd 6869), (Green Paper), London, HMSO, July.

DEPARTMENT OF EDUCATION AND SCIENCE (1977c) *Local Education Authority Arrangements for the School Curriculum* (Circular 14/77), London, HMSO, November.

DEPARTMENT OF EDUCATION AND SCIENCE (1977d) *Curriculum 11-16* (HMI Red Book 1), London, HMSO.

DEPARTMENT OF EDUCATION AND SCIENCE (1978a) *Primary Education in England: A Survey by HM Inspectors of Schools*, London, HMSO, September.

DEPARTMENT OF EDUCATION AND SCIENCE (1978b) *Secondary School Examinations: A Single System at 16 +* (Cmnd 6869) (White Paper), London, HMSO.

DEPARTMENT OF EDUCATION AND SCIENCE (1979a) *Local Authority Arrangements for the School Curriculum: Report on the Circular 14/77 Review*, London, HMSO, November.

DEPARTMENT OF EDUCATION AND SCIENCE (1979b) *Aspects of Secondary Education in England: A Survey by HM Inspectors of Schools*, London, HMSO, December.

DEPARTMENT OF EDUCATION AND SCIENCE (1980a) *A Framework for the School Curriculum*, London, HMSO, January.

DEPARTMENT OF EDUCATION AND SCIENCE (1980b) *A View of the Curriculum* (HMI Series: Matters for Discussion 11), London, HMSO.

DEPARTMENT OF EDUCATION AND SCIENCE (1981a) *The School Curriculum*, London, HMSO, March.

DEPARTMENT OF EDUCATION AND SCIENCE (1981b) *Curriculum 11–16: A Review of Progress* (HMI Red Book 2), London, HMSO.

DEPARTMENT OF EDUCATION AND SCIENCE (1981c) *Memorandum on Education Vouchers*, London, HMSO, December.

DEPARTMENT OF EDUCATION AND SCIENCE (1983a) *Study of HM Inspectorate in England and Wales* (The Rayner Report), London, HMSO.

DEPARTMENT OF EDUCATION AND SCIENCE (1983b) *The Work of HM Inspectorate in England and Wales: A Policy Statement by the Secretary of State for Education and Science and the Secretary of State for Wales*, London, HMSO.

DEPARTMENT OF EDUCATION AND SCIENCE (1983c) *Curriculum 11–16: Towards a Statement of Entitlement: Curricular Reappraisal in Action* (HMI Red Book 3), London, HMSO.

DEPARTMENT OF EDUCATION AND SCIENCE (1984) 'Schools should give balanced view on peace and war: Sir Keith deplores attempts at indoctrination', *Press Release 32/84*, London, HMSO, 3 March.

DEPARTMENT OF EDUCATION AND SCIENCE (1985a) *The Curriculum from 5 to 16* (HMI Series: Curriculum Matters 2), London, HMSO, March.

DEPARTMENT OF EDUCATION AND SCIENCE (1985b) *Science 5–16: A Statement of Policy*, London, HMSO, March.

DEPARTMENT OF EDUCATION AND SCIENCE (1985c) *Better Schools* (Cmnd 9469), London, HMSO, March.

DEPARTMENT OF EDUCATION AND SCIENCE (1986a) *Better Schools: Evaluation and Appraisal Conference: Proceedings* (14–15 November 1985, Birmingham), London, HMSO.

DEPARTMENT OF EDUCATION AND SCIENCE (1986b) *Geography from 5 to 16* (HMI Series: Curriculum Matters 7), London, HMSO.

DEPARTMENT OF EDUCATION AND SCIENCE (1986c) *Report by Her Majesty's Inspectors on the Effects of Local Authority Expenditure Policies on Education Provision in England — 1985*, London HMSO, May.

DEPARTMENT OF EDUCATION AND SCIENCE (1986d) *Report of the Working Party for Pre-vocational Courses Pre-16* (The Johnson Report), London, HMSO, June.

DEPARTMENT OF EDUCATION AND SCIENCE (1986e) *A New Choice of School: City Technology Colleges*, London, HMSO, October.

DEPARTMENT OF EDUCATION AND SCIENCE (1987a) 'Kenneth Baker looks at future of education system', *Press Release 11/87*, London, HMSO, 9 January.

DEPARTMENT OF EDUCATION AND SCIENCE (1987b) 'Kenneth Baker calls for curriculum for pupils of all abilities', *Press Release 22/87*, London, HMSO, 23 January.

DEPARTMENT OF EDUCATION AND SCIENCE (1987c) 'Legislation next Parliament for a national curriculum', *Press Release 115/87*, London, HMSO, 7 April.

DEPARTMENT OF EDUCATION AND SCIENCE (1987d) *Modern Foreign Languages to 16* (HMI Series: Curriculum Matters 8), London, HMSO.

DEPARTMENT OF EDUCATION AND SCIENCE (1987e) *The National Curriculum 5–16: A Consultation Document*, London, DES.

DEPARTMENT OF EDUCATION AND SCIENCE (1988) *English for Ages 5 to 11: Proposals for the Secretary of State for Education and Science and the Secretary of State for Wales*, London, HMSO, November.

DEVON COUNTY COUNCIL/INSTITUTE OF LOCAL GOVERNMENT STUDIES (1984) *Report of a Conference on the Management of Change in the 14–19 Sector*, 24–27 September.

DEPARTMENT OF EMPLOYMENT (1981) *A New Training Initiative: A Programme for Action* (Cmnd 8455), London, HMSO.

DEPARTMENT OF EMPLOYMENT (1982) 'New technical education initiative', *Press Notice*, 12 November.

DOE, B. (1976) 'The end of the middle', *The Times Educational Supplement*, 26 November.

DONALD, J. (1979) 'Green paper: Noise of a crisis', *Screen Education*, 30, spring.

DONOUGHUE, B. (1987) *Prime Minister: The Conduct of Policy under Harold Wilson and James Callaghan*, London, Jonathan Cape.

DOUGLAS, J. W. D. (1964) *The Home and the School*, London, Macgibbon & Kee.

Education Act 1944, London, HMSO.

ELLIOTT, J. (1983) 'A curriculum for the study of human affairs: The contribution of Lawrence Stenhouse', *Journal of Curriculum Studies*, 15, 2, pp. 105–23.

ELLIS, T., MCWHIRTER, J., MCCOLGAN, D. and HADDOW, B. (1976) *William Tyndale: The Teacher's Story*, London, Writers and Readers Publishing Cooperative.

EVANS, K. (1985) *The Development and Structure of the English School System*, Sevenoaks, Hodder & Stoughton.

FENWICK, I. G. K. (1976) *The Comprehensive School 1944–1970: The Politics of Secondary School Reorganization*, London, Methuen.

FINN, D. (1987) *Training Without Jobs: New Deals and Broken Promises*, London, Macmillan.

FLETCHER, C., CARON, M. and WILLIAMS, W. (1985) *Schools on Trial: The Trials of Democratic Comprehensives*, Milton Keynes, Open University Press.

FLOUD, J. E., HALSEY, A. H. and MARTIN, F. M. (1956) *Social Class and Educational Opportunity*, London, Heinemann.

FORD, J. (1969) *Social Class and the Comprehensive School*, London, Routledge & Kegan Paul.

FOWLER, G. (1979) 'The accountability of ministers', in Lello, J. (Ed) *Accountability in Education*, London, Ward Lock Educational, pp. 13–34.

FOWLER, G. (1981) 'The changing nature of educational politics in the 1970s, in BROADFOOT, P. BROCK,C. and TULASIEWICZ, T. (Eds) *Politics and Educational Change: An International Survey*, London, Croom Helm, pp. 13–28.

FRIEDMAN, M. (1955) 'The role of government in education', in SOLO, R. (Ed) *Economics and the Public Interest*, New Brunswick, NJ, Rutgers University Press.

GALTON, M. and MOON, B. (Eds) (1983) *Changing Schools . . . Changing Curriculum*, London, Harper & Row.

GALTON, M., SIMON, B. and CROLL, P. (1980) *Inside the Primary Classroom*, London, Routledge & Kegan Paul.

GAMBLE, A. (1985) *Britain in Decline: Economic Policy, Political Strategy and the British State* (2nd edn), London, Macmillan.

GAMBLE, A. (1988) *The Free Economy and the Strong State: The Politics of Thatcherism*, London, Macmillan.

GIPPS, C. (1986) 'GCSE: Some background', in GIPPS, C. (Ed) *The GCSE: An Uncommon Examination*, Bedford Way Paper 29, Institute of Education, University of London, pp. 11–20.

GLASS, D. V. (Ed) (1954) *Social Mobility in Britain*, London, Routledge.

GLATTER, R. (Ed) (1977) *Control of the Curriculum: Issues and Trends in Britain and Europe*, Proceedings of the fifth annual conference of the British Educational Administration Society, London, September 1976, Studies in Education (new series) 4, Institute of Education, University of London.

GLENNERSTER, H. (1987) 'Goodbye Mr Chips', *New Society*, 9 October, pp. 17–19.

GOLBY, M. (Ed) (1987) *Perspectives on the National Curriculum*, Perspectives 32, School of Education, University of Exeter.

GORDON, T. (1986) *Democracy in One School?: Progressive Education and Restructuring*, Lewes, Falmer Press.

GOW, D. (1988) 'Why the test is far from child's play', *The Guardian*, 29 March.

GRAY, J. and SATTERLY, D. (1976) *Two Statistical Problems in Classroom Research*, Bristol, School of Education, University of Bristol.

GRETTON, J. and JACKSON, M. (1976) *William Tyndale: Collapse of a School — or a System?*, London, George Allen & Unwin.

HALL, J. (1985) 'The centralist tendency', *Forum*, 28, 1, autumn, pp. 4–7.

HALL, J. (1988) 'Supremo of the service', *Times Educational Supplement*, 1 April.

HALSEY, A. H. (1965) 'Education and equality', *New Society*, 17 June, pp. 13–15.

HALSEY, A. H., FLOUD, J. E. and ANDERSON, C. A. (Eds) (1961) *Education, Economy and Society*, New York, Free Press of Glencoe.

HARGREAVES, A. (1986) *Two Cultures of Schooling: The Case of Middle Schools*, Lewes, Falmer Press.

HARGREAVES, D. H. (1972) *Interpersonal Relations and Education*, London, Routledge & Kegan Paul.

HARGREAVES, D. H. (1982) *The Challenge for the Comprehensive School: Culture, Curriculum and Community*, London, Routledge & Kegan Paul.

HAVILAND, J. (Ed) (1988) *Take Care, Mr. Baker!*, London, Fourth Estate.

HENNESSY, P. (1986) *Cabinet*, Oxford, Basil Blackwell.

HILLGATE GROUP (1986) *Whose Schools? A Radical Manifesto*, London, The Hillgate Group, December.

HILLGATE GROUP (1987) *The Reform of British Education: From Principles to Practice*, London, The Hillgate Group, September.

HOLT, M. (1978) *The Common Curriculum: Its Structure and Style in the Comprehensive School*, London, Routledge & Kegan Paul.

HOLT, M. (1983a) *Curriculum Workshop: An Introduction to Whole Curriculum Planning*, London, Routledge & Kegan Paul.

HOLT, M. (1983b) 'Vocationalism: The new threat to universal education', *Forum*, 25, 3, summer, pp. 84–6.

HUGHES, C. (1988) 'Privatizer on parade: A profile of Oliver Letwin', *The Independent*, 6 June.

HUGILL, B. and SURKES, S. (1988) 'Opting out will not guarantee cash', *The Times Educational Supplement*, 15 July.

HUNTER, C. (1981) 'Politicians rule OK? Implications for teacher careers and school management', in BARTON, L. and WALKER, S. (Eds) *Schools, Teachers and Teaching*, Lewes, Falmer Press, pp. 65–75.

HUNTER, C. (1984) 'The political devaluation of comprehensives: What of the future?', in BALL, S. J. (Ed) *Comprehensive Schooling: A Reader*, Lewes, Falmer Press, pp. 273–92.

HUTCHINSON, B. (1986) 'The public image of a DES lower attaining pupils' programme initiative in a local education authority', *Cambridge Journal of Education*, 16, 2, summer, pp. 100–16.

ILLICH, I. (1970) *Deschooling Society*, New York, Harper & Row.

JAMIESON, I. (1985) 'Corporate hegemony or pedagogic liberation? The schools-industry movement in England and Wales', in DALE, R. (Ed) *Education, Training and Employment: Towards a New Vocationalism?*, Oxford, Pergamon Press in association with the Open University Press, pp. 22–39.

JAY, M. (1986) 'The "broken contract" between schools and their pupils', *The Listener*, 20 March, pp. 2–3.

JENCKS, C. *et al* (1972) *Inequality: A Reassessment of the Effect of Family and Schooling in America*, New York, Basic Books.

JENKINS, C. and SHERMAN, B. (1979) *The Collapse of Work*, London, Eyre Methuen.

JONES, G. W. (1985) 'The Prime Minister's aides' in KING, A. (Ed) *The British Prime Minister* (2nd edn), London, Macmillan Education, pp. 72–95.

JOSEPH, K. (1976) *Stranded on the Middle Ground? Reflections on Circumstances and Policies*, London, Centre for Policy Studies.

JOSEPH, K. (1982) Speech to the Institute of Directors, March; printed in full in a supplement to *The Director*, May, pp. 3–5.

JOSEPH, K. (1984) Speech at the North of England education conference, Sheffield, on Friday 6 January 1984, *Oxford Review of Education*, 10, 2, pp. 137–46.

KARABEL, J. and HALSEY, A. H. (1977) 'Educational research: A review and an interpretation' in KARABEL, J. and HALSEY, A. H. (Eds) *Power and Ideology in Education*, New York, Oxford University Press, pp. 1–85.

KAY, B. W. (1975) 'Monitoring pupils' performance', *Trends in Education*, 2.

KELLNER, P. (1988) '1968: The year the revolution got away', *The Observer*, 28 February.

KIRK, G. (1986) *The Core Curriculum*, London, Hodder & Stoughton.

KOGAN, M. *et al* (1973) *County Hall: The Role of the Chief Education Officer*, Harmondsworth, Penguin.

KOGAN, M. (1978) *The Politics of Educational Change*, London, Fontana.

LABOUR PARTY (1976) *Report of the Seventy-Fifth Annual Conference*, London, Labour Party.

LABOUR PARTY (1987) *Britain Will Win* (Labour Party Election Manifesto), London, Labour Party, June.

LABOUR RESEARCH DEPARTMENT (1987) *The Widening Gap: Rich and Poor Today*, London, LRD Publications Ltd.

LAWLOR, S. (1988) *Correct Core: Simple Curricula for English, Maths and Science*, London, Centre for Policy Studies, March.

LAWTON, D. (1969) 'The idea of an integrated curriculum', *University of London Institute of Education Bulletin*, new series, 19, autumn, pp. 5–12.

LAWTON, D. (1973) *Social Change, Educational Theory and Curriculum Planning*, Sevenoaks, Hodder & Stoughton.

LAWTON, D. (1979; 1982) *The End of the 'Secret Garden'? A Study in the Politics of the Curriculum*, Institute of Education, University of London.

LAWTON, D. (1980) *The Politics of the School Curriculum*, London, Routledge & Kegan Paul.

LAWTON, D. (1984) *The Tightening Grip: Growth of Central Control of the School Curriculum*, Bedford Way Paper 21, Institute of Education, University of London.

LAWTON, D. (1985) 'Education and training: Issues for further enquiry', *Report on Proceedings*, Liaison Seminar 1, 10 May, Post-16 Education Centre, Institute of Education, University of London, pp. 3–10.

LAWTON, D. (1987a) 'Cutting the curriculum cloth', *The Times Educational Supplement*, 1 May.

LAWTON, D. (1987b) 'Fundamentally flawed', *The Times Educational Supplement*, 18 September.

LAWTON, D. (1989) *Education, Culture and the National Curriculum*, Sevenoaks, Hodder & Stoughton.

LAWTON, D. and CHITTY, C. (1987) 'Towards a national curriculum', *Forum*, 30, 1, autumn, pp. 4–6.

LAWTON, D. and CHITTY, C. (Eds) (1988) *The National Curriculum*, Bedford Way Paper 33, London, Institute of Education, University of London.

LAWTON, D. and GORDON, P. (1987a) *HMI*, London, Routledge & Kegan Paul.

LAWTON, D. and GORDON, P. (1987b) 'HMI hangs in the balance', *The Times Educational Supplement*, 19 June.

LEACH, A. F. (1911) *Educational Charters and Documents 598–1909*, Cambridge, Cambridge University Press.

LETWIN, O. (1988) *Aims of Schooling: The Importance of Grounding*, Education Quartet Part 3, London, Centre for Policy Studies, March.

LEVITAS, R. (1986) *The Ideology of the New Right*, Cambridge, Polity Press.

LOW, G. (1987) 'Fall of the high-fliers', *The Observer*, 1 November.

LOW, G. (1988) 'The MSC: A failure of democracy', in MORRIS, M. and GRIGGS, C. (Eds) *Education — The Wasted Years? 1973–86*, Lewes, Falmer Press, pp. 215–28.

MACLURE, S. (1987a) *Promises and Piecrust*, Southampton, The Community Unit, TVS.

MACLURE, S. (1987b) 'Leading from the centre', *The Times Educational Supplement*, 3 April.

MACLURE, S. (1988) *Education Re-formed: A Guide to the Education Reform Act 1988*, Sevenoaks, Hodder & Stoughton.

MANZER, R. A. (1970) *Teachers and Politics: The Role of the National Union of Teachers in the Making of National Educational Policy in England and Wales Since 1944*, Manchester, Manchester University Press.

MARENBON, J. (1987) *English Our English: The New Orthodoxy Examined*, London, Centre for Policy Studies.

MARQUAND, D. (1988a) *The Unprincipled Society: New Demands and Old Politics*, London, Jonathan Cape.

MARQUAND, D. (1988b) 'The lure of tradition behind the new right's appeal to the chattering classes', *The Guardian*, 5 April.

MAW, J. (1985) 'Curriculum control and cultural norms: Change and conflict in a British context', *The New Era*, 66, 4, pp. 95–8.

MAW, J. (1988) 'National curriculum policy: Coherence and progression?', in LAWTON, D. and CHITTY, C. (Eds) *The National Curriculum*, Bedford Way Paper 33, Institute of Education, University of London, pp. 49–64.

MSC (1982) 'David Young, Chairman, Manpower Services Commission, welcomes the government's new technical education initiative', *Press Notice*, 12 November.

MSC/TSA (1975) *Vocational Preparation for Young People*, London, TSA.

MINISTRY OF EDUCATION (1945) *The Nation's Schools, Their Plans and Purposes*, pamphlet 1, London, HMSO.

MINISTRY OF EDUCATION (1947) *Organization of Secondary Education* (Circular 144), London, HMSO.

MINISTRY OF EDUCATION (1951) *Education 1900–1950* (Cmnd 8244), London, HMSO.

MINISTRY OF EDUCATION (1963) *Half Our Future* (The Newsom Report), London, HMSO.

MONKS, T. G. (1968) *Comprehensive Education in England and Wales: A Survey of Schools and Their Organization*, Slough, NFER.

MONKS, T. G. (Ed) (1970) *Comprehensive Education in Action*, Slough, NFER.

MOON, B. (Ed) (1981) *Comprehensive Schools: Challenge and Change*, Windsor, NFER-Nelson.

MORGAN, J. (Ed) (1981) *The Backbench Diaries of Richard Crossman*, London, Hamish Hamilton and Jonathan Cape.

MORGAN, K. O. (1981) *Rebirth of a Nation: Wales, 1880–1980*, Oxford and Cardiff, Clarendon Press/University of Wales Press.

MORGAN, K. O. (1984) *Labour in Power: 1945–1951*, Oxford, Clarendon Press.

MORGAN, K. O. (1987) *Labour People: Leaders and Lieutenants, Hardie to Kinnock*, Oxford, Oxford University Press.

MORRIS, M. (1987a) 'Centralized curriculum', *The Times Educational Supplement*, 13 February.

MORRIS, M. (1987b) Review of Bernard Donoughue's *Prime Minister: The Conduct of Policy under Harold Wilson and James Callaghan*, Education, 170, 11, 11 September, p 211.

MORRIS, M. and GRIGGS, C. (1988) 'Thirteen wasted years?', in MORRIS, M. and GRIGGS, C. (Eds) *Education — The Wasted Years? 1973–86*, Lewes, Falmer Press, pp. 1–27.

MORRIS, N. (1976) 'The economics of the voucher system', *Forum*, 19, 1, autumn, pp. 16–19.

MORTIMORE, J., MORTIMORE, P. and CHITTY, C. (1986) *Secondary School Examinations: 'The Helpful Servants, not the Dominating Master'*, Bedford Way Paper 18, Institute of Education, University of London.

NUT (1977) *Education: The Great Debate*, London, NUT.

NUTTALL, D. L. (1984) 'Doomsday or a new dawn? The prospects for a common system of examining at 16 + ' in BROADFOOT, P. (Ed) *Selection, Certification and Control: Social Issues in Education Assessment*, Lewes, Falmer Press, pp. 163–77.

NYEC (1974) *Unqualified, Untrained and Unemployed*, Report of a working party set up by the National Youth Employment Council, London, HMSO.

O'CONNOR, M. (1987a) *Curriculum at the Crossroads*, An account of the SCDC National Conference on Aspects of Curriculum Change, University of Leeds, September 1987, Leeds, School Curriculum Development Committee.

O'CONNOR, M. (1987b) 'Ruskin ten years on', *Contributions*, 11, York, Centre for the Study of Comprehensive Schools, spring, pp. 2–10.

O'CONNOR, M. (1989) 'Steady hands may get the quart into the pint pot', *The Guardian*, 31 January.

OECD (ORGANIZATION FOR ECONOMIC COOPERATION AND DEVELOPMENT) (1975) *Review of National Policies for Education: Educational Development Strategy in England and Wales*, Paris, OECD.

PARKINSON, M. (1970) *The Labour Party and the Organization of Secondary Education, 1918–1965*, London, Routledge & Kegan Paul.

PEACOCK, A. and WISEMAN, J. (1964) *Education for Democrats*, Hobart Paper 25, London, Institute of Economic Affairs.

PEDLEY, R. R. (1969) 'Comprehensive disaster', in COX, C. B. and DYSON, A. E. (Eds) *Fight for Education: A Black Paper*, London, Critical Quarterly Society, pp. 45–8.

PEDLEY, R. (1978) *The Comprehensive School* (3rd edn), Harmondsworth, Penguin.

PILE, W. (1979) *The Department of Education and Science*, London, George Allen & Unwin.

PRICE, C. (1985) 'The politician's view', in PLASKOW, M. (Ed) *Life and Death of the Schools Council*, Lewes, Falmer Press, pp. 169–77.

PRING, R. (1983) *Privatization in Education*, London, RICE, (Right to a Comprehensive Education), February.

PRING, R. (1986) 'Privatization of education', in ROGERS, R. (Ed) *Education and Social Class*, Lewes, Falmer Press, pp. 65–82.

PRING, R. (1987a) 'Privatization in education', *Journal of Education Policy*, 2, 4, October–December, pp. 289–99.

PRING, R. (1987b) 'Free . . . to those who contribute', *The Times Educational Supplement*, 23 October.

PRING, R., WHITE, R. and BROCKINGTON, D. (1988) *14–18 Education and Training: Making Sense of the National Curriculum and the New Vocationalism? A Discussion Document*, Bristol, Youth Education Service.

QUICKE, J. (1988) 'The "new right" and education', *British Journal of Educational Studies*, 36, 1, February, pp. 5–20.

RAGGATT, P. and EVANS, M. (Eds) (1977) *Urban Education 3: The Political Context*, London, Ward Lock Educational in association with the Open University Press.

RAISON, T. (1976) *The Act of the Partnership: An Essay on Educational Administration in England*, Centre for Studies in Social Policy, London, Bedford Square Press.

RAMSAY, R. and DORRIL, S. (1986) *Wilson, MI5 and the Rise of Thatcher: Covert Operations in British Politics 1974–78*, Hull, Voice, Unit 51.

RANSON, S. (1980) 'Changing relations between centre and locality in education', *Local Government Studies*, 6, 6, November/December, pp. 3–23.

REEDER, D. (1979) 'A recurring debate: Education and industry', in BERNBAUM, G. (Ed) *Schooling in Decline*, London, Macmillan, pp. 115–48.

REID, W. A. (1978) *Thinking About the Curriculum: The Nature and Treatment of Curriculum Problems*, London, Routledge & Kegan Paul.

ROSEN, H. (1982) *The Language Monitors*, Bedford Way Paper 11, Institute of Education, University of London.

ROSS, J. M., BUNTON, W. J., EVISON, P. and ROBERTSON, T. S. (1972) *A Critical Appraisal of Comprehensive Education*, Slough, NFER.

RUBINSTEIN, D. and SIMON, B. (1973) *The Evolution of the Comprehensive School, 1926–1972*, London, Routledge & Kegan Paul.

STJOHN-STEVAS, N. (1977) *Better Schools for All: A Conservative Approach to the Problems of the Comprehensive School*, London, Conservative Political Centre.

SALTER, B. and TAPPER, T. (1981) *Education, Politics and the State: The Theory and Practice of Educational Change*, London, Grant McIntyre.

SALTER, B. and TAPPER, T. (1988) 'The politics of reversing the ratchet in secondary education, 1969–1986', *Journal of Educational Administration and History*, 20, 2, July, pp. 57–70.

SARAN, R. (1988) 'School teachers: Salaries and conditions of service', in MORRIS, M. and GRIGGS, C. (Eds) *Education — The Wasted Years? 1973–86*, Lewes, Falmer Press, pp. 145–59.

SCHOOLS COUNCIL (1971) *Choosing a Curriculum for the Young School Leaver* (Working Paper No 33), London, Evans/Methuen.

SCHOOLS COUNCIL (1975) *The Whole Curriculum 13–16* (Working Paper No 53), London, Evans/Methuen Educational.

SCHULTZ, T. (1961) 'Investment in human capital', *American Economic Review*, 51, March, pp. 1–17.

SCRUTON, R. (1980) *The Meaning of Conservatism*, Harmondsworth, Penguin.

SELDON, A. (1986) *The Riddle of the Voucher: An Inquiry into the Obstacles to Introducing Choice and Competition in State Schools*, London, Institute of Economic Affairs.

SELECT COMMITTEE ON EDUCATION AND SIENCE (1967–68) *HM Inspectorate (England and Wales)*, London, HMSO.

SEXTON, S. (1988) 'No nationalized curriculum', *The Times*, 9 May.

SHILLING, C. (1988) 'School to work programmes and the production of alienation', *British Journal of Sociology of Education*, 9, 2, pp. 181–98.

SIMON, B. (1955) *The Common Secondary School*, London, Lawrence & Wishart.

SIMON, B. (1974) *The Politics of Educational Reform, 1920–1940*, London, Lawrence & Wishart.

SIMON, B. (1977) 'The green paper', *Forum*, 20, 1, autumn.

SIMON, B. (1978) 'Problems in contemporary educational theory: A Marxist approach', *Journal of Philosophy of Education*, 12, pp. 29–39.

SIMON, B. (1981) 'The primary school revolution: Myth or reality?', in SIMON, B. and WILLCOCKS, J. (Eds) *Research and Practice in the Primary Classroom*, London, Routledge & Kegan Paul, pp. 7–25.

SIMON, B. (1985) *Does Education Matter?*, London, Lawrence & Wishart.

SIMON, B. (1986) 'The battle of the blackboard', *Marxism Today*, June, pp. 20–6.

SIMON, B. (1988) *Bending the Rules: The Baker 'Reform' of Education*, London, Lawrence & Wishart.

SKIDELSKY, R. (1987) 'Falling through the flaws', *The Guardian*, 21 September.

SKILBECK, M. (Ed) (1970) *John Dewey*, London, Collier-Macmillan.

SMITH, W. O. L. (1957) *Education: An Introductory Survey*, Harmondsworth, Penguin.

SOCIAL DEMOCRATIC PARTY/LIBERAL ALLIANCE (1987) *Britain United: The Time Has Come* (SDP/Liberal Alliance programme for Government), June.

Social Trends (1975) London, HMSO.

SSEC (1943) *Curriculum and Examinations in Secondary Schools* (The Norwood Report), London, HMSO.

START, K. B. and WELLS, B. K. (1972) *The Trend of Reading Standards*, Windsor, NFER.

STONIER, T. (1983) *The Wealth of Information: A Profile of Post-Industrial Society*, London, Methuen.

STUBBS, M. and DELAMONT, S. (Eds) (1976) *Explorations in Classroom Observation*, Chichester, Wiley.

TAWNEY, R. H. (1922) *Secondary Education for All: A Policy for Labour*, London, Allen & Unwin.

TAWNEY, R. H. (1951) *Equality*, London, Allen & Unwin.

TAYLOR, W. (1963) *The Secondary Modern School*, London, Faber & Faber.

TENTH REPORT FROM THE EXPENDITURE COMMITTEE (1976) *Policy Making in the Department of Education and Science*, London, HMSO.

THOMAS, H. (1985) 'Teacher supply: Problems, practice and possibilities', in HUGHES, M., RIBBINS, P. and THOMAS, H. (Eds) *Managing Education: The System and the Institution*, London, Holt, Rinehart and Winston, pp. 68–98.

TOMLINSON, J. (1988) 'Curriculum and market: Are they compatible?', in HAVILAND, J. (Ed) *Take Care, Mr Baker!*, London, Fourth Estate, pp. 9–13.

VAIZEY, J. (1966) *Education for Tomorrow*, Harmondsworth, Penguin.

VERNON, B. D. (1982) *Ellen Wilkinson 1891–1947*, London, Croom Helm.

WADDINGTON, J. (1985) 'The school curriculum in contention: Content and control', in HUGHES, M., RIBBINS, P. and THOMAS, H. (Eds) *Managing Education: The System and the Institution*, London, Holt, Rinehart and Winston, pp. 99–124.

WALFORD, G. and JONES, S. (1986) 'The Solihull adventure: An attempt to reintroduce selective schooling', *Journal of Education Policy*, 1, 3, July–September, pp. 239–53.

WALSH, K., DUNNE, R., STOTEN, B. and STEWART, J. D. (1985) 'Teacher numbers: The framework of government policy', in MCNAY, I. and OZGA, J. (Eds) *Policy Making in Education: The Breakdown of Consensus*, Oxford, Pergamon Press in association with the Open University Press, pp. 251–71.

WARNOCK, M. (1988) *A Common Policy for Education*, Oxford, Oxford University Press.

WEICK, K. E. (1976) 'Educational organization as loosely coupled systems', in *Administrative Science Quarterly*, 21, 1, pp. 1–19.

WELLINGTON, J. (1987) 'Skills for the future? Vocational education and new technology', in HOLT, M. (Ed) *Skills and Vocationalism: The Easy Answer*, Milton Keynes, Open University Press, pp. 21–42.

WESTERGAARD, J. and RESLER, H. (1975) *Class in a Capitalist Society: A Study of Contemporary Britain*, London, Heinemann.

WESTON, P. (1986) 'If success had many faces: Thinking about the lower attaining pupils' programe', *Forum*, 28, 3, summer, pp. 79–81.

WHITE, J. (1975) 'The end of the compulsory curriculum', *The Curriculum* (The Doris Lee Lectures), Studies in Education (new series) 2, Institute of Education, University of London, pp. 22–39.

WHITE, J. (1988) 'An unconstitutional national curriculum', in LAWTON, D. and CHITTY, C. (Eds) *The National Curriculum*, Bedford Way Paper 33, Institute of Education, University of London, pp. 113–22.

WHITTY, G., FITZ, J. and EDWARDS, T. (1986) 'Assisting whom? Benefits and costs of the assisted places scheme', Paper presented to the annual conference of the British Educational Research Association, September.

WILBY, P. (1977) 'Education and equality', *New Statesman*, 16 September, pp. 358–61.

WILBY, P. (1987) 'Close up: Kenneth Baker', *Marxism Today*, April.

WILBY, P. and MIDGLEY, S. (1987) 'As the New Right wields its power', *The Independent*, 23 July.

WILLEY, F. (1971) 'Indifference in the DES', *The Times Educational Supplement*, 21 May.

WILLIAMS, R. (1958) *Culture and Society*, Harmondsworth, Penguin.

WILLIAMS, R. (1961) *The Long Revolution*, Harmondsworth, Penguin.

WOODS, P. (1979) *The Divided School*, London, Routledge & Kegan Paul.

WOODS, P. and HAMMERSLEY, M. (Eds) (1977) *School Experience*, London, Croom Helm.

WRAGG, T. (1976) 'The Lancaster study: Its implications for teacher training', *British Journal of Teacher Education*, 2, 3, pp. 281–90.

WRAGG, T. (1986a) 'Sunny Jim's storm clouds overhead', *The Times Educational Supplement*, 17 October, p. 4.

WRAGG, T. (1986b) 'The parliamentary version of the great debate', in GOLBY, M. (Ed) *Ruskin Plus Ten*, Perspectives 26, School of Education, University of Exeter, pp. 6–14.

WRIGHT, N. (1977) *Progress in Education: A Review of Schooling in England and Wales*, London, Croom Helm.

WRIGHT, P. (1987) *Spycatcher: The Candid Autobiography of a Senior Intelligence Officer*, New York, Viking Penguin Inc.

YOUNE, M.F.D. (Ed) (1971) *Knowledge and Control: New Directions for the Sociology of Education*, London, Collier-Macmillan.

YOUNG, D. (1983) *Circular to Directors of Education on the Technical and Vocational Education Initiative*, Sheffield, MSC, 28 January.

YOUNG, M. and ARMSTRONG, M. (1965) 'The flexible school: The next step for comprehensives', *Where Supplement 5*, Cambridge, ACE, autumn.

Index